PERISHING HEATHENS

Perishing Heathens

Stories of Protestant Missionaries and Christian Indians in Antebellum America

JULIUS H. RUBIN

University of Nebraska Press
LINCOLN AND LONDON

© 2017 by the Board of Regents of
the University of Nebraska
All rights reserved
Manufactured in the United States of America

Library of Congress Control Number: 2017011119

Set in Arno Pro by Rachel Gould.
Designed by N. Putens.

I dedicate this book to my wife, Loretta, to my children, Elise and Joshua, and to my granddaughter, Sydney Tova.

CONTENTS

List of Tables   *ix*

Preface   *xi*

Introduction   *1*

1. The Travails of David Bacon: "A Humble Missionary of the Cross"   *23*

2. The Missionary Vocation of Miss D: A Life Broken by Disease and Disappointment   *47*

3. The Endless Chain of Religious Intelligence: The Emergence of an American Evangelical Identity   *75*

4. The Question of K: "The First Friend of the Osage Nation unto God"   *99*

5. The First Fruits of the Cherokee Nation: Catharine Brown and Sister Margaret Ann   *121*

6. Métis Christian Indian Lives: Jane Johnston Schoolcraft and Mackinaw Mission Converts   *165*

Conclusion   *187*

Notes   *197*

Bibliography   *217*

Index   *231*

ILLUSTRATION

1. Gravestone of Ann Cornelius   *x*

TABLES

1. Composition of the Union Mission to the Osages *58*
2. Number of students enrolled at the Springplace Mission school *143*
3. Christian Indian converts *158*

FIG. 1. Gravestone of Ann Cornelius. Photograph by Julius H. Rubin, Old Durham Cemetery, Durham CT.

PREFACE

At the top of a hill in the southeast corner of Connecticut's Old Durham Cemetery stands a solitary grave marker, set apart from those of whites, the original English settlers and their successors—proprietors, goodwives, children, and servants. It is also sequestered from an adjacent section of graves designated for African American servants and slaves. Located at the margins of this community of the dead, apart from those who enjoyed varying degrees of social standing, property, and privilege in life, the marker reads,

> Ann
> Cornelius
> A Indian Girl
> died Dec' 9th
> 1776 Aged
> 19 Years.

Who was this "Indian girl"? What tribe and natal community did she hail from? How did she come to reside in Durham and with whom? What can we discover about her brief life and the meaning of her Christian Indian identity? How did she die? Who paid the considerable sum for her carved gravestone?

At the time of the Revolution, Durham was a small central Connecticut farming village located on the Coginchuag River. Today, docents provide tours of historical sites in Durham and depict Ann Cornelius as a member of a local tribe, the Wangunk Indians, who were dispossessed of their lands by settler colonialism.[1] However, this tribal identity cannot be substantiated.[2] With the exception of the stone that marks her grave, Ann Cornelius has been erased from the historical record. No evidence exists to answer these questions.[3]

Neither Ann Cornelius nor her family surname appears in the records of Connecticut tribes, such as the Tunxis-Farmingtons, Mohegans, or Mashantucket Pequots, or those for Native groups in Long Island, New York.[4] Nor are they found in Connecticut colony records or in the Durham town records—not in those of freemen; those of births, deaths, and marriages; or those of proprietors; nor in the vital records kept by Reverend Nathaniel Chauncey, the first pastor of Durham's Congregational church.[5] An "Account of the Number of Inhabitants in the County of New-Haven, on the First of January, 1774," a census taken two years before her death, lists no Indian women residing in Durham.[6] This absence suggests that Ann came to Durham sometime between 1774 and her death in 1776.

The sermons, papers, and account books of Reverend Elizur Goodrich, pastor of Durham's Congregational Church from 1755 to 1776, and the account books of other town notables, list the names, dates of service, and wages and compensation paid to scores of day laborers, indentured servants, and apprentices as well as the transactions for numerous African American slaves.[7] There is, however, no mention of Ann. Although many Native children and adolescents in southern New England suffered debt peonage, a form of "judicial slavery" where parents sold their sons and daughters into forced and protracted apprenticeships to settle debt,[8] no contract of indenture exists for Ann Cornelius.[9]

Almost twenty years after Ann's death, Judge John Dickinson, chief of the Middletown Connecticut probate court, appointed Levi Parmalee of Durham as the guardian to an Indian minor, George Cornelius, age fifteen.[10] Parmalee was a town notable serving as a church deacon and justice of the peace. It is unknown whether George, an indigent and possibly orphaned Native youth, was related to Ann Cornelius.

Could Ann Cornelius have succumbed to the smallpox epidemic that ravaged central Connecticut in 1776? Smallpox afflicted combatants in the Revolutionary War during the siege of Boston in the summer of 1775. The epidemic followed the conflict to Quebec in the fall, and by May 1776, American troops routed by British and Canadian forces left behind five hundred sick as the retreating Continental Army brought the contagion to New England and the southern colonies. Governor Trumbull of Connecticut instructed town selectmen to inspect returning soldiers for possible quarantine. "Untold numbers may have died in Pennsylvania and Connecticut where returning soldiers launched epidemics there."[11]

This disease reached Durham in the fall of 1776. The town operated a pest house from 1760 to 1790 and buried many of the victims in a special cemetery adjacent to this place of quarantine. Ann Cornelius is not mentioned in town records of the pest house or among those who died in the epidemic.[12]

Accounts of the life and religious experience of Ann Cornelius have not survived in public and private documents. Was she an evangelical Christian Indian whose encounter with religion resembled the copious tears of repentance and the arduous spiritual pilgrimage that the New Light preacher and missionary Samuel Kirkland recorded in his unpublished journals for Oneidas and other Natives in the Kanonwalohale, New York, congregation? Did she languish in judicial slavery, debt peonage, and indenture to a Durham family? What brought her to Durham? How did she die at nineteen years of age at the beginning of her adult life? These questions remain unanswerable.

Ann Cornelius does exemplify the ubiquitous trope that developed in American culture, literature, and poetry, from the Revolution through the nineteenth century. The "vanishing American" portrayed Native peoples as doomed to the inevitable destiny of extinction, erasure, and replacement by settler colonialism.[13] No minister eulogized her brief life in a written funeral sermon. No documents exist suggesting that she kept a diary or journal of her religious experiences, or sent and received correspondence. Only the grave marker remains to record her death and burial place.

William Chauncey Fowler makes no mention of Ann in his commemorative *History of Durham Connecticut* published during the civil war, although he documents the declining land holdings and presence of the local Wangunk Indians. And Ann Cornelius did not survive in our collective memory as a ghost or apparition to haunt the Euro-American settlers who remained on Native lands and wrote the local histories of New England. As Colleen E. Boyd and Coll Thrush argue in *Phantom Past*, "Native ghosts have in fact shaped and informed colonizing encounters, in significant ways, becoming stock characters in a quotidian North American drama of displacement, transformation, and belonging."[14] Then and now, many Americans have been haunted by Native ghosts as an expression of the anxieties, uncertainties, and moral ambiguities of the country's complex dealings with Native peoples.

Philip Freneau's maudlin poem "The Indian Burying Ground" (1787) laments the passing of indigenous peoples but envisions their continued haunting presence:

> In spite of all the learned have said,
> I still my old opinion keep;
> The posture that we give the dead,
> Points out the soul's eternal sleep.

However, Indians, unlike Euro-Americans, do not enjoy eternal rest, as Freneau's verses conjure the spirits and ghosts of Indian dead who appeared among the graves in spectral forms to resume their past lifeways and identities. The disappearance of local tribes and Native persons haunted many New Englanders during the Revolution, but Ann Cornelius was not among these ghosts.

Despite all that has been lost to historical memory, it is likely that Ann Cornelius was a Christian Indian given her burial in a cemetery associated with members of the First Congregational Church. While the Cornelius surname is not found among Connecticut tribes in this period, it was common among the Oneidas in New York. It is possible that Ann was born and came of age among the Christian Indian settlements of Oquaga on the Susquehanna River or in the principal village of Kanonwalohale, which numbered seven hundred souls and represented more than half of the Oneida population in the late eighteenth century.[15]

The New England Company sponsored the early missions to Oquaga from 1745 to 1753. Reverend Elihu Spencer, Yale educated, aged twenty-seven and trained by Jonathan Edwards, served from 1745 to 1748. He converted Good Peter (Agwrondougwas) and Old Isaac (Dakayenesese) and formed a small Native church.[16] Oquaga was founded in the 1740s and was destroyed by the Patriots during the Revolution in 1779. With a population of 250, this multitribal, polyglot village of Oneidas, Mohawks, Mahicans, Nanticokes, and Shawnees united through an emerging Christian Indian ethnogenesis.[17] Sunday worship consisted of readings from Psalms and scripture, hymn-singing, and a sermon preached by Good Peter. It was "a very lively and agreeable" and orderly assembly where men and women were seated on separate benches along opposite sides of the church.[18]

Edward E. Andrews argues in *Native Apostles* that hundreds of African, African American, and Native American neophytes served as preachers, teachers, and translators who proved indispensable to the missionary enterprise in the British Atlantic world during the seventeenth and eighteenth centuries. He states,

> Why they did this and what these native preachers meant for the development of indigenous Christianities and for the relationships between such diverse peoples is an untold story that helps explain how colonized peoples responded to, rejected, shaped, and appropriated Christianity. Native missionaries, in other words, were at the very core of these cultural exchanges.[19]

Reverend Gideon Hawley briefly served as missionary to Oquaga in 1753 but left during the French and Indian War. Reverend Eleazer Mosely resumed this mission from 1765 to 1773 aided by the Oneida convert and translator James Dean.[20]

The early Protestant missions among the Oneidas gave rise to intratribal factionalism of Christians (Skenandoah Party), themselves divided between

Anglicans and Presbyterians, and pagans (Cornelius Party).[21] Christian Indians, allied with a generation of aspiring young warriors, usurped spiritual and political power from traditional shamans and sachems in their villages that were constituted as model congregational communities of the ingathered faithful. Andrews explains in *Native Apostles*, "Indigenous evangelists believed they had access to spiritual power, but their roles as native preachers often left them abysmally poor, social ostracized, psychologically repressed, and spiritually anxious."[22] Possibly Ann Cornelius and her family converted, switched allegiances from the pagan party, and settled in Connecticut to flee internecine conflict and the dangers of the Oneida nation during the onset of the Revolutionary War.

Ann Cornelius and her family might have come from the Oneida village of Kanonwalohale, which was first settled in the 1760s under the missionary guidance of Reverend Samuel Kirkland. This settlement existed for less than twenty years as the Mohawk military and political leader Joseph Brant, who allied with the British, destroyed Kanonwalohale during a raid in July 1780.

Kirkland championed the New Light teachings of the Great Awakening that espoused extemporaneous fire and brimstone preaching by ministers who were themselves reborn as children of God. Sermons pricked the conscience of each regenerate man or woman with the prospect of damnation, exhorting the faithful to undergo a dramatic and at times excruciatingly painful morphology of conversion: an inward spiritual pilgrimage from despair to the reception of God's grace of the newborn Christian.

Kirkland was the first white student of Eleazar Wheelock's Moor's Charity School in Lebanon, Connecticut, founded on the ideals of the "Grand Design" of Christianizing and civilizing Native children who would as adults return as missionaries to convert and "pacify" their peoples. He later attended Princeton until his senior year, and in 1765 he attempted unsuccessfully to evangelize the Senecas. Kirkland returned to Connecticut in 1766, was ordained by Wheelock, and was commissioned by the Connecticut Board of Correspondents of the Society of Scotland as a missionary to the Oneidas. Known as friend, father, and spiritual director, Kirkland addressed the poverty, hunger, alcohol abuse, and factionalism among the

Oneidas with a plan for agriculture, civilization, and education.[23] He kept school, visited the sick, and doctored them with medicines, sometimes bleeding patients. He catechized, instructed, and consoled Natives who struggled with sin and who sought the path to salvation.

Kirkland reports laboring for nine hours on the Lord's day with services in the morning and afternoon and pastoral visits that extended into the evening. His preaching attempted to awaken slumbering sinners to the depravity of the "natural man," as he urged upon his neophytes the importance of experiential religion of the heart and the necessity of rebirth. Time and again he records in his journals the abundant tears, weeping, and collective anguish of his Native congregation. Writing in December 16, 1770, he observes, "The whole assembly seemed to be melted with the consideration of Christ's great love to us. Scores might be seen weeping."[24] After his preaching on Sunday, December 2, 1767, he notes, "Tears flowed in great plenty. I heard some at noon crying for new hearts, praying that God would take away their old ugly wicked hearts."[25] Later that month Kirkland recounted the religious experience of one Native in the throes of religious despair:

> Tears flowed in abundance from many eyes. One in particular cried out aloud for mercy. Seemed to be almost overwhelmed with a sense of Guilt & Misery, "Brethren, oh hear me, I am miserable beyond all. I beseech you pray to God for me. All my former life rises up. I hate it. I hate it, but much arrows stick fast in my Soul. Oh, my brethren, pray for me, pray for me, I am miserable beyond all."[26]

A generation after Ann's death in 1776, a renewed religious awakening would sweep the new nation in the first decades of the nineteenth century in camp meetings along frontier settlements in Appalachia in Kentucky, Tennessee, and southern Ohio; through the Burned-Over District in central New York; and among the long-settled regions of New England. A surge in female education and literacy and the mass publication of evangelical magazines, tracts, and books accompanied the Second Great Awakening. American national identity was forged, partly, through the ascendancy of Protestant evangelical religion and the exponential growth of Methodist and Baptist denominations. The rise of the missionary spirit—the

Great Commission to convert the world and redeem perishing heathens, at home and abroad—was chronicled by published accounts of Indian conversions and Christian Indian lives. Each story added to the sum of "religious intelligence" and provided compelling evidence that evangelists and missionaries from all denominations were building the Redeemer's Kingdom in America and hastening the millennial day.

Adding a new dimension to the trope of erasure, religious publications in the age of revivals recorded, commemorated, and lauded the lives and religious experiences of Christian Indians, with each new born child of God supporting the creation of the Kingdom of God in America, even as these neophytes also represented what observers believed was the last of their tribe destined to assimilation or extinction.

As a case in point, Thomas Willis published in 1830 *A Short Account of the Religious Exercise and Experience of Betty, An Indian Woman*, transcriptions of a spiritual pilgrimage and exemplary dying that Betty told in her own words to white friends. She died in 1823 at age ninety, which means that Betty was almost seventy in 1795 when she narrated the account of her youthful spiritual journey that had occurred many decades earlier.

Betty was likely an Unkechaug Indian residing in Suffolk County in Long Island, New York, on the reservation at Poospatuck Creek. During the eighteenth century the tribe suffered encroaching English settlement and land dispossession that reduced their holdings from 175 to 50 acres, thus ending their ability to support themselves by traditional lifeways and forcing them to work at the bottom of the local market economy. Indian men labored as whalers, fence builders, wood carvers, and farm laborers. They sold game, hides, fish, firewood, shingles, and split rails for fences. Indian women worked by weaving baskets and as domestics in settler households. Many Indian children and adults suffered judicial slavery as indentured servants to satisfy debt.[27]

In the 1740s, Reverend Azariah Horton brought New Light religion and revivals to tribes on Long Island that fostered the formation of Native congregations like the Unkechaug Church at Poospatuck guided by Native minister Paul Cuffee and later by his grandson, Peter Jones. In the 1760s

Samson Occom, the Mohegan minister and missionary, continued this missionary outreach to Unkechaug, Shinnecock, Islip, and Wading River.[28]

Betty lived in poverty with her young children and a husband who was disabled by rheumatism. She eked out a subsistence living, working hand-to-mouth caning chairs and selling crafts in exchange for meat and supplies. Betty, herself illiterate, relates her story to a white acquaintance and retells her earlier life before her conversion as a time marked by prolonged doubt, suffering, and adversity. Unlike the story of Ann Cornelius, Betty's oral history and narration were transcribed and later published. Her story survives through publication in the 1830s as religious intelligence, as evidence of the conversion of perishing heathens, which presaged the coming of the millennium.

Betty was born in 1733 and came of age during the Great Awakening and the formation of a Christian Indian community among her people. She explains that she was married to a sober, religious man. During the 1760s, during a local epidemic that killed many of her tribe including her mother and two of Betty's children, she fell ill with a fever. Betty had a vision of hell and two small coffins that presaged her children's death. She mourned in sorrow and religious doubt. A year later she experienced a second trance and vision while traveling with an infant strapped on her back as she walked to a nearby town to cane chairs in exchange for meat. Like Paul on the road to Damascus, Betty recounts her conversion experience. She collapsed by the roadside, remaining prostrate from sunrise until sunset, unable to move. While on the side of the road, she experienced a vision, retold as a religious allegory. Betty floated in the air above flames that seemed to have burned her face and blinded her.

> After I had been sometime in this state of fear and distress, I thought I was a poor wicked creature, and ought to be punished, and it would be just in the Lord to permit me to fall into that burning pit.... At length, my whole heart and all within me was entirely given up, resigned to the Lord's will, and even if it was his will that I should go into that dreadful place, that his own will might be done.[29]

She espoused the willingness to suffer damnation and accept the dictates of divine will as evidence of her soul's progress from prideful indifference and enmity toward God to a selfless, agonizing submission.

Betty's journey continued as she approached a great ocean where only the slender thread of a spider's web prevented her from drowning. She floated above the ground until encountering a person who told Betty that she was clothed in sin. Each spot on her skin that she rubbed off symbolized worldliness: "foolish talking and laughing, and doing wickedly."[30]

Betty traveled through an open gate into a marvelous garden where she came upon a tree that was full of luscious fruit. "I was invited to draw near and taste, but thought I was a poor ignorant squaw—was not worthy—felt afraid."[31] She testified to embracing this evangelical humiliation before divine law.

After accepting the instructions of those who wore silver breastplates that were swords of the spirit, Betty ate the fruit and felt joy and strength returning to her body. As the vision concluded and she returned to consciousness, with a heart filled with love, freed of her troubles and restored to health, Betty was invited to sit at a table and enjoy a feast with people of many colors where she received a gift, the word of God.

Betty's story combined the indigenous reliance on visions with the Protestant inward spiritual pilgrimage and resembles the accounts of many other Christian Indians published in the burgeoning literature of evangelical religious intelligence in the early decades of the nineteenth century. Native writings and publications along with the records of white missionaries have made this book possible. While the brief life of Ann Cornelius signifies a lamentable example of the vanishing American and the inexorable destiny of extinction and erasure of Native peoples and persons, much had changed in the new republic. Now, Christian Indian lives and religious experiences like Betty's, together with the memoirs of white missionaries, were recorded and reproduced since they represented for nineteenth century American evangelicals "the signs of the times." This age promised the possibility of building the Kingdom of God in America for missionaries who labored to convert perishing heathens throughout the new republic. And religious intelligence also published the words of Christian Indian neophytes who recounted their spiritual journeys. Many came from mixed-race backgrounds and negotiated the boundaries of their métis culture and tribal identity with the ascendancy of American colonization and missionization. These Christian Indian converts and missionaries also corresponded in magazines and wrote book-length memoirs that brought their experiences before mass publics in America and the Atlantic world.

The research and writing in this study spans the arc of my academic career, beginning with dissertation research conducted in the 1970s that was published by University Microfilms (Proquest) in 1979. A chapter of this thesis, "Crises of Conscience among Missionaries to the Indians during the Second Great Awakening," has been revised for this book. I wish to thank Reverend Dr. James A. Moos, executive minister for Wider Church Ministries, Cleveland, Ohio, for granting permission to publish archival materials from the American Board of Commissioners for Foreign Missions relating to the Union Mission to the Osages. Linda Long, executive assistant of Wider Church Ministries, expedited the process of granting permission, and I am grateful for her assistance.

Over the course of three decades, during sabbaticals at the University of Saint Joseph (formerly Saint Joseph College) in 1988, 1994, and 2002, and during periods when I took breaks from my previous book projects, I have identified stories of missionary men and women and Native converts who are retold in this study. My research has benefited from access to the many libraries of Yale University including the Manuscript and Archives Collection of Sterling Memorial Library, the Special Collections of the Divinity Library, the Beinecke Rare Book and Manuscript Library, and the Henry Cuship/John Hay Whitney Medical Historical Library. I have also used the collections of others libraries: the Library of Congress; the Connecticut State Library; the Oklahoma Historical Society Research Center; the Ingraham Memorial Library of the Litchfield Historical Society, Litchfield, Connecticut; the Olin Library, Wesleyan University; the Houghton Library, Harvard University; the Special Collections and Archives of the Burke Library, Hamilton College, Clinton, New York; and the American Antiquarian Society Library, Worcester, Massachusetts.

Kerry Driscoll, professor of English at the University of Saint Joseph, has provided editorial assistance, and through her friendship and our many conversations she has posed critical questions that have helped me clarify my ideas. Kathy Kelley assisted me by acquiring interlibrary loan materials and microfilms. When my friend Russell Parmelee learned that I was writing a book about Native Americans, he took me on a field trip and introduced me to the graves of his ancestors and to the grave of Ann Cornelius, who is buried near the top of a hill bordering a wooded lot at the southeastern perimeter of the Old Durham Cemetery.

Three anonymous reviewers have raised important questions and have offered insightful suggestions that helped me improve this work. At the University of Nebraska Press, Heather Stauffer, editorial assistant for Native American and Indigenous Studies, has addressed my questions and concerns as I have prepared the manuscript for publication. Matthew Bokovoy, senior acquisitions editor, Native American and Indigenous Studies, has provided encouragement and support from the beginning when I sent him a proposal and sample chapters in 2013, to the completion of this project.

I hope that retelling these compelling and fascinating stories will awaken in contemporary readers a sociological and historical imagination—the capacity to engage with empathy the lived experiences of missionaries and Christian Indians from past times. We need to reflect on what we share in common with those who forged a distinctive evangelical American identity and what we have lost.

PERISHING HEATHENS

Introduction

Harvey Harris Bloom, an undergraduate at Yale College, wrote a private diary entry, "Religious Meditations," on Sabbath evening April 26, 1857. He focused on the condition of the heathen in India and America. Although he would die of consumption at the age of twenty-five in 1864 before he could serve in the Union Army or fulfill his missionary vocation, Bloom articulated the central concerns in antebellum America of the missionary spirit for the fate of "perishing heathens":

> The poor heathen roams in his sin, and his ignorance. No church spire points him to the upper world. No church bell tells him tis the Sabbath, the existence yet to be.... Yet—to be *sure, certain* to which he is hurrying on heedless, unknowing, going down to eternal death. Oh! can we not help them. Doth not God call us to do the work. Doth not the voice of those millions crying out in their sin, in their darkness, reach us far away.... Does it point us to the millions of our own country who are going down to the grave without hope. Oh, God help us that we disregard not these promptings.[1]

This study recounts the stories of missionary men and women in the period from 1800–1830 who responded to the call to save perishing heathens in missions to the Osages in the Arkansas Territory, to the Cherokees in

Tennessee and Georgia, and to Ojibwes in the Michigan Territory. We also recount the lives of Native converts, many from métis (mixed-race) families who were attracted to the benefits of education, literacy, and conversion. Like the story of Bloom—the Yale undergraduate who aspired to a life of ultimate purpose informed by the missionary spirit—the lives of these missionary men and women and Native neophytes offer compelling stories of religious vocation, millennial expectations, and agonizing failure. In striving to save perishing heathens, they also anticipated their own personal salvation and building the Kingdom of God.

No issue better captured the enduring millennial sentimentality of American Protestantism during the first half of the nineteenth century than the cause of missions and the salvation of those perishing in heathen darkness. William Carey challenged believers in the Atlantic world in 1794 in *An Inquiry into the Obligation of Christians to Use the Means for the Conversion of Heathens,* to seize the evangelical imperative of the "Great Commission" and send foreign missionaries to effect the conversion of the world, bringing all peoples to Christ. He estimated that of the 731,000 inhabitants in the world, 420,000 "live in pagan darkness, destitute of knowledge of the gospel."[2]

The Great Commission included foreign missions to Africa and Asia in addition to home missions to new Western settlements and Indian missions to indigenous peoples in the Western Reserve of Ohio, the trans-Appalachian frontier, the upper Midwest, and the trans-Mississippi West. As Perry Miller explains, "in this belief, Protestants of all denominations would come under the influence of the Gospel. The wide world is to be evangelized. The day of slumber is passed. The sacramental host of God's elect are marshaled in arms, and wait for ministers to lead them on to victory."[3] The Great Commission envisioned an American innocence and an emulation of Christ that combined the fervor of nationalistic expansion with the special obligation to build the Kingdom of God in America and evangelize the world.[4]

Sermons and public addresses without number celebrated the spirit of the times, like Abiel Holmes's 1808 address before the Society for Propagating the Gospel among the Indians and Others in North America. Building upon Psalm 72:7, "His name shall endure forever," he annunciated an unfettered hope for propagating the Gospel throughout the world and in America, "when the Indian Powows [sic] shall be silenced by the songs of Zion."[5] The spread of the Gospel to heathens, who perished in ignorance as "impious idolaters" and languished in their "absurd superstitions," would sow the seeds of the Great Commission. "The wilderness and the solitary place shall be glad; the desert shall rejoice and blossom as the rose, and become like the garden of God."[6]

Perry Miller has argued that the millennial aspirations of the era of grand revivals brought masses to salvation. Each new convert would rededicate his or her life to benevolence and reform efforts. Through a "reflex," ever-increasing numbers of "workers in the kingdom" would extend the revival spirit until the ultimate fulfillment of the salvation of all mankind. William Sprague's *Lectures on Revivals of Religion* (1832) captures this sublime expectation:

> Revivals also *lend an important influence to the support of our benevolent institutions*. It is by means of these especially that the Gospel is to be sent abroad to the ends of the earth.... Now, this moral machinery, so far as our own country at least is concerned, is evidently to be sustained and increased chiefly through the influence of revivals. Each individual who is converted to God is a labourer in this glorious cause.[7]

The Second Great Awakening had revived and renewed an extensive interest in the cause of missions. A number of eastern voluntary societies were organized, conducted fundraising campaigns, and opened nearly one hundred new missions between 1787 and 1861. The Society for Propagating the Gospel Among the Indians and Others in North America (1787) and the Society of the United Brethren for Propagating the Gospel Among the Heathen (1787) were among the first of these efforts. By 1807 Congregational groups in Massachusetts (1799), Connecticut (1802), Rhode Island (1801), New Hampshire (1801), Maine (1802), and Vermont (1802) had established state and auxiliary missionary societies. Presbyterians joined together with the Vermont Missionary Society. In addition, Baptists, Methodists, Quakers, and Moravians promoted mission stations to Native Americans.[8]

The American Board of Commissioners for Foreign Missions (ABCFM) was organized in 1810 at Andover Theological Seminary consistent with the New Divinity fervor of Samuel J. Mills Jr., Samuel Worcester, and others. While a student at Williams College in 1806, Mills sought refuge from a summer thunderstorm in a barn, thus beginning the Haystack Prayer Meeting of like-minded evangelicals and missionaries. Worcester would help found the American Board and serve as corresponding secretary until his death in 1821. He lamented the "piteously lost souls in the thrall of the Devil."[9] Leonard Woods, professor of theology at Andover, delivered Worcester's funeral sermon and inquired, what is the grand design? His answer: "the salvation of sinners perishing in the darkness of paganism."[10]

The United Foreign Missionary Society (UFMS), a union of Dutch Reformed, Associate Reform, and Presbyterian synods, began operation in New York City in 1817. In the spirit of interdenominational cooperation missionary groups engaged the attention and commitment of Americans in wide numbers through journals like the *Mission Herald*, the *Connecticut Evangelical Magazine*, and the *Panoplist*.[11]

Missionary groups opened teaching stations throughout the Southeast to evangelize what were called the Five Civilized Tribes (Cherokee, Chickasaw, Choctaw, Creek, and Seminole) in Mississippi, Georgia, Alabama, and Tennessee. The UFMS and the ABCFM founded missions in New York and the Western Reserve of Ohio. However, the preponderance of initiatives from 1820 to 1830 and after the removal of eastern tribes to the trans-Mississippi West involved missionary outreach to Indian groups on the Western frontier and Plains. Thus, the nineteenth-century missionary spirit renewed the mandate of the seventeenth-century Puritans to fulfill their covenant with God to bring the heathen into civilization and salvation. "The challenge to the Puritan ... was not to exterminate, enslave, or ignore the native, but to convert, civilize, and educate him as quickly as possible. This provided more of a task than the Saints had expected, and of course in the long run they failed."[12] We need to view the men and women called to domestic Indian missions as representative lives who forged a distinctive evangelical religious personhood and identity founded upon religious values. These men and women were true believers who pursued the ideals of the Second Great Awakening—a revival of religion that began in the 1790s and persisted through the 1840s.

The Connecticut revival began when teams of New Divinity ministers traveled from village to village in Hartford and Litchfield counties bringing the message of salvation to rural enclaves and into the towns and cities in Connecticut and New England in the ensuing decades. Men like Nathan Strong, Abel Flint, Nathan Perkins, Edward Dorr Griffin, and the itinerant Asahel Nettleton would wins souls for Christ and build churches through their extemporaneous preaching in revivals. They met with "pious youth" and concerned laymen in private homes for "conference meetings" of prayer and exhortation.[13]

Guided by the theology of Jonathan Edwards, Samuel Hopkins, Nathanael Emmons, and other New Divinity thinkers, these revivalists labored to awaken slumbering sinners and rescue backsliders, urging them to embrace a morphology of conversion. New Divinity theology combined several key ideas: the necessity for each believer to undergo a new birth made possible by Christ's unlimited atonement that also promised the possibility of the salvation to Native peoples throughout America. Each reborn man and woman felt duty-bound to toil in the vineyards of the Lord, having appropriated Samuel Hopkins's ethical prescription of disinterested benevolence that rejected self-interest for Christ's sake. In this manner, the revival produced new born men and women who would dedicate their lives to the cause of missions, the commission to evangelize the world.[14] Committed to the dictates of evangelical Protestant religious personhood and the mentalities of an age of divine wonders, they viewed their lives through sublime millennial expectations as builders of a Redeemer's Kingdom in their lifetime.[15] James A. De Jong identifies a pervasive ideal where "millennial hopes were stimulated wherever evangelical Protestantism, particularly in those denominations most influenced by the Edwardsean tradition, experienced new revivals. Millennial hopes in turn created a new sense of urgency and responsibility for missions culminating in the formation of new societies."[16]

Most evangelicals supported Sprague's "moral machinery of the awakening" through contributions made after continual solicitations for funds by missionary agents and representatives of the empire of benevolent organizations. However, a few extraordinary individuals responded to the spirit of the times by abandoning more mundane and routine lives and accepting the call to missionary life. For those who embraced the call to missions, the burden of their vocation involved nothing less than the realization of seemingly impossible utopian values—the civilization and conversion of heathens. They confronted many vexing perplexities in the quest for the realization of their utopian goals: how to respond to adversity, indifference, or failure; how to measure their individual progress in implementing seemingly infinite ends; how to assuage feelings of anxiety, doubt, and discouragement. Many missionaries came to see themselves as failures, in part an accurate evaluation of their effect on particular indigenous groups. They succumbed to seasons of despair and religious melancholy. As such these melancholiacs need to be understood against the background of the strains placed upon Protestant believers as they attempted to devote their lives in full measure as instruments of God through the missionary vocation.

New birth required a spiritual journey where the sinner was slain by God's law—the excruciating realization of guilt, worthlessness, and depravity. At this stage, the awakened sinner might chafe at the severity of God's law and condemnation. He or she frequently rebelled against God and uttered exclamations of anger and enmity toward divine justice—the prospect of eternal damnation. Next, the sinner entered a stage of agonized selflessness and acceptance of divine power. The humbled soul, stripped of pride and repentant of sin, opened his or her heart to receive the ravishing seal of grace through the infusion of the Holy Spirit. With a new heart turned toward godly affections, the sinner received new birth as a child of God who would devote life to progressive sanctification in obedience to divine law and universal disinterested benevolence to build the Redeemer's Kingdom in America. These new men and women embodied the ideals of republican liberty—a dutiful willingness to sacrifice self-interest for the commonweal. The regenerate would embrace godly living and virtue in a society that was increasingly characterized by the individualism of a competitive market economy.[17]

The revival envisioned the formation of a new imagined community of saints across two continents in the Atlantic world and specifically devoted to building the Kingdom of God in America. New Divinity theology championed an unbridled optimism as believers anticipated the dawning of a millennial age where regenerate Christians worked indefatigably to wins souls to Christ and remake and reform society in voluntary societies that institutionalized Christian benevolence.[18] Thus, the Second Great Awakening provided the impetus for numerous religious innovations, including the Sunday School Movement, domestic and foreign missions, temperance societies, and other charitable and reform initiatives.[19]

Connecticut had experienced more than two generations of population exodus as succeeding generations migrated to the frontiers of Vermont, New Hampshire, and central and western New York. These migrations paralleled the voluntary Indian removals to Brothertown and New Stockbridge in New York. White settlers desired inexpensive land and economic opportunity. For the Congregational orthodoxy left behind, this exodus from New England meant the loss of kin, friends, and congregants and anxiety about how to "keep the covenant" with these migrants on the frontier "wilderness."[20] By the 1790s, more than two hundred settlements that Connecticut evangelicals viewed as their "destitute children and neighbors" were without settled ministers who would transmit the faith of the fathers and reaffirm the Puritan ethic of collective responsibility, self-control, and communal harmony.[21] From 1790 to 1830, more than eight hundred thousand New Englanders had migrated to the frontier from the Hudson to the Mississippi Rivers.[22] To remedy this situation and promote the Redeemer's Kingdom, the Connecticut Missionary Society (CMS) was formed in 1795. Domestic ministers who traveled to the "wilderness" as missionaries expected to find heathens, infidels, scoffers, ministers of Satan from opposing denominations, and a hostile anticlerical climate of irreligion. The CMS employed 148 missionaries in Vermont, New York, Pennsylvania, Ohio, and the Northwest Territory in this period in their struggle to transplant Congregational orthodoxy when confronted with Methodist and Baptist proselytizers and the indifference of the emigrants to religion.[23]

Missionaries imagined their journey as an epic adventure that would test their mettle and their commitment to disinterested benevolence as they labored in the spirit of David Brainerd.[24] As Joseph A. Conforti explains, "the *Life of Brainerd* thus became a spiritual touchstone for missionaries who used it to test the genuineness of their commitment to disinterested benevolence. Enduring the physical and emotional hardships of missionary work, as Brainerd had, was one element of this test; facing the prospect of death, especially from disease, was another."[25]

The sublime hopes of the religious awakening rested upon the foundation of winning souls en masse. However, conversion and the new birth represented only one moment in forging a godly life. Christians needed to devote themselves methodically and tirelessly to making a life of spiritual pilgrimage. Ever vigilant of human frailty and sinfulness, the regenerate practiced daily piety through self-examination, prayer, meditation, and reading the Bible and other devotional books. Only after a life of godly living could the believer find what Richard Baxter termed the saint's everlasting rest and the psychological comfort of assurance of salvation. Until then, each believer was at times beset with an awareness of the tentativeness of the state of grace. Not infrequently, the newly regenerate lapsed into agonized doubt about self-deception and hypocrisy.[26] This spiritual pilgrimage and the travail of making a godly life structured the marrow of divinity for evangelical personhood.

The *Connecticut Evangelical Magazine* and many other periodicals published accounts of local revivals and testimonials of conversion, authenticating the awakening as an outpouring of the Holy Spirit that avoided the excesses and religious enthusiasm of the Great Awakening in the 1740s. These published conversion narratives and spiritual biographies provided the models of the sinner's pilgrimage to new birth, charting the spiritual itinerary for others to follow.

Asahel Nettleton's (1783–1844) reconversion while at Yale during a college revival of religion in 1808 captured the lived experience of new birth that was later published for the edification of all inquirers. Nettleton, already reborn after a ten-month struggle in 1800, intended to commit his life to missionary work. He labored in the college revival, exhorting his fellow students. In the midst of this spiritual hothouse, Nettleton began to question the genuineness of his own conversion and sought comfort in the works of Edwards's *On Religious Affections* and Edwards's unpublished sermons on regeneration provided to him by President Timothy Dwight of Yale. Bennett Tyler writes, "The all-absorbing question resting on his mind by day and night, mingled with many sighs, tears, and groans, was, am I a child of God?"[27]

Nettleton lapsed into a spiritual despondency, taking to bed and refusing to eat. He charged himself with hypocrisy and deceit. "A few Christian friends lingered about the bed of the agonizing and despairing sinner; and many were the prayers offered, that the balm of Gilead might be applied to the wounded spirit."[28] After a week of starvation and suffering, Nettleton was near death. President Dwight was summoned to the bedside and offered pastoral care, reassuring Nettleton of the infinite fullness of Jesus. "A sweet serenity seemed to steal over the agitated sinner's mind—a serenity which was the harbinger of a joy . . . and was 'unspeakable and full of glory.'"[29] Nettleton took a leave of absence to convalesce before returning to complete his studies at Yale.

This study reconstructs the lives, mentalities, and aspirations of people who embraced the evangelical piety exemplified by Nettleton. These men and women became missionaries and willingly shouldered the arduous demands of conversion. They forged lives devoted to disinterested benevolence and the missionary spirit of the New Divinity and embraced the highest ideals of religious identity and vocation. Converted and reborn through the moral machinery in an era of revivals, their religious personhood was forged in the crucible of evangelical culture. They wanted to devote their lives to the fulfillment of ultimate values: embracing a religious vocation of disinterested benevolence as missionaries who would redeem the souls of perishing heathens and thus help build the Kingdom of God in America.

Irving D. Yalom, a contemporary existential psychotherapist, can assist us in understanding the lived experience and predicaments of the Protestant missionaries in this study. Drawing upon insights from psychotherapy, philosophy, and medicine, he maintains existential psychotherapy "ministers to human despair" that is inextricably connected to the human condition: death, isolation, the search for meaning, and the pursuit of human agency and freedom.[30] He suggests that our relationships in families, kinship networks, and communities as well as the directives of our cultural milieu frequently fail to protect us from death anxiety. Yalom explains in *Staring at the Sun* that those who suffer debilitating anxiety over death "might have encountered too much death at too early a stage of life; they may have failed to experience a center of love, caring, and safety in their home, they may have been isolated as individuals who never shared their intimate moral concerns; they may have been hypersensitive, particularly self-aware individuals who have rejected the death-denying religious myths proffered by their culture."[31]

While existential psychotherapy adopts a perspective that speaks to a universal, invariant human condition, ethnohistory investigates the particulars of intercultural encounters between groups who are the carriers of distinctive cultures and social orders situated in a particular time and place. In the antebellum period, American Protestant missionaries embraced highly individuated structures of religious personhood that cultivated a heightened sensitivity to the brevity of life and the obsessive need to seek otherworldly salvation. A common diary notation for New Year's Day might read, "Another year closer to the grave." Would the faithful be ready when death found them?

In Yalom's terms, it is ironic that those "death-denying religious myths" intended to assuage existential anxiety about mortality exacerbated death anxiety. Evangelical culture placed a premium on becoming a hypersensitive, self-aware, and introspective believer who cultivated an inner spiritual life through the daily practice of piety and methodical self-examination. As a result, many who embraced evangelical religious personhood suffered from acute, unremitting death anxiety. Reverend David Brainerd (1718–1747) became an important exemplar of evangelical religious personhood, a life devoted to the missionary spirit, and one who had embarked on a spiritual pilgrimage characterized by the extremes of devotional piety: recurring religious melancholy and self-loathing and death anxiety punctuated by interludes of religious ecstasy—contemplations of the savior. Norman Pettit describes Brainerd's "joyless determination to persevere as a missionary. He appeared at times to crave death more that he cherished life."[32] The diaries reveal a life fraught with melancholy, anguish, and despair.

Brainerd was born in Haddam, Connecticut, in 1718, entered Yale College in 1739, and was expelled in 1742 for questioning the grace of a college tutor during Brainerd's participation in a college revival and New Light enthusiasm. In the remaining six years of life before his death from tuberculosis, he completed his preparation for the ministry, received ordination, and worked as a Presbyterian missionary to Mahicans in Kaunaumeek (near Stockbridge, Massachusetts) and to Leni Lenapes (Delawares) in Forks of the Delaware (near present-day Easton, Pennsylvania) and Crossweeksung and Bethel near Trenton, New Jersey.[33]

He embodied Yalom's characterization of those who suffer from acute death anxiety. Brainerd was a hypersensitive child, marked by a religious precocity. He remembers that at eight years of age, "[he] became something concerned for my soul, and terrified at the thoughts of death." At age sixteen, in 1832, he witnessed too much death in a local epidemic and the untimely death of his mother. Consistent with evangelical child-rearing practices, he did not experience what Yalom identifies as "a center of love, caring, and safety" at home.[34]

Brainerd practiced methodical self-examination that revealed indwelling sin that was resolved by interludes of selfless submission to God. Chronicling the maturation of his piety at age twenty following his conversion experience, he languished for months with unrelieved heroic inner torment, tortured with self-loathing, alienation from God, and the vileness of his sin. Secret prayer, meditation, fasting, self-examination, and wrestling with God revealed fresh evidence of sin, pride, wickedness in his heart, and an abandonment by God. This practice of piety prepared Brainerd for the eventual resolution of this spiritual distress that he found in "the sweetness of communion with my dear Saviour."[35] He wrote of numerous interludes of religious ecstasy: "My soul was so captivated and delighted with the excellency, the loveliness and the greatness and other perfections of God that I was even swallowed up in him."[36] While at Yale College in 1740, he enjoyed a release from religious melancholy through the contemplation of the crucified Christ: "My soul was filled with light and love, indeed I was almost in an ecstasy and my body so weak I could scarcely stand. Oh, the tenderness and endearing love I felt toward all mankind."[37]

The moments of assurance and spiritual comfort did not abide and the alternation between religious melancholy and ecstasy continued for the remainder of his life. As a result of these spiritual exercises, Brainerd's heart overflowed with acosmic love, and he frequently reported a renewed commitment to his religious vocation of converting the heathen, of redoubling his efforts at godly conduct (progressive sanctification) as captured by Edwards's notion of universal disinterested benevolence. He welcomed the great sufferings in the cause of Christ among the heathen, anticipating the creation of "a mountain of holiness"—an evangelical Christian Indian commonwealth forged in the religious excitement of the Great Awakening.[38] He exclaimed early in his missionary career, "Had raised hopes today respecting the heathen. Oh, that God would bring in great numbers of them to Jesus Christ! I can't but hope I shall see that glorious day."[39]

Jonathan Edwards published *The Life of David Brainerd* in 1749, editing and compiling Brainerd's diaries with the purpose of demonstrating an authentic New Light conversion. Edwards's publication became an evangelical classic, achieving mass appeal more than seventy-five years later during the Second Great Awakening with the American Tract Society 1833 edition. Conforti argues that this work influenced John Wesley and American Methodists and shaped the experience and expectations of a generation of foreign and domestic missionaries who trained at Yale and Andover Theological Seminary.[40] James R. Rohrer argues in *Keepers of the Covenant*,

> Brainerd's example inspired missionary efforts on two continents. In 1798 John Love, Secretary of the London Missionary Society, expressed his hope that New England might produce a "host" of Brainerds, "by whose exertions the whole American wilderness may become a field of blessings, a vineyard of red wine, a garden of heavenly pleasures and fruit."[41]

Succeeding generations of missionaries published memoirs and letters in the burgeoning evangelical press and religious periodicals. They forged new links in an unending chain of religious intelligence that credited David Brainerd as their model of inner piety and missionary vocation. Brainerd's temperament and proclivity to religious melancholy and meditative retreat from the world, combined with the prescriptions of evangelical personhood, provided an exemplar of how to forge a godly life.

This model of piety shaped the experiences and aspirations of countless foreign and domestic Protestant missionaries. David W. Kling argues, "For ABCMF missionaries, the *Life of Brainerd* became the spiritual yardstick by which to measure the fidelity of their own willingness to endure physical, emotional, and spiritual hardship—and yes, even a Hopkinsian willingness to die for the greater glory of God."[42]

Brainerd's model of evangelical personality consisted of four distinctive elements:

1. After traversing the morphology of conversion—turning away from worldly depravity and toward God through new birth (regeneration of the heart), each neophyte continued an inward spiritual pilgrimage alternating between hope and despair, at times experiencing an innerworldly mystical illumination of the Holy Spirit only to later encounter times of abandonment by God. Believers were denied the comfort of the unwavering assurance of grace.
2. Believers imposed upon themselves a harsh ascetic discipline, refusing to surrender to the sensuous pleasures of the world. They practiced a piety that prescribed methodical self-examination to identify evidence of sin and declension and, through evangelical humiliation, sought renewed repentance and reconciliation with God.
3. Those who emulated Brainerd lived in dynamic tension between longing for seasons of private prayer and meditative withdrawal from the world and the need for active missionary engagement.
4. Brainerd provided an exemplar of spiritual discipline that fostered the growth of personal piety and progressive sanctification given the everpresent realization of the brevity and fragility of human existence.

Max Weber's definition of the religious virtuoso and inner-worldly asceticism applied to David Brainerd. The virtuoso adopted a type of religious life order and stance toward the world where the believer commits the entirety of his or her life to the fulfillment of a vocation. He explains,

> The religious virtuoso can be placed in the world as an instrument of a God and cut off from all magical means of salvation. At the same time, it is imperative for the virtuoso that he "prove" himself before God as being called *solely* through the ethical quality of his conduct in this world. This actually means that he "prove" himself to himself as well. No matter how much of the "world" as such is religiously devalued and rejected as being creatural and a vessel of sin, yet psychologically the world is all the more affirmed as the theatre of God-willed activity in one's worldly "calling."[43]

Religious virtuosity demanded heroism and the cultivation of an intense and unrelenting spirituality that could not be sustained by most believers who emulated Brainerd. As a case in point, Reverend Gideon Hawley (1727–1807) graduated from Yale College in 1749, and after ordination in 1755 he served as a schoolteacher at the Mahican Stockbridge Mission in 1752 under the sponsorship of Jonathan Edwards, where Hawley embraced Brainerd's practice of piety. Hawley forged his religious identity on Brainerd's model of piety during an unsuccessful mission to the Oneidas at Oquaga in 1753 and at the start of his mission to the Mashpee Plantation in 1757. As a young man approaching thirty, his diaries reveal the piety of a melancholy saint: meditation and prayer, self-examination, repentance, and continued humiliation before divine law and Providence. Writing on February 16, 1757, he reports, "My spirits are down. . . . I have observed the conduct of Divine Providence respecting my mission and I think that a multitude of coincident circumstances conspired to give me sufficient sight to quit it."[44]

Hawley kept this spiritual journal for two years, in the spirit of Brainerd, chronicling his inner journey, recording a seemingly endless story of self-doubt and despondency, meditating on living each day with the awareness that death was near. At times Hawley found serenity when he submitted to God's will. However, after two years, he married and entered into the arduous roles of householder, minister, missionary, and tribal overseer to the Mashpees. Hawley no longer kept a spiritual diary. In the face of the arduous labors of preaching and pastoral care, riding horseback hours each day to tend to his congregation and fulfill his duties as colonial administrator, Hawley no longer wrote of the inward struggles of religious melancholy or the practice of piety in the spirit of David Brainerd. He now kept meticulous accounts of church construction, funds received and spent on indigent Mashpees, lumber and goods sold from tribal lands, and other secular, administrative matters. Hawley no longer pursued the spiritual hothouse and religious virtuosity in the spirit of David Brainerd.

The stories of Reverends David Bacon, Samuel Allis, William Hervey, Edmund Franklin Ely, and others that we will examine in this study suggest that these true believers ventured forth with a copy of *The Life of Brainerd* as their companion and guide. They emulated Brainerd's devotional piety and embraced his unwavering devotion to a missionary vocation in the service of acosmic love as they struggled to civilize and Christianize perishing heathens.

In this manner, missionary men and women championed the zeitgeist of evangelical America, anticipating that the conversion of Native peoples would help build a millennial Redeemer's Kingdom of God. Without a calculation of the costs, they left the comfort of church, family, and friends in their natal communities for the arduous conditions of the frontier, ever mindful of the perils of sickness, early death, and religious melancholy. They devoted their lives to quixotic journeys westward to distant frontiers in Indian lands in the upper Midwest and the Arkansas Territory, seeking to fulfill these ultimate concerns. Brainerd's model of devotional piety alternated religious melancholy and ecstasy, which exacerbated their death anxiety while simultaneously reassuring believers that their heroic suffering would hasten the millennial day, thus creating a sublime vision of collective salvation. We will inquire: how successful were these missionaries in sustaining Brainerd's ideal of religious virtuosity and innerworldly asceticism?

The first three chapters of this study are devoted to the stories and travails of Protestant missionary men and women. Chapter 1 retells the life of David Bacon and his wife, Alice, lay missionaries sent by the Connecticut Missionary Society to evangelize Ojibwes in Mackinaw in Michigan's Lower Peninsula from 1802 to 1804. When this mission failed, Bacon worked briefly as a domestic missionary in the Ohio Reserve and helped found the town of Tallmadge, Ohio, as an experiment to create a covenanted church community for migrants from Connecticut and New England.

Chapter 2 uncovers the story of a missionary woman from the Union Mission to the Osages (founded in 1820 by the UFMS and later absorbed by the ABCFM). She returned to Connecticut in 1825 suffering from the debilitating effects of malaria and religious melancholy and was admitted for care at the Hartford Retreat, a newly opened private asylum for the insane.

Chapter 3 investigates the endless chain of religious intelligence, the mass publications of memoirs, correspondence, and accounts of foreign and domestic missions published in the evangelical press about ventures to India, the Middle East, South Africa, and Hawaii and among Indians in the Southeast and throughout America. Each inspirational tale provided a familiar formula: religious fervor in the spirit of Brainerd, sacrifice and suffering as champions of the missionary spirit, and illness frequently resulting in untimely death. We will recover the lives of Sarah Smith, Reverend Henry Martyn, Mrs. Harriet Newell, Adoniram and Ann Hasseltine Judson, Samuel John Mills, William Hervey, Mrs. Susanna Champion, Hannah Moore, and many others. Sublime hope as workers in the vineyard of the Lord and religious melancholy characterized these missionary lives. We will explore the varieties of religious virtuosity for women who appropriated Brainerd's model of a missionary vocation. How did the experience of gender and the ideals of femininity in this era differentiate the experiences of these missionary women from those of the men?

Today, in an age marked by growing disaffiliation from organized religion in America, we marvel at religious vocation, at identities forged in the crucible of revivals by those committed to reshaping their selves, communities, and society guided by transcendent and ultimate concerns. The heroics of religious virtuosity and the tortured religious psychology inspired by Brainerd's model of piety appear foreign to contemporary sensibilities.

Yet, despite the distance of two centuries and the pervasive secularism of our contemporary civil society, nineteenth-century missionaries and neophytes achieved "modern identities" that share elements in common with those of contemporary Americans.

Charles Taylor's *Sources of the Self* identifies the distinctive characteristics of the culture of modernity built upon a foundation of the Protestant Reformation, the Enlightenment, and other depth-historical developments in the West, what the French Annales School term the longue durée. Modern selves, dating from the seventeenth century, share three distinguishing features: first, a capacity for self-reflection, inwardness and interiority; second, incessant self-expression through written memoirs, diary-keeping, correspondence, poetry, and other modalities; and third, self-realization and emotional fulfillment in intimate friendships, companionate marriages, parenting, and the asceticism of work in a mundane calling.[45]

Today, the content of self-reflection, self-expression, and self-actualization are decidedly different. But the dynamics of selfhood and identity persist. Like contemporary selves, the lives and identities of white and Indian Protestants in this study are constituted by self-reflection, self-expression, and self-actualization through family, kinship, and a mundane calling or vocation. Then and now, narcissism characterized self and identity.

The devotional piety of Brainerd and Edwardsean divinity cultivated a continual personal relationship with God through the elaboration of the transmoral conscience—a personal conscience and spiritual consciousness informed by the soul's inner light that was independent of pastoral direction or control by denominational or local church and community authority. As I have written, "like the romantic lover caught in the throes of passion and misery, pining and longing for the lost or unattainable love object, so the narcissism of the transmoral conscience evokes a litany of self-absorbed, self-reflective emotions, experiences, joy, and agonies, alone on the stage in the cosmic drama with God."[46]

Today, after two centuries have passed, we have difficulty developing an empathetic understanding of this religious intelligence and the aspirations, expectations, and lived experiences of missionary men and women who committed their lives to the fulfillment of the Great Commission.

But we need to engage these missionaries who forged their identities in the crucible of revivals and the emulation of Brainerd. What then did they anticipate in the encounter with Native peoples on the frontier? In their estimation, how would indigenous peoples receive these messages of evangelical religion and "civilization?" A work of contemporary fiction can assist us.

Michel Faber's *The Book of Strange New Things* is a contemporary novel about the colonization of an alien planet that was given the place name Oasis, and their indigenous inhabitants were called Oasans by a global corporate conglomerate, USIC. The Earth colonists depended upon indigenous labor for their food supply. In exchange, the Oasans made two demands: the services of a non-denominational Protestant missionary to instruct them in the Bible that they referred to as "the book of strange new things" and deliveries of over-the-counter pain medications.

The Oasans readily accepted the Christian narrative of a savior-prophet who came to redeem all of creation from sin, suffering, and the finality of death. Oasans eagerly and without resistance read and committed to memory portions of the King James Bible provided for them. With great individual and collective sacrifice, these neophytes who identified themselves as "Jesus Lovers" labored to build a church in their settlement.

Language differences would not prove an impediment to Oasans and colonists. Speaking to their new missionary, pastor Peter, in a heavily accented English, the Jesus Lovers proclaim an abiding faith: "We will have no other God but God our Saviour. In Him alone we have hope of Life."[47] This uncritical and open-hearted acceptance of Christian cosmology and the role that Jesus played in redeeming all of creation that included humanity and extra-terrestrial aliens, fulfilled the sublime aspirations that have motivated missionaries in all times and places. Peter voices a missionary rationale—an idealized, almost fantastical account of his effortless success with the Oasans:

> It was what any Christian pastor might yearn to hear from a new convert, yet hearing it so baldly stated, so calmly, was a bit unsettling. Ministering to Oasans was a joy, but Peter couldn't help thinking that it was

too easy. Or was it? Why *shouldn't* it be easy? When the window of the soul was clear, not smeared and tarnished with the accumulated muck of deviousness and egomania and self-loathing, there was nothing to stop the light from shinning in. Yes, maybe that was it.[48]

Peter examines this issue from the point of view of the individual neophyte, stripped of artifice, open to the manifest truth of doctrine. What Peter fails to acknowledge is a cultural dimension where indigenous peoples have their own cosmology, spirituality, theodicy, and systems of meaning that address the ultimate concerns of existence: good and evil, suffering and ill fortune, the purpose of life, and what happens in death. Oasans, caught in these webs of symbolic meanings, are also enmeshed in social worlds of kinship and village and the performance of ritual and ceremony to address the sacred and the numinous. And Oasans would tend to deemphasize solitary individualism and define their identity through a complex nexus of family, extended kinship, and village affiliations.

Faber's fictional depiction of the ethnohistorical encounter between Natives and missionaries is not realistic. However, the novel presents an enduring fantasy of the unquestioning receptivity and acceptance of the Christian message by Natives in a colonial situation from the point of view of the Protestant missionary. Here, Natives acquiesce to invasion by foreigners and land dispossession with a docile acceptance of powerlessness. Oasans toil to produce foodstuffs for the colonists in exchange for medicines and missionaries.

As the story unfolds, Peter discovers that these indigenous creatures have fragile bodies where a seemingly minor injury, cut, or bruise brings catastrophic and often fatal consequences. The Oasans dress in padded, hooded garments, booted and gloved with no exposed skin. Peter observed their caution: "Oasans handle sewing-needles with the same care and respect that humans might handle chainsaws or blowtorches. Each stitch was such a ponderous ritual that he couldn't bear to watch."[49]

The Oasans embraced what they termed "the Technique of Jesus," the promise of salvation and victory over death or "returning to the ground." Peter discovered their affinity for selective passages of scripture. "*Nothing shall hurt you*, said Luke. *When thou walkest through the fire, thou shalt not be burned*, said Isaiah. *The Lord healeth all thy diseases*, said *Psalms*. There it was: there it was[,] . . . the perpetual reprieve the Oasans called 'The Technique of Jesus.'"⁵⁰

While conversion offered salvation from the terrors of death and bodily suffering, USIC pain medications helped sufferers palliate suffering and manage the injuries that ended their brief lives. Christian teachings provided for the Native population what Max Weber terms the rational theodicy of suffering and dying. Weber argues, "The idea of redemption, as such, is very old, if one understands by it a liberation from distress, hunger, drought, sickness, and ultimately from suffering and death."⁵¹

Faber's novel captures with clarity and consistency not a twenty-first-century sensibility but rather the logic of the missionary spirit and the mentalities of missionaries who ventured forth to redeem perishing heathens in the nineteenth century. In past times, missionaries discounted Native belief and ceremony and anticipated that, when confronted with the manifest superiority of Christian teachings, indigenous peoples would eagerly abandon their religious worldview, cosmology, theodicy of good and evil, understanding of the meaning of life, and what happens to the person following death. Protestant theology and teachings would thus expunge "false beliefs" and superstitions and inscribe true religion on the tabula rasa of Native minds. Missionaries understood their vocation: they endeavored to bring the light of the Gospel to illuminate "heathen darkness," to offer a handbook for godly living that sanctified Native lives, and to assist neophytes in the morphology of conversion with the joyous anticipation of salvation and Christian paradise after death. Unlike the fictional super-receptive Oasans, those whom missionaries in the nineteenth century encountered were not eager, receptive, and uncritical Natives who abandoned all traditional belief and lifeways in favor of the teachings of a book of strange new things. Actual indigenous communities proved recalcitrant or selectively appropriated parts of the Christianization and the plan of civilization. The majority of Natives tenaciously clung to their lifeways and traditional practices and ceremonial life, hoping to remain on ancestral lands. The book of strange new things captivated few, although a mixed-race elite and so-called progressives desired mission schools and literacy for themselves and their children for personal advancement in the market-commercial economy as American hegemony replaced the waning of French and British influence. Many adopted Christian Indian identities as an accommodation and defensive strategy when confronted with settler colonialism and the threat of dispossession and removal.

The final three chapters of this study are devoted to Native neophytes, Christian Indians who represented the first fruits of these missionary endeavors. Chapter 4 recounts the story of an Osage youth given to the Union Mission by a peace chief to solidify their alliance. K traveled to the Cornwall Foreign Mission School in Connecticut to further his education, and he was admitted in 1827 to an asylum for the insane, suffering from religious mania and melancholy following the scandal and controversy occasioned by the interracial marriage of the Cherokee scholar Elias Boudinot to the daughter of a local merchant that resulted in the closing of the school. Eventually K completed his education, experienced conversion, and returned to his tribe to work as a missionary, only to succumb to an early death from tuberculosis. Chapter 5 revisits the lives of Cherokee neophytes, the first converts of the Brainerd Mission in Tennessee that included Catharine and David Brown and John Arch. The first fruit of the Springplace Moravian mission to the Cherokees in Georgia reconstructs the life of Margaret Scott Vann, a member of a mixed-race elite group, and her subsequent conversion as Sister Margaret Ann. She envisioned creating a Christian Indian church community, a *Brüdergemeine* that might resist forced removal and revitalize Cherokee community and sovereignty. Chapter 6 explores the Chippewa-Métis (mixed-race) elite groups in Mackinaw and the Michigan Territory in the 1820s with a focus on the Native women who converted in the revival of 1829 and the remarkable life of the métis author, poet, and folklorist Jane Johnston Schoolcraft.

Religious intelligence in this age of revivals published the letters, memoirs, and writings of many Native converts, capturing the marrow of their divinity and their aspirations, in their own words, as they forged evangelical Protestant selves. They encountered the national policy initiatives of the plan of civilization and missionization and Indian removal to the lands on the Western frontier. Christian Indians struggled with the these public issues and the challenges of their new identities as they advocated for their kindred, community, and tribe given the transformations of colonization and Americanization that threatened their ancestral homelands and traditional lifeways.

As a historical sociologist, I have delighted in discovering and recovering interesting and significant stories of patients treated in early nineteenth-century asylums and the lives of missionaries and neophytes from publications and archives long removed from our collective memory. Some of these missionaries and Native neophytes are the subjects of important new scholarship, while others have remained hidden in the historical record. But together they need to be seen as representative lives, as men and women who appropriated aspects of an emerging American identity—evangelical personhood informed by the missionary spirit. They devoted their lives to convert perishing heathens. And those Christian Indian converts, in turn, would strive as missionaries and interpreters to complete the conversion of their families, villages and bands. White missionary men and women and indigenous neophytes, respectively, lived with heroic, tragic, and melodramatic fervor. Their stories merit retelling to remind us of how evangelical Protestant culture helped shape American identity—how missionaries and Christian Indians, respectively, forged their lives and found meaning and purpose in the fulfillment of religious values of ultimate concern.

1

The Travails of David Bacon

"A Humble Missionary of the Cross"

Reverend David Bacon's headstone contains the following epitaph:

A HUMBLE MISSIONARY OF THE CROSS,
who, having passed through
many scenes of suffering in his efforts to extend
THE REDEEMER'S KINGDOM,
entered into his rest
August 27th, A. D. 1817,
IN THE 46th YEAR OF HIS AGE.[1]

Bacon exemplified the sublime millennial aspirations of building the Redeemer's Kingdom in America as an early missionary licensed and commissioned by the Connecticut Missionary Society (CMS) to evangelize and convert Indians. He set his sights on the Ojibwes from L'Arbre Croche, a settlement on Lake Michigan, who made the thirty-mile seasonal migration each spring to Mickilimakinac (Mackinaw Island), Michigan, to sell furs in order to acquire trade goods. Mackinaw was located at the tip of Michigan's Lower Peninsula on a strait strategically situated between Lake Huron and Lake Michigan. From 1802 until 1804, Bacon resided in Mackinaw Village each fall and winter and struggled without success to build a mission station and farm in the interior of the island during the spring and summer. Writing to Nathan Strong of the CMS, Bacon expressed a "hope of eventual success," knowing that excerpts from his quarterly correspondence would reach publics in America and across the Atlantic. He explains, "We make publick through the Christian world, by means of our [Connecticut] Evangelical Magazine. You will obtain the approbation of the good wishes of all good people especially of those who are contributing for my support, and earnestly praying for my success."[2]

Consistent with the divine commandment to seek the Kingdom of Heaven and salvation, he intended to change Native peoples into temperate and industrious "*real Christians.*" It was Bacon's belief that "Christ has commanded ministers to go into all the world, & preach the gospel." Despite "the unfavorable appearances which I shall probably meet with at first," he remained confident the mission would bring Natives "out of heathenish darkness into marvelous light."[3]

However, less than one year later, in July 1804, he would welcome being recalled from Michigan to assist in home missions of New England emigrants in New Connecticut in the Western Reserve of Ohio. Bacon wrote, "I am disposed to make almost any sacrifice rather than remain much longer in this ungodly place, where I can have no hope of doing good, & must be living at a great expense. I am also heartsick of worldly entanglements."[4] These worldly entanglements included failing as a farmer and abandoning an unfinished log cabin in the woods that was planned as a mission station. Bacon was continually rebuffed when he appealed to Ojibwes, who had little interest in this mission. He never became proficient in their language and failed to secure an interpreter to facilitate his preaching. He staggered under the burden of supporting his wife and children on a frontier island populated by an American military garrison, Yankee and French fur traders and voyageurs, and settlers who were indifferent to evangelical outreach.

Not surprisingly his evangelical fervor turned to despair. Despite the CMS expenditure of almost twenty-five hundred dollars, he had little to show for his years in the field. He had repeatedly promised to establish a mission school, church, or model farming village (like the Moravian settlement in Fairfield, on the Thames River in Ontario) that would attract Indian neophytes. Leonard Bacon, David's brother, informed him that the CMS board had lost faith in their missionary. Writing on September 10, 1804, Leonard Bacon explained,

> The fact is that they [the CMS board] have for a long time been dissatisfied with your conduct—the continued series of disappointments which have uniformly succeeded to the prospects of success you have so frequently and sanguinely announced—tended to beget and strengthen in their mind a conviction that your schemes were *visionary & chimerical*, and that you were wasting their funds.[5] (emphasis added)

David Bacon's life and journey exemplify the central ideals of the missionary spirit and the fate of the religious fervor of many true believers whose schemes did seem unrealistic and chimerical to those looking for tangible results. His story bears retelling. He was born in Woodstock, Connecticut, in 1771 as the third son and fifth of six children to Joseph Bacon of Stoughton, Massachusetts, and Abigail Holmes of Woodstock; little is known of his childhood. During his youth he was a partner in a spinning wheel factory in Troy, New York, and when this business failed, he taught school in Washington County, New York. In 1799 he returned to Mansfield, Connecticut, to reside with his family. During a religious awakening in this local congregation, fostered by Reverend John Sherman and Richard Salter, Bacon "owned" the covenant of grace and joined the church.[6] As recounted by his son, David embraced the evangelical classic *The Life of David Brainerd* as a guide to vital, experiential piety, and as a model for making an authentic Christian life. Leonard Bacon explains of his father that "from the beginning of his own new life his soul was fired by the example of Brainerd's self-consecration and self-sacrifice. He felt that to labor, like Brainerd, in the service of the Gospel among the most benighted of his fellow-men, was the highest vocation to which he could aspire. He determined that, if it were possible, he would be a missionary to the Indians."[7]

At the age of twenty-eight with no formal training in divinity or a college education, he could not work as a minister or missionary in a Congregational or Presbyterian congregation. However, the trustees of the CMS in the inaugural issue of the *Connecticut Evangelical Magazine*, in July 1800, published their plan to send a missionary to the Indian tribes bordering Lake Erie. They wished to recruit an emissary who would first visit Reverend John Sergeant Jr. in Stockbridge, Massachusetts, who would provide a guide and interpreter. Next, the pilgrim would travel to Seneca lands and receive a formal message of welcome and exhortation that he would later deliver to persuade these tribes in the Western Reserve to accept a mission. Since New Light ministers with settled congregations were reluctant to leave Connecticut for the frontier, the trustees decided "that a discreet man, animated by the love of God and souls, of a good common education, who can be obtained for a moderate compensation, be sought to travel among the Indian tribes south and west of Lake Erie, to explore their situation, and learn their feelings with respect to Christianity, and, so far as he has opportunity, to teach them its doctrines and duties."[8]

Bacon was to be named as this emissary and eagerly prepared for this unusual licensure and missionary vocation by studying theology with three ministers: Levi Hart, Samuel Nott, and Zebulon Ely. Reverend Ely's son wrote, "I have a fresh remembrance of your father, in his black deer-skin breeches, where he studied theology with my father."[9]

David wrote to his brother in a letter dated August 7, 1800, as he began a four-month journey, explaining that the trustees of the CMS licensed him as a missionary after careful examination "with respect to his knowledge of the doctrines of Christianity and his experiential acquaintance with the truth, were fully satisfied with his answers."[10] Modestly prepared in New Divinity theology and acknowledged as a new born child of God, he began his religious vocation, carefully recording his receipt of a salary of one hundred ten cents per day, additional money provided for an interpreter, a one-hundred-dollar draft for expenses, and a small Bible presented to him by the CMS (valued at $2.12 ½).

Those who attended his examination and prayer service openly wept as Dr. Benjamin Trumbull began the first prayer. Bacon recounted this affecting scene as he prepared for his solitary journey on foot: "They were all in tears, and expressed the tenderest affection and concern for me, and the most ardent desires for the salvation of the heathen. But I was insensible as steel. . . . But hope I shall ere long reap the happy fruits of their prayers, and praise God for the health of his countenance."[11]

The *Connecticut Evangelical Magazine* published his first letter from the field, dated September 4, announcing that he had arrived in Buffalo Creek (Buffalo, New York). Bacon had spent nearly a month traveling on foot about twenty-five miles each day, relying on the kindness of "both the friends and enemies of religion."[12] He arranged with the superintendent of Indian Affairs at Canandaigua, Captain Israel Chapin Jr., for an introduction to Seneca chiefs, who after two days of oratory, gift exchange and deliberation, provided Bacon with a string of wampum and a transcribed oratory of welcome that the minister intended to use to convince the Western Indians to accept Christianity. He reported, "They then shook hands with me, very affectionately wished me the blessing of the Great Spirit, and retired to their council house. The next day they met with me as they had proposed, their great orator [Red Jacket] in the midst of a large concourse of Indians delivered a speech to me, and another to write down to their Western brethren."[13] Unbeknownst to Bacon, Red Jacket's ceremonial salutation, gift exchange, and oratory were modeled after a condolence ceremony—ritual actions that wiped away the tears, cleared the eyes, and lifted sorrow from the hearts of those bereaved. These ceremonies also created or renewed bonds of friendship.[14]

The record of this address does not survive. Was Bacon aware of Red Jacket's cultural nativism and abiding rejection of Christianity?[15] Was the welcoming oratory intended to appease Bacon and hasten his departure from the Seneca reservation?

It is unclear whether Bacon knew about the Haudenosaunee, the six tribes of the People of the Longhouse: Oneidas, Cayugas, Onondagas, Mohawks, Tuscaroras, and Senecas who served as "keepers of the western door." During the War of Independence, the unity of the League of Peace and Power of the Six Nations was fractured as Oneida and Tuscarora tribes allied with the Patriot cause while Mohawks, Cayugas, Onondagas, and Senecas moved from neutrality to alliance with the British. In 1779 General George Washington ordered the invasion of Haudenosaunee lands in western New York by General John Sullivan and Colonel Daniel Brodhead. This "squaw campaign" amounted to total warfare that killed hundreds of women and children and destroyed entire villages, crops, orchards, and food caches.[16] The casualties, the starvation winter of 1779–80, and dysentery, measles, and smallpox resulted in a 50 percent loss of population between 1770 and 1797.[17]

The Treaty of Paris in 1783 viewed the Senecas as a conquered people and began a series of treaties that hastened land dispossession. In the Treaties of Fort Stanwix (1784), Canandaigua (1794), and Big Tree (1797) the Senecas relinquished all land claims to the Ohio country, acknowledged the sovereignty of the United States, and permitted the building of forts, roads, and trading houses. In exchange for the loss of many millions of acres of land in western New York, Ohio, and Pennsylvania, the Haudenosaunee received small cash payments and annuities for land purchases (Phelps-Gorham, 1788; Big Tree, 1797). The language of these treaties included the logic of forced acculturation through the process of "civilization": missions, schools, and the reliance on an agrarian economy in a reduced land base that prevented seasonal migration.

Red Jacket visited Hartford in 1795 and received fifteen hundred dollars from the Connecticut Land Company, extinguishing Seneca claims to "New Connecticut."[18] By the time of David Bacon's visit, the Seneca land base had been reduced to six small reserves, ranging from two to sixteen square miles along the Genesee River, and the larger reservations of Cattaraugus, Allegheny, Tonawanda, and Buffalo Creek.[19] Anthony F. C. Wallace describes these reserves as "slums in the wilderness" that suffered from depopulation, alcoholism, internecine violence, fear of witches, and a pervasive anomie and loss of confidence.[20]

His brief sojourn at Buffalo Creek did not call into question Bacon's distorted perception of Native groups as willing recipients of the Gospel who were eager to reap the benefits of schooling and literacy, and who demonstrated receptivity to a settled reservation life. Had Bacon tarried a few weeks longer until October he would have observed the encounter between Red Jacket and Reverend Elkanah Holmes, a missionary sent by the New York Missionary Society to evangelize, educate, and "civilize" the Senecas.

Holmes arrived at Seneca Castle on the Buffalo Creek reservation, a tract approximately fifty thousand acres bordering the shores of Lake Ontario, a remnant from the recent decades of land dispossession of the once vast holdings of Seneca land in western New York, Pennsylvania, and the Western Reserve of Ohio. Holmes requested permission to preach, which prompted laughter and ridicule, and as a gesture of disrespect, one young Seneca farted. The chiefs deliberated and permitted Holmes to preach. Red Jacket, known as Sagoyewatha ("He Keeps Them Awake") seemed obsequious as he lavished hospitality upon the missionary and introduced him with oratory of praise and forbearance:

> FATHER,
> WE are extremely happy that the Great Good Spirit has permitted us to meet together this day.... We thank the Great Spirit, who has put it into the minds of the great society of friendship at New-York, to send you to visit us. We also hope that the Great Spirit will always have his eyes over that good society, to strengthen their minds to have friendship towards the poor natives of this Island.... We are convinced that what they say of you is true, that you come purely out of love to do us good, and for nothing else; and that there is no deceit in your business, or in the good people that sent you.[21]

After Holmes delivered his message, Sagoyewatha continued his oratory by affirming the existence of a good and loving Great Spirit, a powerful omniscient creator deity. He questioned why white people had long ago condemned Jesus to death. Sagoyewatha disavowed any Native responsibility for this and other sins. He excoriated whites for taking Indian lands. He uttered this lament to Holmes: "Father, perhaps if we had such good people as you and your Society to have stepped in and advised us Indians, we and our forefathers would not have been so deceived by the white people for you have the great and good God always in your sight."[22] He lifted a fathom of wampum and promised to continue to polish bright the chain of friendship with the missionary society.

However, Sagoyewatha recounted the unending land dispossession that neither treaty nor schooling had prevented. He was astonished that whites, who themselves possessed the Bible, behaved with deceit and "do so many wicked things."[23] In this manner, speaking for the tribal council, he rebuffed Holmes and rejected the proposed mission and school.

Sagoyewatha delivered his most famous and best-articulated oratory of cultural nativism before a council of chiefs of the Six Nations in the summer of 1805 in response to Reverend Cram, who proposed a mission. Sagoyewatha articulated an account of the "separate creation"[24] by the Great Spirit of two races, red and white:

> There was a time when our forefathers owned this great island. Their seats extended from the rising to the setting sun. The Great Spirit had made it for the use of Indians. HE had created the buffalo, the deer, and other animals for food. HE had made the bear and the beaver. Their skins served us for clothing. HE had scattered them over the country, and taught us how to take them. HE had caused the earth to produce corn for bread. All this HE had done for is red children, because HE loved them. *But an evil day came upon us. Your forefathers crossed the great water and landed on this island.*[25] (emphasis added)

He retells the story of Native hospitality and generosity. "We gave them corn and meat, they gave us poison [ardent spirits] in return."[26] Whites invaded Iroquois homelands dispossessing the tribes. Wars and the ravages of liquor killed thousands. Sagoyewatha laments, "*Brother*; Our seats were once large and yours were small. You have now become a great people, and we have scarcely a place left to spread our blankets. You have got our country, but are not satisfied; you want to force your religion upon us."[27]

David Bacon left Buffalo Creek with his fathom of wampum, apparently having learned little about his Seneca hosts that would alter his abiding belief about the receptivity of Native peoples to missionary outreach. In actuality, however, the Senecas at Buffalo Creek as well as Native groups in the Western Reserve of Ohio and on the Great Lakes had little interest in missions and conversion, and only a practical interest in schools and English literacy for their children.

Bacon arranged passage on a boat that would take him to Detroit and on to Harson's Island on the St. Clair River by September 29. He reflected in his correspondence intended for publication the spirit of David Brainerd's introspective piety: "I have had nothing to trouble me since I left home but a hard and ungrateful heart. I do not recollect that I have had the least desire to turn back, but have felt as though I was going home."[28] He learned that an Ottawa village at L'Arbre Croche and Chippewa settlements on Lake Huron at Saginaw under the sachemship of Nanga might welcome a mission like the Moravian mission at Fairfield.

Moravians had built the Fairfield Mission (1792–1813) on a remote location on the Thames River in Ontario for Delawares, Nanticokes, Mahicans, Mohawks, and Chippewas. Sponsored by a land grant from the Anglican Society for the Propagation of the Gospel in Foreign Parts and located on Chippewa homelands, the mission began with one hundred and fifty Delaware Indians and six missionaries who found asylum when expelled from the United States during the Revolution. This pacifist, multicultural, and polyglot farming community resembled a traditional Native village. Christian Indians resided in extended households in the central village and farmed adjacent common cornfields. With a population that never exceeded two hundred, Fairfield's Christian Indians continued traditional seasonal lifeways of hunting, gathering, fishing, and maple sugaring. By 1813 when Fairfield was burned by American forces during the War of 1812, the mission had grown to forty-seven buildings including residences, a church, a smokehouse, a storehouse, stables, and hogsties.[29] Although Fairfield might offer the promise of material well-being and prosperity, the Moravian missionaries championed a religion of brotherliness that imposed a comprehensive system of rules for godly living and waged a relentless struggle against alcohol abuse as missionaries attempted to suppress traditional "heathen" practices of powwows, dances, feasts, and curing ceremonies.[30]

Nanga expressed his admiration for this mission. Bacon wrote, "He says that the Moravians have been the means of making the Delaware's sober, industrious, and happy, like the white people, and that he hopes that my endeavours will have the same effect on his Indians."[31] Bacon considered the Moravian mission enclave as a model for his future work.

Aided by General Uriah Tracey, formerly of Litchfield, Connecticut, and then Indian commissioner for the United States, and Indian agent Schieffelin, Bacon met with a "great council of Indians" on October 7. They expressed interest in a mission school. Writing for the evangelical public after this meeting, and unaware of Native resistance to evangelization, he exclaimed, "I have everything to support and animate me. I think the most sanguine have never dreamed of such an encouraging prospect. Surely the fields are white already to harvest!"[32]

However, he cut short his planned six-month survey of the field and began the arduous journey home, reaching Hartford early in December. Apparently, he did not have everything to support and animate him, as he had written in his published correspondence. He lacked a wife and helpmate and returned to marry Alice Parks.

The first issue of the *Connecticut Evangelical Magazine* in July 1800 published "A Letter from a Young Woman to Her Pastor Giving Some Account of the Exercises of Her Mind." The young woman, aged seventeen, was Alice Parks, and the pastor was Reverend Zebulon Ely, who was preparing Bacon for the ministry. Thus began their acquaintance, brief courtship, and marriage on December 24. Alice's letter penned in March recounts her morphology of conversion, which begins with a torturous three months of religious melancholy marked by a heightened consciousness of her sin and damnation. In this exemplary and formulaic testimony, Alice admits to possessing a hardened and vile heart. She cannot help herself and will her own salvation, and she expresses enmity that she must surrender to the will of God. She grew more despondent, mired in the belief that she had committed the unpardonable sin, having sinned away the possibility of grace. Alice lamented, "I thought myself to be the worst, the vilest of creatures. I was confident that never was such a monster on earth before.... I thought that I had grieved the Holy Spirit."[33]

She spent nearly a week in unrelenting mental anguish, despairing of life, when in a moment of selfless ecstasy, clutching her Bible, she found the infusion of grace in the contemplation of Jesus: "Worthy is the Lamb that was slain." Vowing to rededicate her life to serving God with her whole heart, she exclaimed, "O I saw such glory, such love in the sufferings of Christ that I cannot describe!"[34]

As Nancy Cott argues in *The Bonds of Womanhood*, many New England women in the period from 1780–1835 embraced the spiritual pilgrimage of forging religious personhood in the crucible of religious melancholy and conversion. The reborn child of God understood that the submission of self as an instrument of God's will was also an act of profound agency and self-assertion.[35] In 1800, before pervasive missionary intelligence, exemplars of missionary women, and the crystallization of the female religious role as missionary sister or wife, Alice Parks chose to leave the comforts of her family and New England home for a compelling vocation when she married David Bacon. Despite the struggles ahead, she agreed to assist him as a pious "true woman" in domesticity as his wife, a mother to his children, a helpmate, and a schoolteacher on the frontier. Cott is correct when she describes the feminization of Protestantism in the era of revivals, when women like Alice Parks embraced "a lifetime of purposeful struggle holding out heartening rewards. It provided a way to order one's life and priorities."[36]

The Missionary Society ordained Bacon on December 31 and gave him a commission to labor as an evangelist among the Indian Tribes, providing him with modest funding. He departed on February 11, 1801, with his bride and Beaumont Parks, Alice's brother, aged fifteen, who intended to learn Native languages and work as an interpreter. Traveling on horseback to Buffalo and through upper Canada before the spring thaw, delayed by poor weather and impassable roads, they arrived in Detroit in late May after visiting Fairfield or "Moravian Town."

Bacon recounts being inspired at meeting an elderly Delaware woman at Fairfield who as a child had been baptized by David Brainerd at the Forks of the Delaware Mission in Pennsylvania in the early 1740s. He wrote, "Having occasion to speak of Brainerd, as they were giving the character of some of their missionaries, they observed that they had two Christian squaws in their society who were baptized by him, and that one of them had showed them a Bible a few days before, which she said she received as a present from him."[37]

The Bacons opened a school in Detroit, an academy for girls run by Alice and David, and David preached as a home missionary to local congregations. Together they earned enough money to sustain themselves without support from the CMS. Beaumont Parks wrote nearly five decades later of Detroit as a city defended by a palisade wall that was closed each night to Indians:

> Detroit, at the time we were there, was the largest and most important city west of Albany. It was the great emporium of the fur trade. The Indian traders, as they were called, were men of great wealth and highly cultivated minds.... The inhabitants were English, Scotch, Irish, and French, all of whom hated the Yankees most cordially. I am sure there was not an American in the place except the officers and soldiers of the garrison, which was composed of a regiment of infantry and one company of artillery.[38]

The Bacons spent a year in Detroit, but their principal concern was finding an appropriate site for a mission. He considered a mission near Fairfield and a site on the Miami (Maumee) seventy-five miles south of Detroit near the place destroyed by General Wayne in 1794 near the Battle of Fallen Timbers. Unknown to Bacon, as the correspondence had failed to reach him, there was an order by the trustees of the CMS to travel to Michilimackinack and open a mission to the Ojibwe at L'Arbre Croche.

Parks relates his journey in April 1802, with Bacon and a hired man in a dugout canoe loaded with provisions and gifts. They paddled for twenty miles the first day, arriving at Brownstown. Parks described this adventure: "We arrived safely at Maumee Bay in three or four days. Here was an old Indian village on a beautiful elevated place covered with blue grass. The Indians had just returned from Detroit, where they had been selling their furs and peltry. They received in payment whiskey, bread, flour, and meat, and were preparing for a grand drunken *powwow*. I think there were about 1,500 Indians on the river."[39]

Bacon was at the site of present-day Toledo and traveled up river to Fort Miami where he unloaded food and farming tools that he would later present as gifts to Little Otter. (Most likely this chief was the renowned Miami leader Little Turtle and Bacon misunderstood the translator.) However, the missionaries were forced to wait for almost a week while the Natives enjoyed an unending series of ceremonies: "conjuring," feasting, and dancing. He reported Natives smoking pipes and intemperate use of whiskey that kept them in a state of continued intoxication. While observing a ceremony, Bacon was accosted by a conjurer (shaman), who threatened him with his fists. An interpreter told Bacon that the shaman accused him of making sport of the Natives and their rituals. Bacon wrote, "He added that the Great Spirit had made him an Indian, made him red, made him everyway just as he was, and placed him there on that ground, and he said that he meant to remain just as he was."[40] Here, as during the encounter with Red Jacket, Bacon encountered cultural nativism—the wholesale rejection of his missionary outreach by a ritual specialist who angrily declared the separate creation of white and red and the refusal to relinquish Native ground, lifeways, and beliefs.

On Friday, May 14, 1802, Bacon delivered through an interpreter the prepared remarks written by Connecticut's Governor Treadwell in 1800, "To the Indian Tribes Bordering on Lake Erie." The ponderous remarks introduced the constitutional government of the state, the nature of religion, and the history, organization, and functionaries of the Missionary Society. After what must have seemed an interminable, incomprehensible tedium, the address concluded with the endorsement that the society had sent a good man and a good Christian who should be received in friendship. Bacon continued his address pleading that the white man's religion was fitting for Indians and would benefit their communities by educating children, promoting godly conduct, and providing legal and political protection under the rule of law. Bacon faced the stiffest opposition when he advocated permanent settlements that prohibited the consumption of alcohol.

David Bacon was part of what David Andrew Nichols terms "the revolution of 1800 in Indian Country." After decades of warfare that continued after the Treaty of Paris, the confederation of northwestern tribes, Delawares, Potawatomis, Chippewas, Miamis, Shawnees, Weas, Wyandots, Ottawas, and Kickapoos assembled ninety chiefs as signatories of the Treaty of Greenville in 1795. The treaty ratified land cessions in Trans-Appalachian areas of Ohio extending south to Kentucky. Because of war in Europe, the British were forced to abandon military support for the Northwest Indian confederacy and surrender their forts to American control, thus prompting Native groups to seek peace after the Battle of Fallen Timbers. By 1801, the newly elected president, Thomas Jefferson, supported a civilization project that attempted to transform Natives into settled farmers who would adopt an agrarian economy and sell or cede "surplus" land that was no longer required for hunting and seasonal migration. Citing a "coincidence of interests," the civilization policy envisioned the sale of land to pay for tools, plows, and trade goods supervised by government trading posts (factories) created by the Indian Trade and Intercourse Acts.[41]

Bacon championed the plan of civilization as he pled his case before the Miami chief and the hundreds assembled:

> I showed them the advantages of adopting the plan,—that they would live in peace, as they never quarrelled [sic] when they were sober; that with my assistance they would be able to give their children an education[;] ... that I would show them and assist them what I could, about making carts and ploughs, and about ploughing their ground; so that they might improve [employ] their horses, which were then almost useless to them, and raise a plenty of corn and wheat, potatoes, squashes and tobacco, horses and cattle, sheep, hogs, and poultry; that I would show them and assist them for what I could about building a mill, building houses, and making furniture for their house; that I would make them wheels and show them about making looms.[42]

The plan of civilization would produce literate children who could read, write, and speak English, and who could promote their individual and tribal self-interests. He promised them prosperity, comfort for the sick and elderly, and "a religion of God's Word, which if they would rightfully attend to it, would make them unspeakably happy forever."[43]

Bacon professed a disinterested benevolence but gave them a warning of the consequences should he be rebuffed: "You will exceedingly grieve the hearts of God's ministers and people, and what is infinitely worse, you will dreadfully offend God who has sent me, and will make Him very angry with you."[44] Speaking with great condescension in the spirit of religious paternalism, Bacon explained to the assembled Natives:

> I might have lived much happier at home among my dear friends and acquaintance[sic], where we had everything that was comfortable around

us; but knowing how much you need my assistance, and having a great love for you, and being commanded by God, I have forsaken all, and have come a great distance to spend my days with you in order to make you happy in this world and in the world to come.[45]

The following day the Miami chief rejected Bacon's assistance and gave his reply that Bacon summarized from the interpreter. "Your religion is very good, but only for white people; it will not do for Indians." He explained the Great Spirit gave to whites farms, livestock, and religion written in a book. However, he made Indians wild and placed them in woods to hunt for game.[46]

Within two weeks Bacon had reunited with his family in Detroit and removed to Mackinaw Island, where he would remain for two years until his recall to New Connecticut in 1804. The Ojibwes at L'Arbre Croche refused to accept a mission in their home village but held out the possibility of sending their youth to a mission school.[47]

For two years, David Bacon, Alice, and their growing family expressed public confidence of the eventual success of their mission, but in private correspondence they recorded the familiar litany of complaints and impediments to the conversion of the heathen: failure to learn their language or secure an interpreter, a continual shortage of funds, the rarity of the visits of Natives who arrived to sell furs, whiskey, and trade goods, and the failure to build a mission station and farm. All of these issues prevented Bacon from building a mission.

Mackinaw was a diverse frontier outpost, a polyglot assemblage of French, British, Yankee, American military, and various Native groups from the upper Midwest. Bacon and his family rented housing for two years in this village. Alice kept a school and dairy, and David attempted to preach to the locals. He would complain in February 1803 about "a want of Christian society, quickening, grace & opportunities for more intensive usefulness are the greatest, & about the only evils we have experienced."[48] Writing that same month to a friend in Connecticut, Alice acknowledged the hardship of missionary life but explained that excellent books, faith in God, and happiness with her "family connection" and her infant son, Leonard, sustained her. Speaking with the solicitude of the burdens of "true womanhood," she wrote, "O that I possess that grace which is sufficient to enable me to train him up for God."⁴⁹

In the context of the profanity, drunkenness, licentiousness, and indifference to religion of soldiers, traders, and white settlers, Alice echoed her husband's complaint regarding the inhabitants of Mackinaw: "These are as generally destitute of religion as their heathen neighbors. What a place this must be! Could you for a moment be transported hither, and hear the awful language which I daily hear methinks you would be filled with horror and imagine that this was the place where infidels rave." Alice penned this poem:

> What do I see? Nought but a savage train
> Of men who never heard of Jesus's name
> Or those who once have heard but now despise
> The God that made them, God who built the skies.⁵⁰

Alice endured hardship as the mistress of her household, caring for her husband and young children. She also shouldered the responsibility of teaching school and operating a small dairy, earning money and producing goods and services for the local barter economy. And Alice suffered a growing disillusionment about the prospects for success of a missionary outreach to settlers and Natives in these frontier settlements. She looked inward for the signs of grace and the strength to persevere against such adversity. However, Alice confronted vexing concerns: could she sustain her missionary vocation? Would the model of Brainerd's evangelical piety and personhood endure?

After many refusals by the Ojibwes to receive Bacon or to visit Mackinaw, in October of 1803, Pemenechaugun, chief sachem, and his retinue presented Bacon with a string of wampum and an oration that rejected the possibility of a mission or school for his people. Like the oration of Sagoyewatha and Little Turtle, the Ojibwe leader spoke of separate creations that made white lifeways and religion undesirable for Natives. This speech was committed to memory, translated, and delivered by Sigenog, a member of the visiting party. The oration referred to Reverend Bacon by the kinship designation of "my father":

My father, I have spoken to your children, to get them to listen to you, but they tell me that they think they are too foolish to learn.

My father, we think the Great Spirit did not put us on the ground to learn such things as the white people learn.... My father, we cannot live together so as to attend to these things like the white people. The Great Spirit has given them cattle and everything about them that they live upon. If they are hungry they have only to go into their yard and kill a creature. But he gave us no such things. He put us upon the ground to run in the woods to get our living. When we are hungry, we have to go away and hunt something to eat.[51]

Sigenog concluded that Bacon might teach the children. "But I do not know that it would be best.... If we were to get to know so much, perhaps the Great Spirit would not let us live."[52]

Bacon reported what had transpired in a lengthy letter to the CMS trustees in November, enumerating several reasons for Native resistance to a mission. These factors included the proximity of this Ojibwe band to the British fort at St. Joseph Island where the British offered generous gifts and a free trade in whiskey to encourage the fur trade. Fur traders opposed a plan of civilization, permanent agricultural villages, and schooling that would diminish Native reliance on hunting and peltry. In addition, Natives had been catechized by Jesuits and maintained friendship with the French Canadian "fathers." However, in Bacon's estimation, the most serious obstacle to forming a mission was Native rejection of Christianity. Bacon lamented, "It is an objection that is in the mouth of everyone in this country, and it is thought to be so conclusive as to make any further attempts is the height to folly. Pemenechaugun gave me this as a reason for his concluding that I should not be successful; and I believe it is so considered by the Indians in general."[53]

Bacon was undeterred by rejection and proposed in his correspondence to the Connecticut trustees a grandiose plan to build a Moravian-style village and school on Mackinaw Island with the anticipation that the CMS would educate promising Native scholars in New England and prepare them to return and evangelize their people. Bacon's plan anticipated the missions sponsored by the ABCFM in the 1820s and the Foreign Mission School in Cornwall, Connecticut. In reality, Bacon could not complete a small log house (twenty by thirty feet), and he and his family lived in a hut on the mission site from May through September while renting quarters in Mackinaw village during the fall and winter months.

Later in November, he wrote to the trustees of the CMS requesting a loan of one hundred dollars, explaining the crushing debts owed to banking agents in Detroit, despite his austere economies and meager diet. He recounted that

> our common diet for morning and evening, last winter, was bread and tea; that but twenty weight of butter was used in the family from November till May. . . . I do not recollect that I have purchased a fowl since we have been here, except in the case of sickness, and six pounds of poor beef (for which I paid a dollar) and about as much pork, at a quarter of a dollar a pound, is all the fresh meat I remember to have bought since last winter.
>
> But so it is, my money is gone, and I am so much in debt that I shall need all my pay for the ensuing year, and must practise [sic] the strictest economy in order to be clear of debt at the end of the year.[54]

Although Bacon received a modest stipend and funds for an interpreter, he was expected to earn money and support himself and his family by teaching, farming, and itinerant preaching at local congregations. He paid transportation expenses and purchased lumber and building materials, tools, farming implements, horses, and livestock. The CMS did not provide sufficient funds to support these initiatives and by January 1804 voted to end this mission and recall Bacon and his family to New Connecticut, where he would labor as a domestic missionary to frontier churches composed of white emigrants from New England.

Because the Great Lakes were frozen over in the winter, navigation and mail resumed in May. However, this written notification failed to reach him. Instead, Colonel Kingsbury, an emissary from the CMS, personally informed Bacon of the decision to close the mission. Bacon proceeded to sell his tools, household furnishings, and livestock, attempted to settle his debts, and removed with his wife and two children to Cleveland by October. He was directed to join Reverends Thomas Robbins and Joseph Badger as itinerant missionaries.

After a long and arduous journey delayed by sickness, Bacon was greeted by news that the CMS board had refused to honor his promissory notes and pay the debts from the Mackinaw mission, exposing him to possible arrest and imprisonment for debt. He was invited to return to Hartford to offer a financial accounting. He left his wife and children in Hudson, Ohio, and set out on foot for Hartford in November, pale and emaciated from "a very serious attack of intermittent fever" (malaria), arriving in Hartford in late December.[55]

Joseph Badger wrote to the CMS board in Bacon's defense. Badger explained,

> He feels himself extremely wounded and injured by the official communications.... In regard to Mr. Bacon, I have no doubt but his necessary expenses far exceeded the calculations of the Board. The knowledge and experience I have had of expenses in this part and about Detroit lead me to believe his expenses have not been extravagant.[56]

Bacon met with the board on January 9, 1805, and gave a detailed accounting of the mission expenditures, thus clearing his reputation. They voted funds to pay his promissory notes in Detroit and paid him seven hundred dollars for his past expenses.[57]

Bacon presented a letter from David Hudson, founder of Hudson, Ohio, who agreed to pay half of Bacon's salary as a missionary. This letter, in addition to the letter from Reverend Badger, convinced the board to authorize Bacon's immediate return to New Connecticut. He arrived in Hudson in March and began his work as an itinerant circuit preacher who served the settlements of Warren, Nelson, Mantua, and Aurora as well as the frontier settlements in Pennsylvania. However, after five months of exhausting travel, he tendered his resignation on July 22. He explained, "For many years it has been my ardent desire to serve God in the gospel of his Son, as a labourer in the missionary cause." He acknowledged his failure as a missionary and his inability to preach to Natives in their language.

He questioned his qualifications for service as a domestic missionary, as he lacked sufficient "wisdom piety & prudence, aided by good natural and acquired abilities."[58] Bacon stated that he intended to remain in New Connecticut and preach "supply" to congregations that lacked a settled minister, but he had more grandiose ambitions.

Bacon began his next utopian religious venture founded on the home missionary ideal of the CMS as exemplified by Hudson, Ohio—the creation of an idealized Puritan village to offset the moral dangers of the American frontier. Each new town would be structured as a well-organized settlement plotted in a grid of household farmstead lots that surrounded a village green, church, and school, a planned community that would structure a "moral geography" where emigrants from New England voluntarily embraced godly living. In this manner, national expansion would progress through the establishment of church communities composed of evangelical believers who would labor to fulfill the providential idea of building America as the Redeemer's Kingdom.[59]

The prosperity and success of Hudson proved atypical. Most settlements were a bricolage of diverse homesteads where the new settlers lacked a defining religious purpose and were not committed to the ideals of a godly church community of the ingathered faithful. New settlements were rife with disease, intemperance, poverty, violence, extreme weather conditions, and great adversity. The CMS ideal championed by David Hudson and Bacon, however, envisioned a nostalgic recreation of New England villages: the construction of orderly towns that promoted a cohesive moral community, family government, prayer, piety, Sabbath-keeping, public worship, and the moral education of children and youth.[60]

David Hudson, who hailed from Goshen, Connecticut, at age thirty-nine and newly converted in the white heat of the local revivals, founded his eponymous settlement in 1799. He wrote about his spiritual pilgrimage from sinner to saved, from the places of his youth to the promise of a new beginning: "I, like Jonah of old, formed a design of fleeing from the presence of the Lord, and removing myself to the solitary wilds of the Connecticut western reserve, and there commenced a life of religion."[61] Hudson was motivated by religious and financial ambitions, and with four other investors he purchased seven thousand acres in New Connecticut that they planned to sell at $2.50 per acre.

The town prospered with the addition of many new settlers and the founding in 1801 of a Congregational Church where Bacon preached as an itinerant. Hudson, Ohio, began as a church community where townspeople embraced a church covenant and submitted to religious discipline, Sabbath-keeping, and measures of fraternal correction for drunkenness, disturbing the peace, lying, and profanity.[62]

Ten miles south of Hudson was a tract of undeveloped land, twelve thousand acres owned by Ephraim Starr of Goshen and Benjamin Tallmadge of Litchfield. Bacon purchased these lands for $1.50 an acre with a promissory note in 1805, thus establishing the planned community that he named Tallmadge. Bacon spent two years traveling throughout Connecticut in an attempt to recruit emigrants before he removed there and built a rude log cabin in the woods in 1807.[63] His son Leonard wrote, "The next thing in carrying out the plan to which Mr. Bacon had devoted himself was to bring in, from whatever quarter, such families as would enter into his views and would cooperate with him for the early and permanent establishment of Christian order."[64]

By 1808 twelve families had settled in the new town, and their number grew to thirty families by 1811. They formed a Congregational Society and church in 1809. However, monies from the purchase of thirty lots did not permit Bacon to satisfy his creditors. The business stagnation and financial freeze created by the Napoleonic Wars and Jefferson's trade embargo prevented potential buyers from selling their Connecticut property and purchasing lots in Tallmadge. Facing default and the alienation of townsfolk who were in danger of losing their investments, Bacon, ever hopeful, returned to Connecticut in April 1811 in a futile attempt to restructure his debt.[65]

Alice wrote to her husband in May to inform him of her postpartum depression after she had given birth to their fifth child: "You know I am always feeble when I nurse in warm weather. I suffer greatly from a depression of spirits which I cannot shake off. I think I never felt so unable to endure your absence as at present. I most sensibly feel the want of your soothing hand to administer the balm of consolation to my wounded spirit."[66]

Although she appealed to God for support, she remained distressed at their financial crisis and the burden this has placed on her husband. Alice wrote,

> God is able to raise us up friends in the midst of enemies and to provide us with every strait and difficulty. How often hath he appeared for us in darkness and distress and wrought out deliverance for us. . . . I am not anxious *how* if it is only done. I long to have you free from such embarrassments and such a load of cares. You have almost worn out yourself in the arduous employment.[67]

Alice would delay sending the letter for three weeks, opening the envelope and adding a melancholy postscript: "My spirits are so depressed that it seems to wear me out. My heart is full of sorrow, and my eyes are overflowing with tears."[68]

Alice revealed her sense of longing for her absent husband and her feelings of loneliness and despair as they again faced failure and financial ruin. During her decade of marriage she had endured his many leave-takings and extended absences, having to cope with deprivation and rely on the generosity of friends and neighbors to support their growing family. In September, Bacon sent a peculiar letter in reply that proffered pastoral care—words intended to console, sustain, and guide his afflicted wife to trust in the assurance of God's love and the consolation of Psalm 25. However, he could not send money to Alice or return home despite his continuing encouragement and promises.

Bacon wrote a detailed account of the stellar success of his itinerant preaching in Connecticut at Canton, Torrington, Cornwall, Warren, and Litchfield and his abiding hope that he would succeed in satisfying his creditors. Bacon recruited evangelical Christian proprietors, who agreed to transfer their Connecticut holdings to the mortgage holders in exchange for homestead lots in Tallmadge. In November, Colonel Benjamin Tallmadge rejected this settlement and demanded payment in cash.

Bacon arrived at his brother Leonard's house in Litchfield, penniless, overwhelmed by new debt, and in default of his obligation to Benjamin Tallmadge. His brother wrote this reply about David Bacon to Benjamin

Tallmadge, pleading for more time, and for understanding, and leniency, describing David Bacon's "mental depression": "His state of mind is such that though he has made several attempts he has not been able to write. . . . He feels that his last earthly friend on whom he could depend for succor, and in whose constancy he had utmost confidence has now forsaken him." Sleepless, agitated, and wretched, he ruminated over the past five years of struggle and failure, and over the burden of a debt of one thousand dollars that he contracted in addition to the unpaid mortgage. Leonard continued, "He is now 600 miles from home and destitute of money; if aided by his friends to return to what will it introduce him but to scenes of more complicated woe—to behold a beloved wife of feeble health & five helpless children who look to him for bread—but look in vain, for he must immediately resign himself to a host of disappointed creditors whose tender mercies are cruelty, and who will probably seek revenge in attempts to vilify his character."[69]

Like the missionary adventures to the Ojibwes, this venture to build a planned religious community did not end well. Bacon returned to Tallmadge to retrieve his family, and together they returned to Connecticut in May 1811. He subsequently taught school in Litchfield, and in 1813–14 he preached in parishes in Prospect and in the rural fringe of Middletown (Westfield). In 1815, he moved to Hartford and worked as a traveling Bible salesman until his retirement due to ill health in 1816, a year before his death.[70]

He had failed as a missionary to the Indians, as a home missionary in New Connecticut, and in his endeavor to build a planned religious community in Tallmadge. In part, he lacked sufficient means to establish a mission or fund the church community in Ohio. And despite his fervor and unending devotion to the benevolent ideals of evangelical religion and the millennial aspiration to help build the Redeemer's kingdom, David Bacon lacked the organizational skills to realize his utopian visions. In the end, his sublime expectations as a missionary and his youthful evangelical piety in the spirit of David Brainerd did not abide as he ended his career, worn down and in broken heath, peddling expensive leather-bound Bibles that kept the genealogical records for families of wealth and social standing in New England. By abandoning the practice of evangelical piety,

Reverend Bacon failed to realize the ideals of his past religious vocation. Failure also entailed the renunciation of the religio-political aspirations of American nationalism: building a moral geography of Protestant church communities of New England's emigrants on the frontier and bringing perishing heathens into the new republic as Christian Indians who might help create the Redeemer's Kingdom in America.

David Bacon ended his career as a salesman, no longer in pursuit of the millennium but in a new role as an American huckster. He hoped to profit from the sale of lands in Tallmadge, and he was filled with "chimerical schemes" of pecuniary success that continually eluded him. Alexis De Tocqueville in *Democracy in America* identified this trait of the pursuit of material comfort in the chapter "Why Americans Are So Restless in the Midst of Their Prosperity." He explains the American pursuit of happiness as measured by the frenetic quest for material success: "Death at length overtakes him, but it is before he is weary of his bootless chase of that complete felicity which forever escapes him."[71] The special genius of America to commodify ideas, values, and lifestyles, as evidenced by Reverend Bacon's evolution from missionary and utopian to traveling Bible salesman, is indicative of the renunciation of his religious vocation. The huckster proved antithetical to Brainerd's ideal of evangelical personhood and piety.

We will permit Alice Bacon the last word as she penned a letter to her absent husband who was away from home traveling his circuit in Connecticut and Massachusetts, peddling *Scott's Family Bible*. Forced to depend on the support of family and friends, she had long abandoned her vocation as a missionary wife, helpmate, and partner in a utopian intentional community in Tallmadge as well as hopes of being a companionate wife who enjoyed intimacy with her husband. Left alone and in straitened circumstances, afflicted with melancholy and feeling forsaken by God, Alice wrote this lament as she cared for another newborn, their sixth child: "I am almost worn down with fatigue and am frequently on the point of giving up. But I still keep about and try to get along as well as I can—I have been and still am afflicted with Job's torments which has made it very difficult for me to take care of the babe."[72]

2

The Missionary Vocation of Miss D

A Life Broken by Disease and Disappointment

The Hartford Retreat, a small private asylum for the insane, was founded in Hartford, Connecticut, in 1821 and began admitting patients in April 1824. A little more than a year later, in May 1825, the retreat admitted a charity patient, a young woman, aged twenty-seven from Litchfield, Connecticut, who had recently returned from her work as a missionary "sister" at the Union Mission to the Osage in the Arkansas Territory.[1] Concerned neighbors and family collected donations and paid the thirty-nine dollars for the initial three months of her treatment. After suffering from the effects of a virulent malarial infection and contracting pulmonary tuberculosis, she was afflicted with delirium, a protracted religious melancholy, and a wasting physical disease. This essay reconstructs the life of this woman prior to admission and the meaning of her melancholy. Her life reflected and exemplified the central themes and contradictions of the missionary spirit in the era of grand revivals.

By the early decades of the nineteenth century the idea of the Indian as a racially inferior primitive destined "to be destroyed by God, Nature, and Progress to make way for Civilized man" informed both the secular ideology of Manifest Destiny and the evangelical missionary spirit.[2] So little time remained to rescue Native Americans who perished in savage darkness. Whites viewed Native peoples as "vanishing Americans" seemingly destined to extinction as the inevitable "natural" outcome of contact with white civilization, which undermined Indian peoples through warfare, alcohol abuse, epidemics of infectious diseases, and the progressive encroachment of white settlement onto western Indian lands. The poet William Cullen Bryant enunciated the theme of the vanishing American in the 1824 piece "An Indian at the Burying-place of His Fathers":

> They waste us—aye—like April snow
>   In the warm noon, we shrink away;
> And fast they follow, as we go
>   Towards the setting day,—
> Till they shall fill the land, and we
> Are driven into the western sea.[3]

The theme of the vanishing American reflects the broader question of how Americans conceptualized indigenous cultures from what might be termed "Christian anthropology." Christian missionary outreach encountered indigenous groups in America and throughout the world. How would missionaries conceptualize these cultures (anthropology)? Today, Christianity is a world religion that espouses theologies, doctrines, and ethical codes of *caritas* that accept and affirm cultural and religious relativism in the encounter with indigenous peoples. However, in the early nineteenth century Protestant missionaries frequently viewed themselves as representatives of the one true religion, albeit divided by denominational differences and competition. Native beliefs and ceremonies were labeled as erroneous and harmful superstitions that missionaries debunked, ridiculed, and attempted to eradicate to prepare neophytes for the reception of doctrinal truths. In this manner, missionaries ignored the diversity and complexity of distinct cultures and tribes and classified all Native peoples under a single stereotypical category—Indian, heathen, and racial Other. Indians were perceived to be savages and heathens. Whites understood the Indian as either the "noble savage" living in an idealized harmony in a state of nature or alternatively as an "ignoble savage"—an atavistic evil barbarian running wild and untamed in the midst of depravity, violence, and lust. Either version of the Indian savage judged him as deficient when measured against the standards of white civilization and the institutions of law, government, arts, trade, marriage, morality, technology, and especially religion. According to the logic of this Christian anthropology, Indians needed to be rescued from a rude and undomesticated state of nature, reduced, degraded, and forced to bear the yoke of civility. This reduction and degradation pertained to learning Euro-American ways of living, embracing a vocational work ethic, and abandoning Indian ways of family, economy, and political organization in order to emulate white Americans. Once civilized, Indians could be converted and could dedicate their bodies, souls, lands, and lives to the "higher" purposes of the evangelical pursuit of the millennium. The Christian anthropology of missionaries in America, however motivated by ideals of charity and benevolence, supported a program of the forced acculturation of Native peoples and the use of Indians as instruments and examples of divine Providence.

The trope of "perishing heathens" structured the thought and perception of Protestant evangelicals and Christian anthropology as they viewed Native cultures in America and peoples throughout the world—in the Middle East and the Indian subcontinent. The ubiquitous lament of perishing heathens pervades the endless chain of published religious intelligence in periodicals, memoirs, and tracts as well as unpublished diaries, letters, and religious reflections.

Images of heathens—denied the light of Gospel truth, practicing sinful paganism, and living the irregular life of the savage hunter—came to mind when depicting Native Americans. So little time remained for the vanishing Americans. Evangelicals anguished over the prospect of perishing heathens who could be converted and civilized if only the organizational arm of the revival could reach them in time. Zachariah Lewis, domestic secretary of the United Foreign Missionary Society, published a letter in defense of missions sent to Congress in 1822. He argued that mission stations could civilize and convert Indians. He anticipated a time

> when the savage shall be converted into the citizen; when the hunter shall be changed to the agriculturalist or the mechanic; when the farm, the workshop, the school-house, and the church shall adorn every

Indian village, [when] . . . the red man and the white man shall every where be found mingling in the same pursuits, cherishing the same benevolent and friendly views, fellow citizens of the same civil and religious community, and fellow heirs to an eternal inheritance in the kingdom of glory.[4]

The policy of the federal government utilized missionary initiatives for distinctly military and political goals. Following the military defeat of the Iroquois tribes who allied with the British during the Revolution and of the tribes loyal to Tecumseh during the War of 1812, Congress viewed Indians as conquered peoples and their lands as conquered territory and no longer accorded tribes the sovereignty of nations. Indians were increasingly viewed as impediments to white settlement and western expansion, incompatible with homogenous nationalism, forced to assimilate or face removal or extinction. The Trade and Intercourse Acts of 1796, 1799, and 1802 intended to restrict Indian contact with white society by establishing a system of Indian agents, garrisons, and cantonments on the frontiers as well as trading outposts or factories to regulate Indian-white fur trade, resolve disputes and treaty violations, prevent white encroachment upon Indian lands and game, and restrict the sale of alcohol and firearms to Native peoples. The Indian Bureau also supervised the distribution of federal annuities and agricultural supplies. These efforts envisioned the voluntary transformation of Indians into settled agriculturalists who would relinquish title to "surplus" tribal lands, thus freeing millions of acres for white settlement.[5] Indians would relinquish lands, whether peacefully as assimilated farmers, by treaty, by conquest, or by removal.

Legislation enacted on March 3, 1819, authorized the expenditure of ten thousand dollars annually to civilize Indian tribes of the southwestern frontier. This legislation provided for President James Monroe to designate an agency to perform the legislative mandate. Monroe chose Christian missions to bring civilization to the heathen. Missions, in cooperation with Indian agents and garrison soldiers in strategically located forts established by the War Department, would pacify, regulate, and assimilate Indian groups in the new nation.[6] The "civilization fund" was intended to transform indigenous peoples into republican freeholders consistent with Thomas Jefferson's agrarian ideal of the hard-laboring property owner whose labor transformed the land, produced abundance for the commonweal, and conferred dignity upon each individual.

Secretary of war John C. Calhoun commissioned Jedidiah Morse to undertake a survey of Indian tribes during the summer of 1820 and to prepare a report to Congress proposing how best to appropriate the civilization fund. Morse in his *Report on Indian Affairs* called for the creation of model utopian communities of Christian missionaries united together as "education families." These missionary communities that were to be established in Indian territory would also include detribalized Indian families or youths who would receive training, education, and guidance toward salvation. Morse describes the education families as

> an association of individual families, formed of one or more men regularly qualified to preach the Gospel, to be at the head of such a family; of school-masters and mistresses; of farmers, blacksmiths, carpenters, cabinet-makers, mill-wrights, and other mechanics—of women capable of teaching the use of the needle, the spinning-wheel, the loom, and all kinds of domestic manufactures, cooking, etc. common in civilized families. This family is to consist of men and women in a married state, with their children, all possessing talents for their respective offices, with a missionary spirit, devoted to their work; contented to labor without salary.... These bodies are to be the great instruments in the hands of government for educating and civilizing the Indians.[7]

Using the mission station as a model, Indians were expected to emulate the white families, forsake Native lifeways, and build new identities and communities. Morse and the Baptist missionary Isaac McCoy believed that within a generation successful education families would be founded throughout Indian territory in the West and produce self-sufficient Indian agrarian communities. Indian converts would preach the Gospel to their people. Indian teachers would instruct their youth in agriculture and mechanics. Indian statesmen would confederate these model communities into an Indian state. Thus, missionary utopianism held that civilized, detribalized groups could join together in a pan-Indian movement to establish in the West, separate from the corruption of white influence, an "Indian Canaan" of planned communities administered by educated Indians who would participate as coequals within a national federalism. Indian missions, in the space of one generation, could ensure a just fate for Native peoples.[8]

The concept of the education family as the instrument of civilizing and Christianizing the savage culminating in an Indian Canaan was derived from Morse's survey of Protestant mission stations in the West, particularly the UFMS mission stations to the Osages. Based on the expected success of these first experiments, Americans could foresee the future "gentle extinction" of the vanishing American not with pity or censure but with the sublime optimism anticipating the winning of Indian souls for Christ and the creation of an Indian state.[9]

Morse reiterated these sentiments in the first report of the American Society for Promoting the Civilization and General Improvement of the Indian Tribes in the United States, published in 1824. He wrote of the prospect of

> raising half a million up from a state of ignorance, heathenism and wretchedness, to the possession of innumerable blessings, which result from Civilization and Christianity. To be instrumental in imparting these blessings to the destitute is Godlike. It is the only sure way of securing for our country, the favour and protection of heaven. In carrying forth such a work, who can refuse his aid? Who, in a Christian community, will deny themselves the privilege and happiness of receiving the "blessings of thousands, who are ready to perish?"[10]

So much depended upon the success of these first education families. So clearly did the millennial hopes of the awakening and the national concerns charged with the ideology of progress and Manifest Destiny devolve to the Union Mission. The board of managers of the UFMS published a statement of purpose for the Union Mission, charging them to "ever keep in view the great objects of your mission, which are to evangelize the Indians; and to teach them the arts of civilized life.... You must labour effectively to wean them from the hunter's life, and to bring them into the habits of patient industry, and a regular pursuit of the farmer's occupation of civilized men."[11]

The board had sent the Reverends Job Vinall and Epaphras Chapman as their agents to the Missouri and Arkansas Territories. In the summer of 1819, they arrived at the frontier and set about the task of obtaining permission from the chiefs of the Osage and Cherokee tribes to establish missions. Vinall died of malarial fevers, but Chapman did succeed in gaining the consent of Clermont, chief of the Osage village in Verdigris. Plans were made to establish a mission in what is today Maze County, Oklahoma, to be called Union Mission. A second Osage mission, Harmony (1820), situated on the Grand River in southern Missouri, and Dwight Mission to the Cherokees in Arkansas were also contemplated and later established.

Vinall and Chapman carried the following introduction from John C. Calhoun, secretary of war, extending the mandate of the president and protection of the War Department in the cause of the Union Mission. He described the missionaries as

> friendly and benevolent, and have the approbation of your Great Father, the President of the United States, and he expects you will receive them kindly. Their object is to teach your children to read and write; your young women to spin and weave, and make clothing for you, and prepare food like white people; to show your young men how to make axes, hoes, and ploughs, and how to use them in tilling your land ... and to introduce among you, generally, the arts of civilized life.[12]

Upon his return to New York in the spring of 1820, Chapman reported his success to the board of managers of the UFMS, who solicited nominations for service in the Union Mission family. Thus began an adventure of evangelical utopians who intended to civilize and convert the Osages to demonstrate the feasibility of an Indian Canaan and hasten the Kingdom of God in America. The story of this utopian adventure and the subsequent failure of the Union Mission is reconstructed in the sections to follow through the narrative of the experiences of a missionary sister afflicted by religious melancholy, who became a patient at the Hartford Retreat. Her life was shaped by the missionary movement and awakening. In recounting her life-crisis, the narrative moves from biography to public history, from the personal documents of this individual to the institutional initiatives of missionary groups, congressional legislation, and national policy.

MISS D'S MISSIONARY VOCATION

D was born in Litchfield on April 9, 1798, the third of six daughters. Her father and mother were married by Reverend Judiah Champion on July 15, 1793, and affiliated with the Litchfield Congregational Church.[13]

The father worked as a barber and earned scarcely enough to provide for his large family. Her mother was engaged in domestic pursuits as mistress of the household and directed the education of her daughters. She died after a prolonged illness on August 25, 1816, at the age of fifty-two.[14]

Miss D's personal documents, such as journals or letters, have not survived. In reconstructing her early life and childhood, we do not have first-person accounts but must rely upon town records, asylum and biographical accounts, and public sources.

D came of age in a cultural center of Connecticut. Litchfield (town and county), although a sparsely settled and prosperous agricultural district located in the northwest corner of the state, championed the various initiatives of the Second Great Awakening and the foundation of many educational and benevolent institutions. Tapping Reeve established a distinguished law school in Litchfield. Miss Sarah Pierce opened the Litchfield Academy devoted to the progressive education of young women. Lyman Beecher, that staunch defender of Congregational orthodoxy, preached from 1810 until 1826 in the town's Congregational Church and promoted the effervescence of evangelical religion and benevolent institutions as experiments worthy of emulation in New England and America.[15]

Litchfield was then one center of revivals of religion promoted by the Congregational and Episcopal churches during the years 1807–8, 1812, 1815–16, and 1825–26 and, through Beecher's efforts, a model for other communities to follow.[16] The Reverends Champion and Huntington worked steadfastly in these efforts as Lyman Beecher reported, writing in April of 1807, "The ministry of the latter [Huntington] had been blessed with a powerful revival, the fruits of which were yet visible, and the memory warm in the hearts of Christians. Three hundred persons were said at that time to have been converted."[17]

Lyman Beecher labored to effect revivals by conducting periodic prayer meetings and evening meetings, sometimes offering nine sermons weekly to prepare the community for the visitation of the Holy Spirit. Reverend H. C. Vaill offers this account of these extraordinary times of community-wide spiritual awakening: "In 1812 there were indications of a revival, which in 1813 became marked and hopeful. It continued as a revival first in the centre of town, next in the west, then in the east, and on the extreme outskirts of the society, and till 1817 there was scarcely a communion season at which there were not additions to the church."[18]

Although it was a village of fewer than five thousand inhabitants, the innovative social institutions of the awakening flourished in this close-knit community.[19] Here, through the new principles of interdenominational cooperation, all might find salvation, enter church covenants, and dedicate their lives, in some measure, to the benevolent and reform initiatives of the awakening: temperance societies, Sunday School Unions, charities to educate indigent youth for the ministry, and foreign and domestic missionary societies.[20]

The Litchfield Foreign Missionary Society, chartered in 1811 as the first chapter of the Boston-based American Board of Commissioners to Foreign Missions (ABCFM), sent more than thirty town residents into missionary service during its first fifty years of service. Members of the Litchfield chapter labored in India, Ceylon, Syria, and Hawaii and as missionaries to the Choctaws, Cherokees, Dakotas, Ojibwes, and the Osages in the trans-Mississippi West.

Lyman Beecher could point to his town and congregation with the proud assurance that the new principles of evangelical piety would bring all peoples to Christ and that the institutional moralism of voluntary societies would reform individual conduct and social institutions. Litchfield, "that delightful village, on a fruitful hill, richly endowed with schools both professional and scientific . . . with a population enlightened and respectable[,] . . . was now in its glory."[21]

Miss D's exemplary piety and decision to enter the vocation of missionary to the heathen reflected the highest ideals of the awakening and the most profound personal aspirations to dedicate her life as a Christian soldier. She came under the powerful influence of Reverend Beecher as a youth in his church, as a participant in revivals, and in 1816 as a communicant in Beecher's First Congregational Church.[22] In addition to being pious, Miss D was a literate and bookish young woman. Her name appears on the published list of subscribers to the first edition of Sarah Pierce's *Universal History*, published in 1814.[23] School records indicate that four of her sisters attended Miss Pierce's School during the summer sessions between the years 1814 and 1822. Miss D probably attended this school or another common school, as she was a literate, well-read, and accomplished young woman.

During the winter of 1820, at the age of twenty-one, Miss D embarked upon a critical life-course. She decided to pursue the vocation of a Christian missionary devoting her life to unpaid service in the cause of converting the heathen. The UFMS publicized their intention to establish mission stations on the western frontier of the Arkansas Territory among the Osage and Cherokee tribes. Circulars were mailed to Congregational, Presbyterian, and allied denominations soliciting funds and nominations of candidates who might serve in this initiative. The board of managers of the UFMS received on March 27, 1820, "a letter from Rev. Dr. Beecher recommending Miss D. to the service of the Board."[24]

On April 15, 1820, twenty members of the newly formed Union Mission to the Osage gathered in New York City for two days of prayer, dedication, instruction, and fundraising prior to their departure. Each candidate brought testimonial letters of nomination certifying their piety and steadfast dedication to the missionary cause. The board questioned each applicant and, after assurances of their sincerity and fitness, admitted them into a full commission as missionaries. The board of managers published the following account:

> The persons having presented to the Committee of Missions the most satisfactory testimonials of their good standing as members in full

communion of the Church, and of their qualifications to fill the respective stations to be assigned them, and the Committee having particularly conversed with them on their views on desiring to go out on this mission, did unanimously agree to recommend them to the Board of Managers, which was accordingly done, and they were severally appointed members of the Missionary family.[25]

The Union Mission, named as a symbol of the three constituent denominations of the UFMS, met in Presbyterian and Dutch Reformed churches in New York City and publicly consecrated their lives together as a "family" united in fictive kinship and through the common bonds of faith and collective purpose. Reverend Philip Milledoler, director of the board of managers, addressed the Union Mission family in the Dutch Church on Nassau Street on Monday evening, April 17. On the eve of their departure, Milledoler reminded the family of their vocation as missionaries. Each felt called upon to go preach and evangelize the heathen. This commission, "coming from the highest authority,"[26] directed the family to rededicate their lives as tools of the divine purpose for the improvement and salvation of the Osages: "There can be no doubt that all the sensibilities of your souls have been awakened, and all their feelings tried on this occasion—But O, delightful thought, you are going to do it for the sake of Christ and of the Gospel, the love of Christ constraineth [sic] us."[27]

Although they came from different towns, congregations, and backgrounds, the members of the Union Mission pledged themselves to unite as a family of Christians who addressed one another as "Brother" and "Sister" respectively. This fictive kinship and the constitution of a family united by *caritas* gave the mission a particularly intense and sentimental emotional foundation. The board of managers urged upon them the importance of brotherly mutual aid and concern. "Your happiness and usefulness essentially depends on the preservation of harmony among yourselves.... Maintain a kind and courteous deportment towards each other, and be a family of brothers and sisters indeed."[28] Table 1 provides the organization of the Union Mission.[29]

Table 1. Composition of the Union Mission to the Osages

NAME	OCCUPATION	ADDRESS
Rev. William Vaill	superintendent	North Guilford CT
Rev. Epaphras Chapman	assistant superintendent	East Haddam CT
Dr. Marcus Palmer	physician and surgeon	Greenwich CT
Stephen Fuller	farmer	East Haddam CT
John Spaulding	teacher and farmer	Colchester CT
William Requa	teacher and farmer	Tarrytown NY
George Requa	carpenter	Tarrytown NY
Alexander Woodruff	blacksmith	Newark NJ
Abraham Redfield	carpenter	Orange County NY
Mrs. Asenath Vaill	housekeeper and teacher	North Guilford CT
Mrs. Hannah Chapman	housekeeper and teacher	East Haddam CT
Miss Sarah Lines	seamstress and teacher	Reading CT
Miss Mary Foster	housekeeper and teacher	New York NY
Miss Dolly E. Hoyt	housekeeper and teacher	Danbury CT
Miss Phoebe Beach	housekeeper and teacher	Newburg NY
Miss D	housekeeper and teacher	Litchfield CT
Four children with Rev. Vaill's family		

Source: *Religious Intelligencer* 5, July 1820, 25.

The Union Mission family came from communities along the Eastern Shoreline and the northwestern region of Connecticut, and from several communities in New York and New Jersey. The Union Mission, formed as a mission family, represented an amalgamation of the families of procreation of Vaill and Chapman and unmarried men and women known to the ministers either as members of their local church communities or through nomination from personal networks of evangelicals in New England and New York. Under the leadership of the Yale-educated Reverend William F. Vaill, who adopted the Edwardsean ideas of disinterested benevolence, with the ideas about education and moralism of Lyman Beecher, and with carefully selected candidates who were themselves products of the Connecticut revival, the Union Mission would seek to transplant the ideals of Eastern evangelism to the West. Indeed, the mission family embarked upon a self-consciously utopian adventure as a God-willed instrument to civilize and Christianize the savage, promote the ideas of republican nationalism, and hasten the advent of the Kingdom of God in America. The ideals of the missionary spirit inspired and directed the Union family.

The proposed division of labor specified that Reverends Vaill and Chapman would serve as superintendents, exercising executive control over the mission, maintaining a mission journal, and corresponding from the field with the board regarding the activities and finances of the mission station. Most important of all, they would establish a mission church to evangelize and a school and farm to educate and civilize the Osages, concentrating their efforts upon Indian youth. Marcus Palmer would serve as physician and surgeon. William Requa and John Spaulding would learn the Osage language and serve as translators and teachers to Indian boys in the mission school. The remaining men would work and teach mechanics, agriculture, carpentry, and other useful skills. The women were to serve as instructors in domestic arts to Osage girls and provide meals and clothing and assume other household tasks for both missionaries and Indian scholars in residence. In addition, the men would work on the mission farm, planting and harvesting crops, tending livestock, and building shelters and other structures. With the combined work as farmers, blacksmiths, carpenters, teachers, housekeepers, ministers, and interpreters, they would collectively build a mission, transforming the prairie into a self-sufficient plantation.[30] The Union Mission would become a model Christian community based on a model New England farming village that represented the agrarian ideals of civilization and piety as an exemplar for the Osages, who ostensibly would acknowledge the superiority of the Christian ways, abandon Indian ways, and eagerly transform themselves through conversion and civilization.

Zachariah Lewis, domestic secretary of the UFMS, instituted this model of the mission family as the organization for all of the society's missions to the western Indians, arguing, "Whether the object, therefore, be to civilize or Christianize. Both must be carried on with an equal and united effort, through teaching Indian youth the arts of civilized life, common school education, agriculture and mechanical arts for boys and girls instructed in spinning, weaving, sewing and household business."[31]

The extensive publication of missionary journals, tracts, autobiographies, and correspondence from the field served the purpose of promoting the cause of missions among communities in New England. The stories of heathen superstition, darkness, and degradation, of missionary trials, setbacks, and triumphs, reached New Englanders who opened their hearts and pocketbooks for this cause. These publications, part propaganda and part hero's tale, dramatized missionary lives. Readers could vicariously experience the travels to exotic places, the strange contact with heathen peoples, and identify with the abiding, urgent need to evangelize and civilize these vanishing races. No other life-course held such dramatic appeal, particularly to a single young woman, as did the sentimental portrayal of a missionary's vocation. As Charles Roy Keller maintains, "there was glamour to the foreign-mission movement. . . . The American Indian living close to the white man, had long been viewed with interest and concern by Christian forces, and it was dramatic and romantic to help in converting the heathen in distant places."[32]

Religious publications, that endless chain of religious intelligence, included with each issue numerous examples of the heroic, selfless struggles of missionaries. Even the accounts of persons whose illnesses and deaths prevented them from ever reaching the field were published to depict and reanimate the missionary spirit. For example, Miss Eliza Brainerd, aged twenty, was also appointed to the Union Mission family, but illness, probably pulmonary consumption, prevented her from traveling to New York to receive her commission. She resided in East Haddam, Connecticut, and died in November 1820. Her published obituary, consistent with the genre of religious intelligence, provides a testimonial to her character and represents the passionate resolve of those who would dedicate their lives to the cause of missions.

> She had an ardent love of the discriminating doctrine of the Gospel, of holy duties, of prayer, of the Sabbath and the communion, and in reproving sinners, in quickening saints in the private prayer meeting, and the Sabbath School her usefulness was not surpassed by any. She sacredly devoted her days to the glory of God and salvation of souls; and when a door of usefulness seemed to be opened, the last spring among the Osage Indians, it was her ardent desire to go to carry to these poor pagans the word of life. She received an appointment from New York as a member of the mission family, but obstacles arose to her going which could not be overruled; and she yielded up with reluctance this favorite object, though she remained determined to devote her life, when Providence should permit, to missionary labours. But it has pleased the All-wise Disposer of events to change her countenance and send her away.[33]

During this era, religious intelligence—correspondence, diaries, and memoirs—created the genre of the missionary memoir that helped codify the tenets of Edwardsean piety based upon the principles of self-denial and self-abasement found in *The Life of David Brainerd*. In this spirit, the evangelical devoted selflessly to disinterested benevolence, seeking to bring Gospel light to heathen darkness, might "burn out in one continuous flame for God."[34]

New Divinity theologians built upon the work of Edwards to create a doctrine of universal disinterested benevolence as a signpost of the believer's growing sanctification and spiritual maturation, and as an ethical doctrine of brotherly conduct. Nathanael Emmons draws a parallel between the new born's renovated heart that manifests a true love to God and the brotherly conduct of true love to men and women. He explains, "All true love to man is disinterested, and all true love to God is disinterested. True disinterested benevolence is always the first exercise of a new heart."[35] Samuel Hopkins speaks of the holy affections of the reborn sinner who has confronted the "infinite odiousness" and "unsearchable wickedness" of total depravity in his or her heart to find evidence of holiness in disinterested benevolence.[36] The godly will craft an active, engaged life of vocational asceticism in the imitation of Christ, balancing enlightened self-interest with the ethical demands of contributing to the commonweal. Hopkins writes, "This disinterested benevolence will lead everyone to take his proper place, and to be industrious, active, prudent, and faithful in his own business, and honest, upright, sincere, and true in all his concerns and dealings with his fellow men. This love is kind; it is mercy, humility, condescension, meekness, peaceableness, temperance, long-suffering, and brotherly kindness."[37]

Missionaries embraced these New Light doctrines of conversion and the ethics of benevolence. Even though they might fail to win converts and see their efforts languish, like Brainerd, they were inclined to turn inward and interpret setbacks and failures as opportunities for redoubling their benevolent acts and for spiritual growth. Paradoxically, disinterested and selfless benevolence served the inward psychological needs of assurance for each believer. Joseph Conforti observes, "Thus, like Brainerd, nineteenth-century Edwardsean missionaries often seemed disproportionately concerned with their own spiritual lives and quest for true holiness and only secondarily with the salvation of non-Christians."[38] We will discover how after repeated frustrations and failures in missionary enterprises that were freighted with seemingly impossible millenarian goals, that assurance turned into doubt and melancholy.

Missionary religious intelligence, whether read sympathetically by evangelicals imbued with faith in their cause or critically by those opposed to missions, did not minimize the dangers attendant to both domestic and foreign missions. The Union Mission itself would add to the sum of intelligence by sending correspondence and excerpts from the mission journal for publication in the East. From the beginning of their journey westward, Union added additional names to the toll of disease, death, and despondency.

The Union Mission family departed from New York City on April 20 and proceeded by steam packet to New Brunswick, New Jersey, and then by carriage to Trenton and Philadelphia. At each city they attended local worship services, solicited funds, and met with local ministers and dignitaries. Reverend Vaill interpreted the good fortune and successes in light of a pastoral theology that exhorted the family to rededicate themselves to their purpose as Christian soldiers and avoid the temptations of complacency or worldliness. Writing in the mission journal from Philadelphia he instructed the family,

> What meaneth this prosperity. Is it that we may be led heedlessly along into the wilderness to be perplexed and defeated? God forbid. May we not suffer mercies to lead us away from Him. May we not forget our own hearts and relapse into the enjoyment of this world, but may we be prepared to endure hardship as good soldiers of Jesus Christ and to go where no hand of Christian kindness can be found to welcome our arrival and give us comfort.[39]

This spiritual direction would help sustain the mission family during their travels westward as only Christian soldiers could bear the discomforts, sicknesses, frustrations, and disappointments they would encounter. Reverend Vaill would be called upon, repeatedly, to reaffirm God's special Providence in the face of the adversity, to render their suffering bearable. The themes of the cause of missions, the missionary spirit, and the travails of Christian soldiers would fill many of Reverend Vaill's sermons to the mission family and punctuate his writings in the mission journal. Both Vaill and Chapman constantly directed and charged the family to keep their ultimate purposes and vocation ever in mind—to bear success and adversity with the single-minded purpose of the Christian pilgrim.

The mission family included single missionary "brothers" and "sisters" who accepted the spiritual direction of the paternal guidance and authority of Reverends Vaill and Chapman. These superintendents appealed to the "education family" through bonds of affection, companionship, and emotional intimacy founded upon evangelical piety and missionary vocation. These bonds permitted them to bear the lack of privacy in their journey and new settlement as well as the poor sanitation, hunger, cold, and drought. However, many of these missionary brothers and sisters discovered that their loving family connection could not endure torturous and calamitous events that awaited them in their journey.

Arriving in Philadelphia on April 22, the mission family tarried three days in preparation for the long wagon ride across Pennsylvania to Pittsburgh and the Ohio River. The family arrived at this western port on May 12 and immediately set about the tasks of fundraising and purchasing two kneel boats and twenty tons of provisions and tools. They hired three boat hands and two river pilots and accepted for service Mr. John Ranson, who had volunteered to join the mission as a millwright. Vaill reports in the mission journal that the people of Pittsburgh received them with hospitality and generosity. Vaill collected five hundred dollars in cash and goods.[40]

The family had grown into an enterprise of twenty-four people that included missionaries, children, and hired hands. They embarked upon the Ohio River on the morning of May 24. This would begin a twenty-eight-day journey down the Ohio to the Mississippi River, stopping along the river ports in Ohio and Kentucky. Vaill reports that the family traveled this eleven hundred miles of waterway in a manner that was "particularly pleasing." Writing in the journal from port in Cincinnati, June 8, 1820, Vaill stated,

> We have two boats, and yet are one family. We take our regular meals together on the roof of one of the boats, where we have a large dining hall, covered with awning and eat while we are floating down smooth stream. We rise by the ringing of the bell at 4. Within half an hour, we assemble for morning prayer, and then proceed immediately on our voyage. We have order, peace, and plenty; and we trust, the presence of God, and the consciousness of doing good.[41]

However, as they proceeded along the Mississippi to the Arkansas River, the mission family encountered conditions that were far from pleasing or salubrious. Throughout the month of July, each member of the family fell ill to either typhus or malarial fevers. Prior to their arrival in Little Rock, Arkansas, on July 23, one hired hand and Sisters Hoyt and Lines had died on the river. In view of the raging fevers, the debilitated state of the crew, and the low water level, Vaill decided to unload the boats and remain in Little Rock for the next four months. He wrote, "From the close of July to the beginning of December, there was not a week in which there were not some of the family, or of the hired men, stretched upon the bed of sickness."[42]

Reverend Chapman, the assistant superintendent of the mission, searched for the significance of the family's sickness. He adopted the familiar theology of consolation that admonished each victim, individually, and the family collectively. God had visited them with sickness as a chastisement for their sins and complacency. God humbled and tested each missionary through trial as a preparation for their missionary vocation. Search inward for the significance of your suffering. Chapman wrote,

> Where have we gone astray? Have we not the greatest reason to be humble before God? The answer to these solemn queries is obvious. We have been too much elated with our prosperity. We have lost in a measure the spirit of Christians and we have never had, as we ought, the spirit of missionaries. God is putting us into the school of affliction to prepare us for our work.[43]

During the summer and autumn in Little Rock, Sister D succumbed to the ague, or bilious remittent fever. These nineteenth-century medical terms refer to malarial infection.[44] With each of the repeated bouts of fever, Sister D lapsed into delirium. Reverend Vaill reported in his correspondence: "The removal of her fever, and the recovery of her general health, were, unhappily, unaccompanied by the restoration of her intellectual powers. She sunk into a state of mental imbecility."[45] Unlike Sisters Johnson and Hoyt and Mrs. Requa, who became delirious and unbalanced during malarial fevers but eventually regained their reason, Sister D remained melancholy and withdrawn.

Dr. Daniel Drake (1785–1852), a noted nineteenth-century authority on malaria and a physician in practice in the Upper Mississippi Valley, describes malaria or "autumnal fever" by citing the following symptoms: chills alternating with high fever and sweats, yellowing of the skin, delirium and coma, and at times death.[46] Drake discovered that many patients, after severe and repeated episodes of delirium associated with malaria, suffered mental impairment. Writing in *A Systematic Treatise, Historical, Etiological, and Practical, on the Principal Diseases of the Interior Valley of North America* (1856) he states, "The intellectual functions, and the feelings and affections of the mind are passive; and the expression of the countenance is vacant and stupid. In some cases, a considerable degree of delirium supervenes; but in others, the facilities of the mind, almost up to the moment of dissolution, show nothing more than inactivity."[47]

Sister D's course of illness resembled that described in Drake's clinical account. She fell victim to an epidemic disease that ravaged the Upper Mississippi Valley and the southeastern frontier from 1810 until 1870. John McCulloh's *An Essay on the Remittent and Intermittent Diseases* (1830) questioned the possibility of settling this area so ridden with disease and detrimental to the health of migrants. Ackerknecht, drawing upon nineteenth-century textbooks, medical geographies, memoirs, travel reports, army statistics, and medical journals, reveals the pervasive malariousness of the prairies and western frontier, afflicting Indians and white settlers alike.[48]

Thomas Nuttall's *A Journal of Travels into the Arkansa Territory* (1819) describes the conditions prevailing at the times of the Union Mission's arrival. Nuttall succumbed to a virulent attack of malaria on August 14, 1819, and his illness continued until the late fall. Nuttall needed to convalesce at the army garrison of Fort Smith on the Grand River. He wrote,

> In consequence of sickness, and an extreme debility, which deprived me of the pleasure of my usual excursions, I remained at the garrison until the 16th of October.... Amongst my associates in affliction were numbered two missionaries, who had intended to proceed to the Osages. One of them, (Mr. Viner), after the attacks of a lingering fever, paid the debt of nature. From July to October, the ague and bilious fever spread throughout the territory in a very unusual manner.[49]

Nuttall had a chance encounter with the advance party of the Union Mission and had witnessed the death of Vinall and the recovery of Assistant Superintendent Chapman. Doubtless, Chapman had warned the mission family of their risk. However, malaria would be accepted as one form of adversity, among many, characteristic of a missionary's life. Reverends Chapman and Vaill viewed illness and other adversities as the inevitable sufferings of missionaries. They counseled the mission family to bear this suffering as an opportunity for humiliation and the reaffirmation of faith and spiritual growth, and they urged upon each missionary the metaphor of the pilgrim in temporary sojourn in this world. Vaill wrote on January 1, 1821, "We are now travelers, weary indeed, but walking through such grace assisting us, to what the appointed time of our arrival. O, that we might all learn to feel and to act more and more as pilgrims and strangers on the earth."[50]

Historically, malaria had stricken missionaries in the seventeenth century in Virginia, the Carolinas, and New Jersey.[51] Missionary intelligence published monthly obituaries of domestic and foreign missionaries felled by attacks of cholera, consumption, dysentery, malaria, and other pestilences. Reverend Vaill offered the following supplication and pastoral care, endeavoring to make their suffering bearable. He termed their troubles "our light afflictions,"

> because we hope they will work out for us a far more exceeding and eternal weight of glory. The Mission Family have, by these trials, been called to bear the yoke; but it is only suffering affliction with other missionaries who have gone before us—yea, with Christ, the Captain of our salvation. We have already seen them needful, and we have no reasons to doubt that this school is the best for missionaries entering this field.[52]

Vaill's spiritual direction proved essential in helping to sustain a fragile community prostrated by sickness and death. From 1820 to 1827, the mission lost ten persons. Reverend Chapman died in 1825 of typhus, Mrs. George Requa died from malaria in 1826, and eight of the missionary's children perished.[53] Miss D, George Requa, and Mrs. Fuller never regained sufficient strength and health to work in any capacity. Stephen Fuller's letter to Jeremiah Evarts petitioned the board of managers for dismissal due to the continued sickness of his wife. Fuller spent most of his time caring for his invalid wife and could devote little attention to the mission. He wrote on September 11, 1826, "After mature deliberation and ardent prayer for direction it appears to be duty for me to leave this mission on account of the ill health of my family. Mrs. F. for nearly five years has been visited with sickness, which, notwithstanding her ardent desire to be useful has rendered her incapable of active service."[54]

Despite many setbacks—the epidemics that produced universal sickness, all-too-common death, or disability that necessitated the hiring of outsiders to build the mission and run the farm—the mission family never lapsed into despair. Not even the intertribal warfare between the Osages and Cherokees or the untimely death of Indian students dampened their spirit. Writing a summation of their experiences as of May 25, 1822, Reverend Vaill could point with satisfaction to the formation of a mission church and the steadfastness of the faithful. "Neither the severe and protracted sicknesses of the family, nor the confused noise of the battle of the warrior, appears to have arrested their zeal, or impeded their progress. Under all their trials and adversities they have put their trust in their Covenant God, and have, thus far, been sustained by his omnipresent arm."[55]

For nearly three years, from July 1820 until March 1823, the mission family had accepted the burdensome task of providing around-the-clock care for Sister D. She was unable to feed or dress herself and manifested what were termed mental imbecility, somatic rigidity, and social withdrawal as a helpless invalid. She could not assist in her duties in the kitchen, and illness prevented her from partaking in public or "social worship" and communion in the mission church. The mission journal records the following entry for Sunday, November 4, 1821:

> Sister D has been for several months in a deranged state of mind. Her derangement came on during her sickness last year, and has continued to this time to a greater or lesser degree. Not only has she refrained from social worship, but much of the time has required the watchful attention of some of the family. We think it our duty to make her case known to the Board. We have delayed this unpleasant task, hoping she might be restored. This afflictive providence God has sent upon us for wise and holy purposes. We thought our trials great before, still we do not complain.[56]

Vaill wrote to Reverend Gillet of Branford, Connecticut, in December 1821, stating, "Sister D has been for some time deranged in mind, which is our greatest trial, at present, within."[57] She had become so burdensome that by June of 1822, two mission sisters devoted their full attention to her care. This deprived the family of adequate female help in the kitchen and Vaill petitioned the UFMS for additional female assistance.

The mission family indulged Sister D by granting her permission to ride on horseback when the weather was fair during the summer and fall of 1823. Her unsupervised excursions relieved the mission of the burden of care and seemed to promote a calm and rational demeanor. However, she failed to return during one outing in mid-November and this provoked a frantic two-day search. The mission journal records the second day of her elopement. "This morning as soon as it was light, proceeded in search of Sister D. Directed by a merciful Providence we found her about three miles distant, wandering at random. She continued on horseback through the night, and had rambled many miles. Thus God preserves his children from harm. We have great occasion for thanksgiving."[58] The situation had deteriorated by August 1823 as evidenced in Vaill's statement in the mission journal:

> Sister D.'s health is at this time low. Her mind is about as much disordered as it has been for a long time past. She is desirous to return to her friends; a favour which the Board have granted, and which she will probably enjoy as soon as the season of the year will admit. The dealings of Providence towards this sister have been mysterious. We have written to her friends, giving them an account of her situation. May God enable them to bear the affliction with Christian resignation.[59]

Miss D was dismissed from service and returned home to Litchfield at the spring thaw in March 1823. The mission journal records the following entry: "Mar. 10 Resolved that Brother Geo. Requa and Sarah Vaill accompany Sister D to New York. Concluded that as Sarah is a discrete youth and one whom Sister D is particularly pleased she would be sufficient unless Sister D's insanity should increase. In that case, Bro. Requa will if possible obtain other help."[60]

Significantly, the mission family had waited for almost four years until they had lost all hope of Sister D's recovery. From their arrival at the mission site in February 13, 1821 until her departure, the family cared for her in the face of the tremendous work required of them. Within the year they had constructed nineteen cabins and structures including a church, dining hall, and school. They established a farm and stocked it with cattle and hogs. Despite repeated outbreaks of malaria, influenza, and typhus, frustrated by shortages of supplies, difficulties in attracting Osage children, and the continual anxiety produced by intertribal warfare, the mission cared for Sister D and prayed for her eventual recovery. Only after they concluded that her insanity and invalidism made continuance at Union detrimental to the well-being of the family were arrangements made for her return to the East.

Reverend Vaill, reflects the loving concern that the family manifested toward Sister D. Writing in May 1823, two months after her removal, he explained,

> In point of health, the members of the family, with the exception of two, have been highly favoured. The exceptions are Mr. George Requa and Miss D; neither of whom has been restored to confirmed health since the severe sicknesses they endured at Little Rock in the summer of 1820. Both have solicited and obtained permission to return.... Her case still excites the commiseration of the family and the Board. At her request, and in accordance with the advice of her physician, she has taken leave of missionary life, and is on her return to her family and friends.[61]

Miss D returned to her father's home in Litchfield under the care of her younger sisters. She became the patient of William Buel, a local physician noted for his treatment of malaria. Dr. Buel served as an important correspondent in a study of intermittent fever in New England conducted by the Massachusetts Medical Society. Oliver Wendell Holmes's *Dissertation on Intermittent Fever in New England* (1838) relied extensively on the accounts of therapeutic procedures and clinical observations made by Buel in 1831.[62] Buel treated patients suffering from malaria with regimes of purgatives, chiefly calomel, followed by the free use of emetics. After the initial depletion of feverish patients, he administered large doses of Peruvian bark (quinine), a highly effective therapeutic agent.[63]

Dr. Buel arranged in the spring of 1825, in an interview with Dr. Eli Todd, superintendent of the Hartford Retreat, to have Miss D admitted as a patient for a three-month trial period. As he stated in a letter to Dr. Todd, "with this will be presented to you by her sister Miss D, the young woman I mentioned to you at Hartford. You will receive with her 39 Dols. payment for one quarter's expenses. . . . This sum has been obtained by donations from her neighbors as she and her father are unable to make the advances."[64]

Buel presents a short account of her past missionary activities, illnesses, and a brief statement of her derangement. Indeed, Dr. Buel, her family, and the UFMS board of managers entered into a conspiracy by developing the ruse that Miss D would enter the asylum, voluntarily, in pursuit of her life's ambition as a missionary agent authorized to evangelize the unredeemed souls among the patients and staff of the retreat. He writes in his letter of introduction,

> The cause of missions I understand still continues to be very much the subject of her reflections and future plans of life, and has been ever since she engaged in the business. Her friends have successfully availed themselves of this state of facts to induce her to go voluntarily and cheerfully to the retreat. She considers herself as in the employment and under the direction of the Board (U.F.M.S.), and has authority (obtained for the purpose to satisfy her) for believing that they have sent a missionary to the retreat with a view to moral and religious agency on the inmates of the institution.[65]

At the age of twenty-seven, single, and suffering from bilious remittent fever and tuberculosis, Miss D entered the asylum broken down in her life and health. She was treated for seven months in 1825 and returned for two weeks in 1826. Miss D was readmitted a chronic and incurable patient in 1830 and remained until 1832.

Miss D lived in three families: her birth family of orientation, the Union Mission "education family," and the retreat "family" of patients and staff committed to the structure of moral treatment for the insane. Moral treatment provided patients with nutritious meals and medications to palliate their despair, soothe their agitation, and treat their physical illness. Dr. Eli Todd, then superintendent, acted as a father figure, hosting afternoon teas, walks in the spacious gardens, and carriage rides in the rural countryside. He encouraged patients to write letters and poetry so that he might assess their returning powers of reason and self-control. Women were expected to sew, knit, and read as evidence of the commitment to the productive use of their time and the return of their reason. This fictive family was meant to emulate an idealized and comfortable urban middle-class household characterized by the bonds of affection and intimacy. The transition from colonial households to the modern family in the antebellum period change in households did not occur because of changes to the size and composition of the family, the age of first marriage, or the number of children that a woman might expect to bear. The beginnings of urbanization and industrialization also did not produce these changes. The modern family was characterized by a cultural revolution of values and sentiment that extolled intimacy, companionship, and loving communication between husband and wife, and parent and child.[66] The ideal of moral treatment initiated by Dr. Todd in the retreat family attempted to recreate this domestic intimacy and affection between patients (children) and paternalistic asylum staff (in loco parentis) for high-functioning patients who lived in the upper floors of the commodious Centre Building.[67] The culture of the retreat also extolled the gender designations for true womanhood: piety, purity, domesticity, and submission. However, the regimen of kindness and moderation of moral management viewed Brainerd's model of evangelical piety and inner-worldly asceticism as symptomatic of religious excitement and religious mania or melancholy. Moral management did not prove efficacious for Miss D.

During her third and final admission, Miss D was treated as a chronic and incurable patient in the terminal phase of pulmonary tuberculosis and languishing in religious despair. She did not live in the domestic intimacy of the retreat family in the Centre Building apartments. Miss D was now sequestered in a ward reserved for chronic and incurable patients. She received support from her sister and charitable donations from concerned neighbors and the ABCFM.

Miss D had agreed to come to the retreat under the ruse that she would evangelize the patients and staff and thus pursue her career as a missionary.

One can imagine her feverish and obsessive exhortation of the doctors, aides, and nursing staff, and her preaching to fellow patients who viewed these rants as evidence of her enduring madness. Throughout her three commitments, she manifested a singular obsession: the haunting desire to return to missionary work—the grief over her failure to succeed in missionary service. In April of 1832, two months after her release from the retreat, Miss D died of consumption with her family in Litchfield. Her missionary vocation, forged in the smithy of Brainerd's evangelical piety, ended in failure, despair, madness, and early death from infectious disease.

Some burdens proved too crushing to sustain for missionary women who had seen their fervent hopes dashed by illness. Even Mrs. Asenath Vaill, the wife of Reverend William F. Vaill of the Union Mission, eventually succumbed to depression, prompting her husband's resignation in 1834 in order to take her east for treatment.[68] The endless chain of missionary intelligence encouraged each missionary to mold his or her character after the self-abasing piety of a Brainerd, to embrace religious melancholy as the impetus to holiness and the foundation of their vocation. When the inevitable frustrations, disappointments, and setbacks befell their mission, they interpreted each adversity through the relentless quest for spiritual victory in the midst of worldly defeat.

For those like D, Asenath Vaill, and countless others imbued with Brainerd's evangelical piety and model of personhood, failure offered a renewed opportunity for self-torture. They blamed their indwelling sin or spiritual inadequacy to account for the chastisement of divine Providence. As always, the melancholy spirit proved a constant companion to their missionary spirit.

The full reckoning and "counting the cost of faith," particularly for missionary women, has yet to be tallied.[69] Lydia Huffman Hoyle identifies five hundred women who were sent to Native American missions from 1815 to 1860. They embarked, as did Miss D, with a sense of calling, of surrendering their lives to the most sacred task of helping to build the Kingdom of God in America.[70] We close with the words of Lydia Purchase of the Oregon mission, who provides a statement of faith and purpose, of melancholy and doubt followed by reconciliation with God:

Oh! How I longed to break the ties that so sinful bound me to the earth and to be loosed from my sin. By my soul was enchained with a heavy chain and all my efforts proved ineffectual. . . . I was led to a full view of the great worth of the Christian cause. I then resolved to trust in the strength of Jesus to live for his sake for the promotion of his kingdom, even if life were a burden. From that time I gradually received strength and evidence of reconciliation with my heavenly father. I was not fill [sic] with inexpressible joy, but with a most ardent desire to do something good.[71]

3

The Endless Chain of Religious Intelligence

The Emergence of an American Evangelical Identity

The lives, travails, and untimely deaths of missionary women like Dolly Hoyt and Miss D need to be seen as exemplars of piety and religious personhood championed by evangelical thought in an age of awakenings. Religious periodicals and published memoirs commemorated each life lost in the cause of domestic and foreign missions, adding another link in the seemingly endless chain of religious intelligence that inspired many readers to dedicate their lives to the cause of extending the light of the Gospel to the darkness of perishing heathens.

This religious intelligence provided a cultural template and idealized model that instructed missionary women about how to forge a life in the crucible of Brainerd's legacy of piety, how to foster a distinctive religious personhood founded upon evangelical Protestant values and purposes. However, we need to consider the fate of evangelical idealism when missionaries entered the field and encountered adversity, where their lived experiences did not conform to the romanticized accounts that first drew them to this religious vocation and adventure.

The endless chain of religious intelligence included countless tracts, devotional literature and pastoral theology, and book-length memoirs of missionaries and epigones of conversion and godly living that reached a national audience. During the first three decades of the nineteenth century, with the rise of literacy, the market revolution, the new technologies of publishing, and the efforts of national, not-for-profit publishing societies, America entered an era of mass media publication and the systematic distribution of printed material.[1] During the 1820s and 1830s the American Bible Society, the American Tract Society (ATS), and the American Sunday School Union pursued the goals of distributing bibles and religious literature to the newly settled regions of the South and West, motivated by the millennial idea that books and the printed word would foster conversion and the Kingdom of God in America. The ATS, founded in New York in 1825 as a nondenominational outreach of Congregational and Presbyterian supporters, created by 1841 a national distribution system of salaried *colporteurs*. By the 1850s, these agents had visited more than 2 million homes and sold or gave away 2.4 million books.[2] The ATS published inexpensive editions of "evangelical classics": Jonathan Edwards's *Treatise Concerning Religious Affections* and *The Life of Brainerd*, Richard Baxter's *The Call to the Unconverted*, John Bunyan's *The Pilgrim's Progress*, Philip Doddridge's *The Rise and Progress of Religion of the Soul*, and John Flavel's *Touchstone of Sincerity*.[3] Mass media publications aided by the growth of literacy, especially among women, fostered a growing national understanding about spirituality, making a godly life, and experiencing authentic religious emotions.

The mass appeal and publication of religious intelligence effectively institutionalized the representations of the missionary spirit and gender. These publications enjoined women to embrace the virtues of piety, purity, domesticity, and submission in the cause of domestic and foreign missions. With self-denying love for those perishing in darkness, missionary women embodied romantic optimism and the heroic mythology of workers sent to convert the world. Even accounts of setbacks born of overwork, internal conflict within the mission, warfare and Native resistance, sickness, and early death did not dampen the zeal of the women and men that was captured in the endless chain of religious intelligence. Exemplary dying and deathbed testimonies recounted the unflagging faith and submission of the missionary to Christ, extolling his or her many virtues. The memoirs were intended to encourage readers to join this cause.[4]

The life of Mrs. Sarah L. Smith proves a case in point. Born Sarah Huntington in 1802 to a prosperous merchant family in Norwich, Connecticut, as a youth she immersed herself in missionary religious intelligence. Her biographer notes she devoted her time to

> listening to preaching on the subject of Christian missions; reading the Missionary Herald, and tracts on missions; attending anniversaries of missionary societies auxiliary to the American Board; attending on the monthly concert, in which she was exemplary for her steadiness; looking at the great field of the world, so desolate and pondering the need for more laborers in the field . . . fixing her attention upon the spiritual condition and wants of a remnant of the Mohegan tribe of Indians living six miles from Norwich; by devoting herself personally to their instruction.[5]

At age twenty-nine, single, living in her parents' home, she met Reverend Eli Smith, who was on leave from his mission to Syria and Persia. After a brief courtship, they married and returned to the Middle East, where she died of consumption in 1836, age thirty-four. Missionary intelligence served as both an advertisement for a religious vocation to embrace an errand into the world and convert the perishing heathen and a theodicy to console and make meaningful the suffering, sickness, and death of missionaries who did not live long enough to realize their sublime aspirations.

Jonathan Edwards published *The Life of David Brainerd* in 1742, which was destined to become an evangelical classic during the Second Great Awakening and a spiritual guide for those who heeded the call to missions. Brainerd's spiritual life was marked, by his own admission, with persistent religious melancholy, obsessive applications of devotional piety—godly sorrow and humiliation, repentance, meditation, fasting, and prayer. Yet this self-torture and mortification built the foundation of an exemplary Christian life of progressive sanctification, selflessness, and disinterested benevolence directed toward the cause of Indian missions. Edwards's *Life of David Brainerd* became a model of authentic conversion and New Divinity spirituality and the chief exemplar for succeeding generations of missionaries and missionary training at colleges devoted to the New Divinity like Yale, Williams, and Middlebury, and Andover Theological Seminary.[6]

Throughout the antebellum period, men trained in divinity and literate laymen read Brainerd's memoir and emulated his exemplary piety and life that was devoted to the conversion of the heathen. Samuel Allis represents one example of Brainerd's influence. Born in 1805 in Conway, Massachusetts, Allis received a common school education and apprenticed as a saddle maker. In 1826 he relocated to Ithaca, New York, and was influenced by Reverend Samuel Parker, an Andover-trained minister who wanted to establish a mission in the Far West. Parker and Allis and Reverend John Dunbar were commissioned in 1834 by the ABCFM to undertake a mission to the Flat Head Indians. When they arrived in Saint Louis late in the season, they were unable to cross the Rocky Mountains in winter. Parker returned to the East, and Dunbar and Allis spent nearly two years traveling with Pawnee bands along the Platte River in Missouri, seeking to learn their language and prepare for a mission station. Allis would remain with the Pawnees as a missionary and interpreter until his retirement in 1861.[7]

Writing to Reverend David Green, corresponding secretary of the American Board in July 1836, Allis invoked the evangelical humility and piety of Brainerd. He wrote,

> I am thankful that my lot has been cast here. I rejoice to look forward to the day when these Indians shall give up their superstitions, and worship the one only living and true God. Although the progress is slow I hope to see them in my day enquiring what they shall do to be saved, although there are many missionaries among the American Indians I fear there are but few who had the spirret [sic] of Branerd (which was the spirret of Christ.) I judge no one but myself, I have to acknowledge that I do not have that spirret I do not possess that high standard of piety that I ought. Oh may I feel more the value of the soul of the poor Indians, and may the love of *him* who has done so much for me melt my hard heart, and separate the dross of sin and pollution which has ascendancy over me.[8]

David W. Kling argues that in the first decades of the republic, a missionary theology unfolded where new born men and women's lives and religious identities were forged in the crucible of revivals. Missionaries aspired to make lives imbued with the values of abiding love and disinterested benevolence, and they felt duty-bound to spread the Gospel to the American frontier and throughout the world. Through Christ's unlimited atonement, a universalism of grace envisioned the salvation of all peoples. In this manner, the spread of missions and the labors of missionary men and women as the instruments God's Providence would hasten the millennial day, a wondrous fulfillment of prophesy that was felt to be imminent.[9]

The chain of religious and missionary intelligence documented the unfolding of a millennial narrative of evangelical and national collective identity, of sentimental and romantic depictions of heroic lives devoted and lost in pursuit of utopian dreams.[10]

Early candidates for missionary service were typically young men and women, in their twenties, well-educated in colleges for men and female seminaries for women, and residents of New England. They made formal application to the American Board of Commissioners for Foreign Missions or other sponsoring Baptist and Methodist societies. Linda M. Clemmons explains in *Conflicted Mission*, "Candidates sent evidence of their educational background, age, and marital status. Most important, applicants forwarded testimonials about their piety from local church officials or theological professors. In the selection process, the potential missionary's piety, faith, devotion and formal theological training received precedence over any secular training."[11]

The ideal missionary women as portrayed in memoirs and religious intelligence entered into service through hastily arranged marriages. Sponsored by their husbands, women embraced the heroic ideal of wife, mother, teacher, and devoted helpmate. Missionary wives reared children, maintained a pious domesticity, catechized Native children, taught domestic arts, and organized praying meetings and Sunday school.[12] The endless chain of religious intelligence promoted self-denial, sacrifice, and humility—a heroic religious personhood characterized by an inward spiritual pilgrimage and outward journey. Missionary wives anticipated a loving emotional intimacy and companionate marriage with their husbands and the potential to enter into a more equal partnership with their husbands in their missionary vocation. Such heightened expectations proved impossible to fulfill.

Additional links in this chain would soon follow. Reverend Henry Martyn, who would distinguish himself as a missionary in India, decided upon a missionary career after reading Edwards's *Life of Brainerd* in 1802. John Sargent, Martyn's biographer writes, of the decision to enter the cause of missions, "his soul was filled with a holy emulation of that extraordinary man [Brainerd], and after deep consideration and fervent prayer, he was at length fixed in a resolution to imitate his example."[13] Martyn embraced Brainerd's regimen of religious melancholy and evangelical humiliation. Only through the depths of self-maceration and self-annihilation could he achieve holiness requisite to labor in the cause of missions. Throughout Martyn's journals, he recorded the familiar cycle that marked Brainerd's struggle—the vileness of sin, alienation from God's love, spiritual desolation, and at times the evanescent experience of meditative rapture. He would write just weeks before embarking upon his mission to India,

> What a sink of corruption is the heart! and yet I can go from day to day in self-seeking and self-pleasing! Lord! show me myself as nothing but wounds and bruises and putrefying sores, and teach me to live by faith on Christ my all.... How much better is it to have a peaceful sense of my own wretchedness, and a humbler waiting upon God for sanctifying grace, than to talk much, and appear to be somebody in religion![14]

Those like Martyn and David Bacon embraced an inward spiritual pilgrimage, a meditative introspection marked by seasons of coldhearted melancholy and distance from the Holy Spirit alternating with seasons of rapture and grace. Trials, afflictions, and failures were recast as special afflictions, providential tests of faith, and opportunities for resignation to God, sanctification, and the growth of piety. The men and women who emulated Brainerd fostered interiority by turning their attention away from the subjects of the mission—perishing heathens—and focusing on a ceaseless, ruminative, and melancholy self-examination.

The dramatic story of the Haystack Prayer Meeting recounts the impetus and founding moment of the foreign mission movement. Williams College students Samuel J. Mills, Samuel Newell, Adoniram Judson, and Luther Rice, under the influence of New Divinity revivals, assembled in the summer of 1806 in a grove for religious inquiry. They sought refuge from a thunderstorm in a haystack and, during prayer, dedicated their lives to the cause of missions.

They were instrumental in establishing the ABCFM in 1810. In 1812, Adoniram and Ann Hasseltine Judson, Samuel and Rosanne Peck Nott, Samuel and Harriet Attwood Newell, Samuel Nott, Luther Rice, and Gordon Hall departed as ABCFM missionaries to India.[15] These pioneers and others who followed in their train suffered illness, debility, early death, and frustration in completing their sublime errand into the world.

Joanna Bowen Gillespie examines the emerging literary genre in the early nineteenth century of the religious memoir. She explains, "The materials of religious self-examination and correspondence written by exemplary Christian women, posthumously compiled and published as their 'memoirs' by husbands, daughters, mothers, or friends, became a literary staple for evangelical readers in the new nation."[16] Protracted and repeated experiences of religious melancholy characterize these memoirs, particularly the accounts of Ann H. Judson, Susan Huntington, and Sarah Huntington.[17] For example, Susan Huntington (1791–1823), a minister's wife who lived in Boston, suffered unending seasons of religious melancholy until her untimely death from consumption. She wrote in her journal,

> February 17, 1815 I feel tonight something of that distressing nervous depression which my God has so graciously prevented for a long time.... Blessed be his name that I have for several months, been almost uniformly cheerful and enjoyed great mental composure! But Oh Should he leave me! A reed shaken with the wind! What should I do![18]

And these memoirs inspired the piety and ambitions of other contemporary young women. Mrs. Sarah Louisa (Foote) Taylor (1809–1836) kept a diary of her spiritual struggles beginning in 1828 until her death from consumption at age twenty-seven. She avidly read the memoirs of Ann Hudson, Sarah Huntington, and other foreign missionary wives, seeking to emulate their piety and disinterested benevolence in the cause of bringing Gospel light to pagan darkness. She shared their spiritual itinerary of melancholy alternating with times of assurance. She would write on November 14, 1830, "In reading the life of Mrs. Huntington, I have been greatly struck with the similarity between many of her feelings and my own. I find her expressing doubts, as to ever having had correct views of the character of God, and his attributes, and of the odiousness of sin in his sight."[19] Earlier that year, she read the memoir of Ann Hasseltine Hudson and remarked, "Never before was I so sensible of the real condition of the heathen. It seems to me that I could calmly, yes, joyfully, leave home and all its endearments, and spend my days amongst them, should the Lord in his Providence prepare the way."[20]

After completing her education at Bacon Academy in Colchester, Connecticut, she removed to New York City in 1826 to keep a school for girls. Miss Foote was baptized in 1829 but continued to suffer doubt and despondency. She was devoted to self-examination and prayer and spent many hours each week in the "secret seasons in the closet." At times she enjoyed selfless surrender to Jesus and the assurance as a child of God. Not infrequently, she lapsed into despondency that lasted days and even weeks. At these times she would observe, "Often when I scan the motives which influence my conduct, I find them such, that I shrink from the investigation and am willing to acknowledge even to myself, the deceit and depravity seated in this heart."[21]

Although marriage and a debilitating, wasting consumption prevented Sarah Louisa Taylor from devoting her life in disinterested benevolence to the missionary cause, the published memoirs helped her shape her own devotional piety and participate vicariously in the building of the Redeemer's Kingdom.

As Lisa Joy Pruitt argues in *A Looking Glass for Ladies*, missionary wives and mothers represented a "living parable of Christian family life in heathen lands," who having had the good fortune of coming of age in a Christian nation with the advantages of family, friends, education, and religious conversion, hoped to bring evangelical religion to the heathen.[22] Committed to the New Divinity theology of evangelical piety, progressive sanctification, and disinterested benevolence, missionary memoirs constituted a literature of consolation that sanctified suffering.[23]

Missionary women, whether married or single, worked as nurses, catechists, and schoolteachers and assisted in domestic affairs while struggling to adapt to an alien culture. They encountered disease, death, and the particularly unsettling death of children. Consistent with the prevailing cultural idea of "true womanhood," they were perceived as the passive receptacles for the Holy Spirit, ever obedient and submissive to God and the authority of their husbands and the mission superintendents.[24] However, new born missionary women were not passive, docile, and submissive. Paradoxically, they employed the character strengths of this gender role allocation of true women to achieve public careers as missionaries. They could claim the attributes of piety and the strengths and virtue of Protestant evangelical character as a cultural legitimation to move from the private domestic sphere (angels of the household) and adapt to public vocations in domestic and foreign missions.

The Memoirs of Mrs. Harriet Newell, Wife of Rev. Samuel Newell, published in 1814, continues the chain of missionary intelligence. Coinciding with the rise of popular evangelical print culture for the masses and literacy among Native-born women in the young republic, Harriet Newell became an iconic figure in the first half of the nineteenth century. As Mary Kupiec Cayton explains, "Newell's story came to symbolize for many women evangelicals the central role they had been called to play in world history. Heroines of a new culture, an 'imagined community' galvanized through the publication and dissemination of missionary narratives, they helped to create a place for middle-class women as influential actors in the public realm."[25] By 1840, the memoir was reprinted in fifty editions throughout America, England, Scotland, and Ireland and the given name Harriet Newell became a popular choice for evangelical daughters in this period.[26]

Born in 1793, this "naturally cheerful and unreserved young woman" came of age in Haverhill, Massachusetts, attended Bradford Academy, and found religion at the age of fourteen in the revival of 1806. The daughter of a prosperous merchant, she agonized for nearly four years about assuming the life of a missionary.

Throughout this period of self-examination and doubt, the previously cheerful and outgoing young woman turned reclusive and melancholy. She wrote in her journal in 1810, "What a dreadful stink of wickedness is my heart. Must I resign the idea of ever feeling the *power* of religion? Surely if I am a child of God, I could not live so stupid."[27] However, her diary and correspondence contained numerous accounts of assurance and joy. She wrote in 1809, "When conversing with a Christian friend upon the love of Jesus, I was lost in rapture."[28] She would write later that year these words after the contemplation of Christ: "Descend thou Holy Spirit: breathe into my soul a flame of ardent love, let not my affections wander from the *one* and *only* thing that is needful."[29]

On October 20, 1810, a week after celebrating her eighteenth birthday, she resolved to dedicate her life to the cause of foreign missions:

> A female friend called this morning. She informed me of her determination to quit her native land, to endure the sufferings of a Christian amongst heathen nations—to spend her days in India's sultry clime. How did this news affect my heart! Is she willing to do all this for God, and shall I refuse to lend my little aid in a land where divine revelation has shed its clearest rays.... What can I do, that the light of gospel may shine upon them [heathens]? They are perishing for lack of knowledge while I enjoy the glorious privileges of a Christian land.[30]

Harriet's resolve did not quiet her scrupulous conscience, and she languished for a year in religious melancholy, asking in her journal entry of February 24, 1811, "My God, why hast thou forsaken me?"[31] She was introduced to Reverend Newell later that year. He needed to marry before assuming his missionary ordination. She needed to marry to receive a proper status within the mission cause as it was a woman's place to tend to the domestic needs of her husband, bear children, and serve as companion and helpmate to her spouse in the cause of missions. After a six-week proper and loveless courtship, they wed. However, Harriet's religious melancholy remained a constant companion. Prior to embarking for India with her new husband she would write, "Depressed with guilt and tired with the vanities of this world. I have retired to my chamber, to seek pleasures within. When blessed with a sense of Immanuel's love, I feel satisfaction in writing, conversing, and thinking on divine things; but when Jesus frowns, all is midnight darkness."[32]

Newell's writings embraced the themes of the shortness of life and passage of time, her self-image taken from Bunyan's *Pilgrim's Progress* as a pilgrim in a strange land, and the need to discern and submit to divine will. Writing on March 26, 1812, in a diary dedicated to her mother while in passage to India, she speaks of a "sweet serenity of mind" as she incorporates these tropes: "I feel this morning like a pilgrim and a traveller in a dry and thirsty land where no water is. Heaven is my home; there I trust my weary soul will sweetly rest, after a tempestuous voyage across the ocean of life."[33]

Harriet Newell died on November 30, 1812, from complications following the birth of her first child. Her last days were memorialized as a model of Christian dying as she suffered the fate of so many missionary wives— untimely death and maternal depletion from the unrelenting burdens of childbearing and missionary domesticity.[34]

Harriet Newell's *Memoir* would inspire others to embrace the necessity of evangelical humiliation and religious melancholy as a spiritual prerequisite for a missionary vocation. Before deciding to become a missionary, Dolly Hoyt of the Union Mission wrote in her diary, "Read the life of Mrs. Newell."[35] Harriet Winslow eagerly read Newell's biography and embraced a "holy emulation" of this model of spirituality. Winslow wrote from New Haven, Connecticut, on September 13, 1814, "Why was Harriet Newell taken from life, and a creature of so little worth as I am continued here? Am I reserved for similar usefulness? I will encourage such a hope. . . . I am thoroughly convinced that no service is so delightful as that of my Saviour—that no privations, no sufferings, are too great for his children to endure for his sake."[36]

The missionary efforts of Adoniram and Ann Hasseltine Judson, Baptist foreign missionaries to Burma, touched the popular imagination, as they became household names by 1850. Ann Judson's, memorialized in 1828 after her early death, drew national attention to the cause of foreign missions and reanimated evangelical sensibility toward Christian women who selflessly exposed themselves to disease and early death in the service of the Redeemer's cause.[37] Even a summary reading of missionary intelligence in this time reveals the great number of missionaries felled by disease, disability, discouragement, and death. Less sympathetic reviewers of the missionary cause and the exploits of Ann Judson remarked in the Unitarian *Christian Examiner* in 1829, "What has been the fruit, or what may reasonably be expected to be the fruit, of all these labors, and sufferings; of all these privations, sacrifices, sicknesses, and deaths? The answer is, as yet, the conversion, real or only external, of a few native heathens."[38]

Adoniram Judson's third wife, a popular novelist in her own right, felt compelled to write *The Kathayan Slave* in 1853 to defend the missionary spirit as founded upon the love of God—not madness, fanaticism, or blind utopian fancy. She argues, "That which is madness and folly in the eyes of one, is regarded by others as but a simple, affectionate, trustful act of obedience to Him."[39] Emily Judson depicts the fictional missionary in her essay as a young woman who announces to her family her intention to evangelize the heathen. "Calmly and deliberately she proposes a sacrifice of all she is now—of all her future earthly prospects."[40] Guided by Christian love for the unredeemed, steadfast in her faith, the young woman proclaims, "The mission enterprise cannot fail until it ushers in that Sabbath of the world—the Christian Jubilee."[41] The symbolism of martyrdom for a utopian cause, although directed to evangelicals sympathetic to missions, inadvertently lends support to anti-missionary criticism.

Isaac McCoy's *History of Baptist Indian Missions* (1840) chronicled the all-too-common cycle of sickness, death, disability, and disaffection that befell missionaries in the Western frontier. After bouts of malaria as in the case of Miss D, missionaries succumbed to melancholy or derangement. McCoy records the case of one such missionary, a Mr. Lewis, who in 1833 "manifested an aberration of mind bordering on insanity."[42]

Accounts of domestic and foreign missionaries have a melancholy sameness. Samuel Nott was born in 1788 in Franklin, Connecticut. A minister's son, he graduated from Union College in 1808 and Andover Theological Seminary in 1810. Nott traveled with Gordon Hall to what was then known as Bombay in 1812, but illness forced his return to America in 1815, thus ending his missionary endeavor.[43]

Samuel John Mills was born in Torrington, Connecticut, in 1783 and graduated from Williams College in 1809. He was a leader of the Haystack

Revival and a revered champion of foreign missions. Mills entered Andover Theological Seminary in 1810 and became a domestic missionary after receiving his license to preach in 1812. He distributed Bibles in the South and West under the auspices of the Massachusetts Missionary Society and Philadelphia Bible Society. During a six-thousand-mile tour with Daniel Smith in 1814–1815, from Lake Erie to the Gulf of Mexico, he estimated a need for seventy-six thousand Bibles—one for each household. He wrote, "The whole country, from Lake Erie to the gulf of Mexico, is as the valley of the shadow of death. Darkness rests upon it. Only here and there, a few rays of gospel light pierce the awful gloom. This vast country contains more than a million inhabitants. Their number is every year increased by a mighty flood of emigration."[44]

Mills turned his attention to foreign missions. He died in 1818 on a return voyage from Sierra Leone while promoting the American Colonization Society and the efforts to return the "free people of color" to an African homeland. His mother eulogized her son with these words: "I have consecrated this child to the service of God as a missionary."[45] He would write to his sister during his voyage to Africa about his devotion to the missionary spirit. "The time will come, when the barbarous tribes of Africa shall worship Jesus as the king of Zion."[46] Gardiner Spring published Mills's memoir in 1819 to extoll his virtues for all to emulate. In Spring's estimation, employing the familiar trope of recounting the exemplary dying and virtues of a departed missionary, Mills demonstrated a deep and uniform piety and was a heavenly minded man of prayer, humble and benevolent.[47] Despite an early death and his failure to realize the goals of mission for freedmen, the publication of this religious intelligence was intended to validate his life and encourage others to follow in his train.

H. W. Pierson published *American Missionary Memorial* in 1853, an ensemble of essays to commemorate the lives and early deaths of twenty-nine missionaries, most from the first generation of American Board–sponsored men and women sent out to Asia, the Middle East, and India. They died young and each essayist needed to find meaning in death. In commemorating the death of Mrs. Catherine H. Scudder, age twenty-three, the following consoling statement is made: "God's way is always in the deep and his paths are not known; but how entirely inscrutable to us is the early death of a useful missionary."[48]

The following encyclopedia entry for William Hervey reveals the considerable time and resources spent on education, the lofty aspirations and futility of a short missionary career. His life was an exemplar of the missionary spirit:

> b. Kingsburgh, Warren Co., N.Y., U.S.A., January 22d, 1799, graduated at Williams College 1824; taught school a year, and then was a tutor in the college. He studied theology at Princeton Theological Seminary, and while there the reading of David Brainerd's Life awakened in him an earnest desire to engage in the foreign-missionary work. He was ordained in Park Street Church, Boston September 1829, as a missionary of the A.B.C.F.M., and sailed August 2d, 1830 for Calcutta, arriving in Bombay March 7th, 1831. He died of cholera in Ahmadnagar May 13th, 1832. Mrs. Hervey died May 3rd of the previous year.[49]

Hervey preached "The Spirit of Missions" in December 1829, three months after his ordination and prior to his departure to India in August 1830. In the preface to the published sermon, written in 1830 by E. D. Griffin of Williams College, Griffin counts Hervey's work as a tutor, his ministry during the college revivals in 1825–26, and the "heavings and melting of soul" as the young man struggled with religious melancholy and forged his missionary vocation in the crucible of the revival. Griffin reveals a telling conversation: "He has devoted himself to die, (*early*, as he told me,) on heathen ground."[50]

Hervey in his sermon inquires, what was the spirit of missions? What would motivate countless men and women to devote their lives in outreach to the six hundred million heathens in obedience to the injunction in Mark 16:15: "Go ye into all the world and preach the gospel to every creature?" What explains this outpouring of acosmic love and self-denial? He maintains that missionaries and those who supported this cause embraced "the missionary spirit" characterized by "the glory of God, the love of Christ, compassion for perishing souls, the unequal diffusion of light, the tried efficacy of the Gospel, the command of the risen Saviour, the promised blessing of God on our efforts, gratitude for past mercies, and the crown of glory prospect."[51]

Recounting the trope of the endless chain of missionary intelligence, he dedicates his life in "the spirit of Brainerd, Whitefield and Wesley, Martyn and Mills, Parsons and Fisk, Hall and Payson, Harriet Newell and Mrs. Judson, and thousands of others whose names are in the book of life. And such, I repeat, should be the spirit of each of us. We all have something to do on this great theatre of missionary operations."[52]

For so many missionary men and women, however noble the sentiment or steadfast their resolve, they did encounter privations and sufferings too great for a child of God to endure. Such was the case for one missionary wife, Mrs. Susana Champion, during her sojourn at one of the first missions to the Zulus in South Africa in 1837. Her husband, Reverend George Champion, attended Yale College from 1828 to 1831, completed his training for the ministry at Andover in 1834, and received an ABCFM appointment in January of that year to establish a pioneering mission in Zulu Land. Like Reverend Newell, Champion needed a wife who shared his evangelical fervor and willingness to abandon New England for the perils of missionary life. The American Board arranged a list of suitable young ladies. After several forays into the list, Champion found Susana Larned, whom he courted without expressions of romantic love. They married on November 14, 1834, and sailed from Boston on December 3.[53]

The Champion party arrived in Cape Town in February 6, 1835. Given the unsettled political situation between the British and Boers, and warfare with the Zulus, Champion was delayed in establishing his inland mission until August 1836 in Umlazi. The mission was named Ginani (I Am With You) and established a rudimentary school, church, and agricultural station. However, disagreements with the Zulu chief Dingaan soured Champion's effectiveness. Dingaan refused to allow children to attend school, workers to assist in mission projects, or tribesmen to receive religious instruction. Susana Champion remained committed to her work among the Zulu women and children. Writing to H. Hill, treasurer of the American Board, on October 2, 1837, she stated, "I think I feel more than ever that souls are perishing around us—we need labourers. You will probably hear from our brethren assembled that the Lord is opening a wide door as we trust in this land. But how few are we"[54]

How few, isolated, and vulnerable, indeed were the missionaries of Ginani, which was located directly in the path of the Boer Trek and Zulu Boer War of 1838. Following Dingaan's participation in the Retief Massacre of Boer settlers in March 1838, Zulus torched the mission station, and Champion and his family were forced to flee for their lives to Port Elizabeth. Susana was afflicted with malaria and lapsed into melancholia. Champion wrote to his brother-in-law Jonathan Edwards of Troy, New York, on March 8, 1838, "S. is not well. I must write it—tho' I did very deliberately—These commotions have affected her nervous system & she is at times quite down hearted."[55] He wrote to another missionary of his wife's illness: "S grew almost deranged with her sleepless nights and loss of appetite, and shattered nervous system. The people too often added to her fears by their strange moves always coming with spear and shield, and staying about us, as if spies on our actions."[56]

Susana anticipated a religious vocation of successful activism in promoting a mission school, educating and catechizing Zulu children, and working as a helpmate and partner with her husband. These expectations were sundered by malaria, religious despondency, and derangement during a time of warfare and indigenous resistance to missionary outreach. It appears that missionary wives whose vocations implied a desire for public religious vocations and yearning to be free from more restrictive gender roles suffered greater disappointments than did their husbands.

George and Susana Champion and their children returned to America in February 1839, arriving in Boston on April 11 of that year. Reverend Champion eventually assumed ministerial duties in Dover, New York, where he remained until his death from consumption in 1841. Susana died of this disease five years later in 1846.

Hannah Moore (1808–1868) was a single missionary woman who served in ABCFM's Dwight Mission to the Cherokee and Mount Pleasant Mission to the Choctaw in the 1840s and later with the American Missionary Association's Kaw Mendi Mission at Sherbro Island in Sierra Leone. Throughout her career, she rejected the model of submissive servant who would not voice her opinions or speak out of turn. Hannah was assertive, outspoken, and guided by conscience when she wrote letters of protest to the missionary societies and mission superintendents who employed her. She employed the attributes of evangelical piety and personhood to strive for agency in influencing mission policy and equal footing with ministers who served as superintendents of the mission station.

Hannah Moore was born in Union Connecticut to Samuel and Amy Moore, the sixth of ten children. She attended a revival conducted by Asahel Nettleton and entered the covenant of grace at the Union Congregational Church in 1829. She worked in a local textile mill and taught school to pay for the tuition at the Nichols Academy, which she attended from 1832 to 1835. At age thirty-one in 1841, the American Board employed her to teach reading, spelling, arithmetic, history, needlework, spinning, and weaving at the Dwight Mission.[57] Hannah wrote of her hopes for her religious vocation in the spirit of Brainerd's inner-worldly asceticism, "that it might please God to use me as an humble instrument of God to this benighted people."[58]

During her seven years of service she contracted malaria and suffered from intermittent fevers and relapses that undermined her health. Hannah also lost vision in one eye from a persistent infection. Writing to her mother during the first month at the mission, Hannah expressed her concern for the injustice of Indian removal and her sublime romanticism regarding the conversion of the heathen in this poem:

> Mother! I'm here in the Cherokee Nation
> With Employment assigned at the Missionary Station
> The work though important, but I wish to pursue
> Though responsible and arduous to make my way through
> There's a glorious prize at the end of the race
> Which will more than repay all the toils of the place
> And the souls of the heathen are worth far more
> Than the wealth of the Indies or Emperor's Store.
>   The poor Aborigines robbed of their rights
> Have traversed the wilderness in fugitive plights

> They were driven from their homes and the farms they did till
> The white man said leave them, they are mine at my will.⁵⁹

These romantic and sentimentalized depictions of mission life and Native peoples did not persist. Hannah found mission life arduous and conflicted as she disagreed with the policy of admitting Native converts in the absence of an ordained minister, and disagreed with superintendent Jacob Hitchcock's educational practices regarding teaching Cherokee young women in the mission boarding school. When Reverend Wiley joined the mission in 1845, his leadership precipitated internal conflicts within the mission family, between those who remained loyal to Hitchcock and teachers like Hannah who allied with the new minister. Hitchcock wrote to Reverend David Green of the American Board, charging Hannah with insubordination. "She was too wise, too selfconfident, selfwilled, and selfconceited [sic] to take advice sometimes."⁶⁰ In October 1845, he formally requested her reassignment, stating, "We may almost as well be without a school as to have Miss Moore teach it. However well she may have done in N. England, she is not a suitable person for this school."⁶¹

In addition, Hannah recoiled from aspects of Native culture as she became more acquainted with the Cherokees. She objected to Cherokee ceremonial life—the Green Corn Dance and ball playing (*anetso*). During a visit to a nearby village, she found ball-playing and Saturday night dances "shocking to humanity." She wrote, "We had not proceeded far before a company of ballplayers overtook us riding full speed whiskey bottles hanging at their sides. Though a great many females attend these plays my guide knew I did not wish for a moment to look on a scene so disgusting to refinement as Indians running in a state of nudity."⁶²

Her staunch abolitionism made Cherokee and Choctaw slave-holding unacceptable to her and put her at odds with the tribes and the American Board, prompting her resignation in 1848. This pattern of assertiveness, internecine conflict within the mission family, and forced resignation would be repeated in her postings in Africa for the American Missionary Association. Claiming her status as an evangelical woman, imbued with the virtues of piety and purity that characterized her gender, Hannah protested against mission policies, confronted others who appeared to have compromised their values, and recoiled against the perceived indecency of Native ceremonies. Evangelical personhood, especially among missionary women, furnished Hannah Moore with a public voice and the personal agency and authority to utter protests based upon her appeal to conscience.

Patricia Grimshaw's *Paths of Duty* examines the fate of American missionary wives in nineteenth-century Hawaii and extends our discussion of the burdens of the missionary spirit, particularly those shouldered by women. Grimshaw seeks to reconstruct the mentalities and experiences of eighty women involved in the ABCFM efforts in Hawaii from 1819 to 1850.[63] These women embraced the central cultural beliefs of the awakening and were called to duty in a Christian vocation as teacher to heathen children. They plainly did not seek a conventional New England marriage and the idea of a woman's sphere confined to the circle of domesticity. Rather, missionary women like Lucy Goodale Thurston and Laura Fish Judd wanted an autonomous life of Christian activism, called to convert the world as teachers of religion and domestic arts. The American Board was reluctant to allow unmarried men or women to work at these mission stations. Single men, it was feared, would not thrive in a celibate life and would succumb to the allure of Native women. Missionary wives would meet the sexual needs of their husbands, serve as friends, counselors, and helpmates, rear children, take care of domestic tasks, and, ideally, participate in the mission school as teachers. As we have seen with George Champion, the American Board maintained a network of contacts—a confidential listing of regenerate, educated, and eager young women who would agree to marry on short notice for evangelical motives and not romantic love.

The lives of these missionary women in Hawaii were filled with frustrations, disappointments, and, for some, despair. They risked the dangers of childbirth and maternal depletion. The drudgery of collective food preparation for the mission station, sewing, and childcare absorbed most of their time and energy.

The fate of idealism for missionary women brought bitter disappointment. They had little time or energy to foster an intimate, loving, and companionate relationship with their husbands. They also suffered disappointment in their public roles as teachers or their work in the American settlement. They isolated themselves from secular Americans and foreigners involved in commerce, rejecting this foreign community as unregenerate sinners, engaged in worldly entertainments, and the wholesale prostitution and demoralization of Native women. The missionary wives were equally distanced from Native groups whom they rejected as heathen. Grimshaw argues that "the women's ethnocentrism, their attachment to their own cultural ways of behaving, their utter inability to make sense of a society so different from their own, drove them to create obstacles which were of their own construction, yet which eluded their conscious control."[64]

The double estrangement from the expatriate community and Native society led missionary wives to establish intimate friendships among the missionary sisters. Here the mission family and the fictive kinship relations among missionary sisters, through which they supported each another through adversity, sickness, and disappointment, helped them persevere. However, the bonds of female friendship could not alleviate the depletion of frequent childbearing and the daily round of drudgery in domestic duties. They feared that their children might revert to Native ways, and the remedy for this threat made the burdens of life even more difficult. The women insisted that they rear their children according to New England habits of dress, education, and demeanor.

Missionary wives were above all else evangelicals who drew inspiration from Brainerd's model of piety and the cultural template of evangelical personhood. They were called to meet each challenge in a spirit of submission, meekness, self-abasement, and not infrequently, religious melancholy.[65] The question of adversity for the evangelical self signified that God had visited his chosen with special chastisements to admonish them for their sin. They properly responded with renewed efforts at evangelical humiliation, repentance, and self-abasement. Religious melancholy and despair attended these souls worn down by the status of women in the missionary cause. Elizabeth Bishop died in such a state:

> She died in a state of despair, calling herself a hypocrite, warning others not to neglect their duty as she had, her mind "dark and often

comfortless." She began to spit up blood and pus, regretting how little she had accomplished in four years as a missionary, and telling Hawaiian women who visited that "I shall soon die, and my unfaithfulness to you makes me afraid to meet God in judgment." The Hawaiians appeared amazed: "If after doing so much for us, *she* is afraid to meet God, how will it be for *us*?"[66]

Others suffered a variety of physical complaints related to these life-crises and stress. Grimshaw relates a litany of psychogenic illnesses for these depressive women who were depleted from child-bearing, domestic overload, and the sense of personal and collective failure of their evangelical mission. What is important is that the capacity of these Hawaiian missionary wives to cope with the burdens and stresses of their lives depended upon support from missionary sisters, a sense of the ultimate religious purpose of their lives that made this suffering bearable, and the ability of exercises of devotional piety to restore a sense of holiness and religious comfort. These measures of coping failed. Indeed, devotional piety actually helped engender religious melancholy that was expressed in bodily-somatic symptoms:

> Women like Sarah Lyman complained of appalling nervous headaches which left them prostrate and scarcely able to sit up in bed, banished to a dark room. Mercy Whitney had pains in her head so acute that her thoughts became confused and wandering. Clarissa Richards described a period of insomnia when she got no more than one-third of her usual sleep: "No one can tell of the misery my wakefulness has occasioned me. It seems at times that the activity of my brain is such that my head will burst—and I am obliged to have something chained across the top of my head to keep my cranium from flying away." Delia Bishop, once so energetic, developed "dyspepsy" and a violent throbbing in the pit of her stomach when she tried even to write. Wrote Juliette Cooke, "I am sadly careworn. I live in the midst of so much noise, my head seems weak from the confusion of ideas—I feel sometimes that I am prematurely old." One night she woke Amos saying she could not breathe and was on the brink of palpitations: He threw water on her

face. Charlotte Baldwin developed asthma of a nervous origin. Sybil Bingham once described herself as a run-down watch—before long, the mainspring would fail.⁶⁷

The endless chain of missionary intelligence encouraged each woman to mold her character after the self-abasing piety of a Brainerd, to embrace religious melancholy as the impetus to holiness and the foundation of their vocation. When the inevitable frustrations, disappointments, and setbacks befell their mission, they interpreted each adversity through the relentless quest for spiritual victory in the midst of worldly defeat. They blamed their indwelling sin to account for the chastisement of divine Providence. As always, the melancholy spirit proved a constant companion to their missionary spirit.

Other women in missionary service suffered a high rate of transience and turnover. Only thirty-seven of the five hundred remained in service after two years. Most petitioned for dismissal from service, citing a desire to marry, or pleading poor health due to typhus, malaria, cancer, and gynecological problems.⁶⁸ Forty-four of one hundred thirty-five ABCFM women died in service.⁶⁹ Many, like Sarah Smith, lapsed into religious melancholy. Here despair prompted the Nez Perce to name her "weeping one."⁷⁰ Elizabeth Morse, a single Baptist missionary to the Delaware, wrote of "hours of despondency."⁷¹ Clary Eddy speaks of her frustration and melancholy: "I have been led to ask the question why I was here, nursing these sick babies, performing more menial service than any slave on the place, I have often felt that God hid his face from me, that his loving kindness was actually withdrawn."⁷²

The endless chain of missionary intelligence was replete with accounts of religious melancholy and madness including those of Dorothy Plackett Carey (1756–1807), wife of the British missionary to India, William Carey, and his colleague Joshua Marshman, who succumbed to three bouts of "morbid depression" that he described as terror and anguish. Carey also provides this account in 1819: "Poor Mr. Wheelock the American missionary from Rangoon in a delirium which was attended with great despondency threw himself overboard last Friday and was drowned."

A "missiology of suffering" suggests that especially for women, pastoral care and evangelical conceptions of theodicy often failed to defend, sustain, and console missionaries as they confronted the myriad forms of adversity in their vocations.[73] So many women entered missionary service with expectations of adventure, the pursuit of an idealized public religious vocation—the wish to be free from the constraints of the domestic sphere. Also, they hoped to find personal satisfaction and happiness in a companionate marriage.

The changing attitudes and growing disenchantment of missionary women is reminiscent of findings of a large survey research study of American soldiers conducted during World War II. Although army training films and propaganda emphasized the broad ideological themes of patriotism and nationalism, the investigating sociologists discovered that soldiers in the combat did not cite these political commitments as motivations to fight the enemy. Rather, they fought to defend their friendship and allegiance to fellow soldiers in their primary group, the platoon. They struggled to protect one another in combat, and to support one another during the times of boredom and isolation from family and friends on the home front.[74] Missionary women in antebellum America might have initially been drawn to the movement by the appeal of the religio-political ideals of American nationalism that sought to extend Protestantism and "civilization" to heathens through foreign and domestic missions. However, for these Christian soldiers, the larger religious and ideological ideas quickly gave way to devising strategies for coping with the exigencies of mission life in the field, and the reliance on the relationships and supports of their primary group of coreligionists in their mission families. The fate of idealism for women when they practiced their vocation within mission families meant the painful acknowledgement of unfulfilled aspirations, drudgery, frustration, and myriad disappointments and conflicts. Many of these disappointments found indirect expression in somaticization through the proliferation of psychosomatic complaints. While a woman's work was never done—tending to their families in the mission's "domestic economy," bearing and rearing children, and teaching indigenous children—men faced far less arduous vocations as preachers, laborers, and administrators.

Contemporary psychiatric interpretation has identified a "missionary syndrome" where persons commit their lives to submission to God's will—like the nineteenth-century Great Commission converting the world and redeeming perishing heathens in the spirit of a David Brainerd or Harriet Newell. When missionaries encounter adversity, frustration, and failure in their religious vocation, they suffer intense guilt and depression.[75] Women in this era seemed particularly susceptible to the missionary syndrome.

The missionary spirit that was fostered and sustained by the endless chain of religious intelligence created heightened expectations of converting the world, saving perishing heathens, and working to hasten the millennium. Religious personhood encouraged an inward piety of selfless, disinterested benevolence in pursuit of personal spiritual attainments and public religious goals. However, for so many women who entered the field of missions, despite the inspirational accounts published in hagiographies, the missionary vocation was fraught with melancholy, madness, disillusionment, sickness, and early death.

4

The Question of K

"The First Friend of the Osage Nation unto God"

On January 26, 1827, an eighteen-year-old Osage Indian was involuntarily committed to a New England asylum for the insane, brought in chains and manifesting cycles of religious mania and melancholy. In this chapter we will explore how this youth, whose father had been killed in the wars with the Cherokees, who was the nephew of the important peace chief Tally, was given at age fourteen as a token of goodwill, diplomacy, and alliance to the Union Mission School. The Osages called him Hal-Bah-Chinto.[1] Reverend William F. Vaill gave him a Christian name, the namesake of an important supporter of the cause of missions; and we will call him K to shield his identity as a psychiatric patient. The Osages recognized his value should he become literate and accomplished. He was expected to return to his people and assist in their trade and negotiations with the U.S. government. The missionaries anticipated that K would become both "civilized" and converted—an invaluable auxiliary to their cause as a bilingual translator, teacher, and missionary who would return to convert and transform the Osages. Sadly, in K's short life, we have nothing in his own voice where he might have related his experience of conflict, anomie, culture shock, confusion, and marginality as he traveled from the familiar Native ground into the perplexing Euro-American worlds.

The title of this chapter is derived from a work of Jonathan D. Spence,

The Question of Hu.[2] His story proves instructive. In 1721 John Hu, aged forty, a widower with one son, lived with his mother and one brother in Canton, China. Hu was employed as a keeper of the gate of the Sacred Congregation for the Propagation of Faith. He became a Christian at age nineteen by the Jesuit mission. Literate in Mandarin and having passed the beginning government civil service examinations, Father Jean-Francois Foucquet, S.J., hired him for a period of five years to work as a copyist and translator, and secured passage for Hu to travel with him to France and later to the Vatican. The Jesuit priest believed that Christian theology provided the master key to unlock the secrets of Confucian and Taoist thought, and he needed Hu's skills to assist in this ambitious project. Hu anticipated that his travels and adventures crossing civilizations and cultures would result in his writing a travelogue and would afford him opportunities for spiritual quickening in an audience with the pope. However, Hu's seemingly irrational conduct, inability to adjust to French customs, religious visions, elopement, and stubborn refusal to work as a copyist or to travel to Rome convinced Foucquet that Hu was mad. The priest prevailed upon the Paris police to take Hu to the asylum for the insane at Chrenton, run by the Brothers of Charity. From 1724 to 1726, he was confined for 658 days against his will as a charity patient, locked in a dark ward without clean clothes or linen, proper sanitation, candles, books, or amusements.[3]

Both Hu and K encountered Christian missionary outreach and converted to a new religion. They both left their natal communities and suffered culture shock and the confusion of strange new worlds. Hu was placed in the service of the religious and cultural ideals of the Counter-Reformation that would convert the world to the one true religion. K was commissioned as a worker in the vineyard to build the Redeemer's Kingdom in America. And both suffered forms of religious insanity that required treatment in an asylum before their returns home. Like Hu's, K's story deserves retelling.

The Osages called themselves "Children of the Middle Waters," a name derived from their myth of creation that depicted the union of the People of the Sky and the Land People.[4] During the early decades of the nineteenth century, they numbered twenty thousand inhabitants distributed within five permanent villages and divided among three distinct tribal groups within the extensive territories of what would become Arkansas, Kansas, Missouri, and Oklahoma.

Kathleen DuVal argues persuasively in *The Native Ground* that in 1803 when the United States acquired their lands in the Louisiana Purchase, Native peoples like the Quapaws, Osages, Shawnees, Miamis, and many others had no need to embrace the Jeffersonian ideal of "civilization" that championed the solitary yeoman household and abandoned traditional lifeways in tribal village communities. Rather, these tribes forged an economy from farming, hunting, horse-breeding, and trading. DuVal explains, "The Osages had established a fur-trading empire, using European trade networks to expand their dominions and gain the upper hand over their Indian neighbors. They received $63,000 in goods from their furs in 1806 alone."[5]

The Osages of the Arkansas River Valley resided on their "Native Ground" as intact, cohesive peoples who exercised a sovereign identity and maintained control over their land and resources, conducting trade, warfare, and diplomacy according to their collective self-interest.[6] They demonstrated masterful diplomacy in their relations with the Spanish, French, English, and finally Americans, using Quapaw settlements as a buffer to shield them from their enemies to the west and south. Willard Hughes Rollings explains in *Unaffected by the Gospel*, "Living among competing colonial frontiers, the Osage skillfully manipulated the imperial competition. They used the fears and jealousies of the French, British, and Americans to obtain power and to maintain the accompanying autonomy throughout the eighteenth and first years of the nineteenth century."[7]

In the eighteenth century, the French administration of the Osages granted a trade monopoly to the Chouteau brothers, who achieved such great influence over part of the tribe as to induce them to move into the Arkansas Territory at the juncture of the Verdigris and Neosho Rivers. The Chouteaus effectively split the tribe and made the Osages vulnerable to white conquest and intertribal warfare.[8] Between 1790 and 1820, five thousand Cherokees who had been removed from their eastern lands invaded Osage territory resulting in decades of land cessions and warfare and a new political order that effectively ended the Osage's claim to "Native Ground" in the Arkansas River Valley. In addition to Cherokees, displaced groups from the east included Potawatomis, Sauks, Mesquakies, Delawares, Kickapoos, Shawnees, Choctaws, and Chickasaws who added to the flood of tribes who competed for land, game, and trade.[9]

The Osage treaty of 1808 ceded fifty thousand square miles of territory between the Arkansas and Missouri Rivers. The United States established forts and trading posts to manage intertribal trade and relations and Protestant missions to prosecute the plan of civilization and conversion. In 1816 the Osages ceded in Lovely's Purchase one hundred miles along the Arkansas River from Fort Smith to the Verdigris Fall, effectively dispossessing the Osage and forcing their removal west in 1822. DuVal concludes, "Militarily defeated, economically depleted, and unable to defend their vast land claims, the Osage agreed in the late summer of 1822 to a peace that surrendered their centuries-old control of access to hunting lands on the Arkansas River."[10]

In the context of invasion, incessant intertribal warfare, dispossession, and the end of their "Native Ground," the United Foreign Missionary Society opened missions at Union (1820), Harmony (1821) at the Marais des Cygnes River, and Hopefield (1823), a model farming village of métis and Osage settlers ten miles from Union. The Union Mission built their station to evangelize the Osages at Verdigris, or Place At The Oaks, a village situated on the banks of the Verdigris River in what is today the state of Oklahoma.

The Osage village consisted of twenty-one clans and an equal number of subclans. Each clan was represented by a totemic emblem, or "life symbol." The Osage encampment formed a ceremonial circle where each clan, confraternity, and moiety was located within a prefigured arrangement. Within the circle of encampment the Osages reenacted a representation of the cosmos, the orders of creation, and the forces of the natural world.[11]

The clans were grouped into five phratries. Two phratries combined to form the *Tsi'Zhu* (House-Peace) moiety. The three remaining phratries formed the *Hanka* (War-Sacred) moiety.[12] Both divisions practiced patrilineal exogamous kinship rules corresponding to the Omaha type.[13]

The village of Place At The Oaks was headed by two hereditary chiefs, one from each moiety. However, the powers of Chief Clermont and Tally

(Peace Chief) were limited to the arbitration of domestic disputes and the selection of hunting areas. Considerable power resided with the council of elders, "the little old men," who ascended into this powerful gerontocracy by virtue of initiation into the seventh, highest rank of the religious secret societies.[14]

The Osages spent summer and winter months living within the long houses of their permanent village encampments. These seasons were periods of tribal reunion characterized by elaborate festivals, ceremonial gift-exchanges, and religious effervescences. However, in the fall months from September until late December, and during the spring thaw of March and April, the village dispersed into smaller, clan-based hunting parties, to pursue deer and bison in fall and beaver and bear in the spring.[15]

Hunting and warfare—the work of men—provided the principal means of winning honor and attaining individual and collective standing with secret societies. The right to wear the badge of honor—the sacred crest of the red-tailed hawk or the brightly colored emblem of the pipe tattooed across the chest, together with the privilege of initiation and advancement within the seven grades of the secret society, depended upon one's prowess as a hunter and warrior.

The opportunity to offer a feast in honor of the little old men and thereby attain new rank or the right to take a wife or undergo the passage into adulthood needed to be won through heroic action. Osage women, on the other hand, traditionally performed the work associated with planting and the cultivation of maize, squash, beans, and pumpkins on the half-acre plots allotted to each household. In addition, women prepared skins, made clothing and tools, and aided in the butchering and preparation of game and provided caches of food for use during the long winter.

Osage men and women valued the profuse ornamentation of their bodies by tattoos, bracelets, belts, and necklaces of buffalo hair and polished stones. A warrior adorned his body with feathers and heavy strings of earrings and beads. Men shaved their heads, leaving only a shaft of hair on the top that they decorated with beadwork and feathers. Dressed in buckskin leggings, loincloth, and moccasins, these warriors presented an imposing "heathen" image of savagery to the Union Mission family.

The Osage and their lands passed from Spanish to French and finally to American jurisdiction in 1803 as a result of the Louisiana Purchase. Known for their fierce warfare, the Osage fought sporadic wars against the encroachment of white settlement and emigrating and displaced Indian tribes. The policy of the federal government, after the War of 1812 and culminating with the Indian Removal Bill of 1830, exacerbated the intertribal struggles. The eastern tribes that were referred to as the Five Civilized Tribes were removed from their lands in Tennessee, Georgia, Mississippi, and Florida and resettled to the territories west of the Mississippi River. The warfare between the Osages and the Cherokees is, in large part, explained by this policy. The Treaty of 1817 provided Cherokees with territory adjacent to the Osages in exchange for lands confiscated in Tennessee. The War Department outfitted the Cherokees with boats, guns, ammunition, and supplies to assist in their removal. The Osages perceived these developments as the influx of newly armed competitors for increasingly scarce game, hunting grounds, and land. The War Department also established cantonments of soldiers at Fort Smith (1817) and Fort Gibson (1823) and Indian agents to regulate Indian-white contact, to prevent Osage depredations against settlers and hunters and to provide a buffer against the clash of Osage and Cherokee hunting and war parties.

Nevertheless, the Osages were involved in intermittent conflicts with Cherokees and other tribes throughout the 1820s. When the Osages sued for peace in 1818, they were forced to relinquished a vast area of land, "Lovely's Purchase," named after the Indian agent who negotiated the terms of settlement. The Osages agreed to cede land to satisfy the claim of four thousand dollars in damages assessed against them for raiding white settlements. This land was later given to the Cherokees in 1828. Through treaties, the pressures of illegal white encroachment, and forced removal, the Osages lost their lands and saw the bison and game decimated by white hunters and fur traders.[16]

The published excerpts of the Union Mission journal provide the following account of an attack upon a village of women, children, and old men at Verdigris: "About the first of November [1821], the Osages were overtaken by the Cherokees and not far from one hundred of the former were either taken or killed. At the time of this defeat, the Osage warriors were absent and the old men, women, and children were in a defenseless condition."[17] The missionaries faced the reluctance of the Osages to permit still more of their children to remain in the undefended mission.

Against this background of conflict and decline, the Union Mission founded their settlement in February 1821 on the banks of the Grand River, twenty-eight miles east of Clermont's Village on the Verdigris River. The mission journal records this description of the Osage settlement: "The place where the village stands is what is usually called a prairie; which is open without trees or shrubs. . . . The village contains about 250 lodges and probably three thousand souls."[18]

The missionaries came with no designs upon Indian lands or game seeking to civilize the tribe through the agency of practical, moral, and religious education. The Mission School provided the keystone to this bridge between the cultures. Initially, Clermont and the Osages would not trust their children to the mission. With prevailing warfare between Osages and Cherokees, Clermont and Tally would not relinquish their people to the care of unarmed and peaceful missionaries.[19] As of October 1821, only three métis children, the sons of an Osage woman and French trapper, were admitted as students. The mission received mostly children of mixed parentage who were already marginal between white and Indian cultures.

On May 13, 1822, the mission accepted their first pupil from Clermont's village. Chief Tally brought his son, age fifteen, to the school. Tally told Reverend Vaill, "Take him, *he is your son*. I will not take him from you."[20] The missionaries named the youth Philip Milledoler, the namesake for one of the wealthy directors of the UFMS. Tally returned to Union again on May 30 and related how others had ridiculed him for giving away his son for adoption. He presented the school with two more youths, age fourteen, saying,

> Take good care of them. Do not let them talk Osage, but teach them English. Don't make them half Osage, but make them white men wholly. Give them a full dress; take off their Humpass [moccasins] and put on stockings and shoes. I want to see them dressed before I leave you, so that I may not weep when I am on my hunt.[21]

The first child was given the name Stephen Van Renssalaer, in honor of another distinguished member of the board of managers. The second youth received the name K in compliance with the request of the Female Missionary Society of Georgetown, who had pledged the sum of thirty dollars annually for the support of an Indian scholar.[22]

Tally's statements reflected the attitudes of missionaries concerning the education of Indian children. The children were separated from their natal communities and considered as given-up for adoption. Mission schools set about the task of acculturating their charges by giving them new Christian names and clothing and teaching them civilized manners. Students were forbidden from speaking in their native language.

Indian youth could no longer feast upon buffalo meat that they believed brought strength and protected their health. They no longer accompanied their families on hunts and raiding parties to win honor. They forfeited the opportunity for rites of initiation, traditional marriage, and passage into manhood. The school stripped them of the foundations of their Indian identity. In place of Indian ways, these young men learned reading, writing, mechanics, carpentry, and farming. However, these civilized activities resembled the "woman's work" of Osage culture and not the traditionally prescribed activities for warriors.

The Osage students learned about the Protestant cosmology and myth of creation depicting a universal creator deity and savior-prophet who proffered otherworldly salvation predicated upon the arduous spiritual itinerary of discovering and nurturing the seeds of indwelling faith. They encountered the duty of individuals obliged to serve God's law and accept the individual responsibility for sin attendant with disobedience and innate depravity. K and the other students needed to embrace a new identity forged within the crucible of the quest for individual salvation and conversion and shaped by a lonely individuated existence that placed premiums on self-reliance and self-control.

Robert F. Berkhofer Jr. in *Salvation and the Savage* presents an important analysis of Protestant missions and Indian responses during the period 1787–1862. Berkhofer's discussion of the Union Mission and numerous other examples identifies the purposes, organization, contradictions, successes, and failures of Indian mission schools. Essentially, these schools attempted to inculcate the social and moral virtues requisite to a civilized and Christianized life. Missionaries selected children rather than adults as scholars, since it was felt that youths might more easily relinquish patterns of heathen life. Thus, schools first promulgated a moral education teaching the habits of sobriety, cleanliness, economy, industry, and honesty. Indian youth were taught injunctions against Sabbath-breaking, sporting, gambling, alcohol consumption, and participation in Native dances, rituals, and hunts. To impress the new valuation of time and the rationalization of personal conduct, schools established a strictly regimented schedule beginning at sunrise and filling the spaces of the day with hygiene, work, lessons, dining, and brief interludes of supervised recreation.[23]

However, these schools faced continual problems. Homesick and rebellious youth frequently eloped and returned to their Native homes. Classroom attendance was sporadic. Parents and Indian leaders opposed and subverted the work of the mission schools. Schools met with only limited success in teaching Indian scholars English, reading, writing, and theology requisite to their conversion. Missionaries attempted to create self-sustaining Native churches populated with Indian converts, yet the preparatory work of education progressed with painful slowness.

Union offered instruction in spelling, New Testament, English reading, geography, arithmetic, and writing. As of February 1827, after instructing sixty-five scholars over a seven-year period, "no Converts from Heathenism have been admitted to the Union Church."[24] Abraham Redfield had served as a schoolmaster at Union for five years. He petitioned for dismissal from his missionary commission in a letter to Jeremiah Evarts sent in August 1827. Redfield's dissatisfaction and despair reflected the difficulties of Indian boarding schools. He wrote, "I need not mention the large sums of money that have been expended on children who are now on the prairie wild as the rest of the Indians.... Now, I ask shall we labour on in this way wasting our lives?"[25] Reverend Vaill penned this explanation, "Remarks on the School," in February 1828:

> The School at Union has had to counter with difficulties, among these I would mention the *variable and fickle feelings of the parents & their*

Wars with other nations of Indians.... It ought to be recollected that the greater part of the children have been absent more than half of the time, or at least more than a third since their first entrance. So that their backwardness proves neither want of ingenuity on the part of the children or of fidelity on the part of the Instructors.... The school has never been fostered by the Nation at large, & yet its prosperity has on the whole increased, and was never greater than at this past time, & the principle of hope benefiting these wild, superstitious people arises from the School by raising of interpreters & teachers. None have left the school who are considered competent for teaching.[26]

The Union Mission wanted educated and converted Indian youths, graduates of the mission school, who would devote their lives alongside the white missionaries in propagating the Gospel among the Osages. The mission had failed to train interpreters from among its own brethren, and after seven years none was fluent in the Osage language. Thus, Native youth who were bilingual and Christians would fill this need. Reverend Vaill explained,

The day it is hoped is not distant, when many of the Indian Tribes on our Western Borders shall be furnished with Legislators, Teachers, and Missionaries, gathered from their own kindred, directing their national concerns, and announcing to them the glad tidings of the gospel in their national tongue.[27]

The Union Mission had reached the point of desperation and resolved in 1828 to "traffic in human beings" by purchasing Indian captives from slavery as war prisoners held by Cherokees and train them as Christian missionaries and interpreters.[28] The difficulty of recruiting Osage youth to train interpreters, teachers, and missionaries who might come voluntarily underscores the Indian experience and evaluation of Protestant civilization. The Protestant ethic of ascetic devotion to vocation and the adoption of a religiously grounded personality appeared to the Osages as repugnant, akin to slavery.[29] The conversion experience that demanded the transformation of self and identity following at times a protracted warfare against the self frequently overwhelmed white Americans. How much more difficult then was conversion for Indians who needed to renounce their indigenous cultures, learn a foreign language, and embrace the harsh and chilling notions of sin, depravity, and otherworldly salvation. How foreign the need to produce "pungent testimonials of sin." "True Indian conversion meant nothing less than a total transformation of Native existence."[30] Protestants demanded a thorough acculturation: the rejection of heathen identity and explicit knowledge and testimonials of the work of faith in each neophyte's heart and life.

Given the difficulty of the process of conversion and the seemingly impossible standards maintained by Protestant missions (in America and elsewhere), not surprisingly few if any Natives met with a saving change. In the face of the energies expended, the adversities overcome, and the need to measure success in terms of the numbers brought to Zion, a missionary might fall into despair. Dr. Marcus Palmer's letter of July 23, 1827, expresses the frustration of the Union Mission family:

> My heart sickening, and deep within my soul is poured out in secret places while I contemplate the discouraging state of these western Missions. I have long prayed and waited for a radical change. . . . Be assured I am not tired of the Mission Cause, nor am I weary of its labors and sufferings, O No! Let my right hand forget the cunning and let my tongue cleave to the roof of my mouth if I do not prefer Jerusalem above my chief joy. Most cheerfully and heartily have I consecrated my better all to the Mission Cause and tho' for the seven years in which I have been employed in its service I have been called in common with my associates in this Family to labor much, to endure much suffering, to see great sumes [sic] of Christian Charity expended, and after all to weep over the lamentable fact—*none converted.*[31]

From 1833 through 1837, the ABCFM closed their Osage missions. Rollings concludes in *Unaffected by the Gospel* that the missionaries failed because the tribes had no need for salvation and conversion and found the message of Protestantism unsatisfying. The missionaries "were asking a people to give up a successful and satisfying way of life, to adopt an alien, and frankly ill-adapted way of life for the prairies. They asked them to adopt a life of loneliness, miserliness, and effete behavior, to ignore their kin, and to challenge the fates by giving up the hunt. As they could only ask, not force, the Osage to change, the Osage could, and did, resist."[32]

The first Protestant missions to the Osage would end in failure in the 1830s as the Osages were removed and relocated from the mission stations. The embattled Osages did value the mission for the material resources—tools, trade goods, and supplies—that might assist the tribe. The missionaries were valued as a political ally who repeatedly interceded with the representatives of the United States to advocate for the Osages in the conduct of warfare and diplomacy in this period. The Osages also recognized the importance of secular education and literacy that schools offered to their children. And the Osages did relinquish a small number of boys and girls to the mission school, which encouraged the missionaries as they persevered in the 1820s, as true believers, ever hopeful that Native converts were portentous of the success of the mission cause.

Reverend Elias Cornelius (1794–1832) published *The Little Osage Captive* in 1822 adding to the encouraging religious intelligence, the sublime hopes penned by a Native student at the Brainerd Mission to the Cherokees in Tennessee: "The Missionary Spirit, which is so now prevalent in this land, is, as I trust, from above I pray that the benign auspices of Heaven may attend the American Board and that the long degraded Indians, whose minds have been held in bondage by the God of this world, may be found in the fold of Christ."[33]

Cornelius was converted in 1813 as a senior at Yale College during a revival. After graduation he continued his studies with Yale president Timothy Dwight, and in 1815 he studied with Reverend Lyman Beecher in Litchfield, Connecticut. Cornelius received a license to preach from the Southern Association of Congregational Ministers and spent the next two years traveling, preaching, and soliciting funds for foreign and domestic missions of the ABCFM.[34]

During his tour of the Southeast in October 1817, he encountered an Osage captive, a girl five years of age taken after her parents had been killed during a Cherokee raid. The Indians proudly displayed the scalps of her mother and father. Cornelius received the support of Lydia Carter of Natchez who donated $150 to ransom the girl. He met with Thomas L. McKenney, agent of Indian trade, and John C. Calhoun, secretary of war, in May 1818, who instructed Colonel Thomas Meigs, Cherokee agent, to obtain the child and transfer her to the Brainerd Mission. The redeemed Osage captive received the name of her benefactress, Lydia Carter. Lydia quickly became proficient in English, accepting religious instruction in the Gospel. Cornelius describes her as obedient, respectful, and grateful for her deliverance from captivity.[35]

Lydia spent two years at Brainerd living in this large Christian mission family of Indian youth and missionary sisters and brothers, learning the "arts of civilized life" that for girls included spinning, weaving, sewing, waiting at the table, and working in the kitchen. In 1820, the Southern Osages demanded that Lydia return. On August 24, 1820, Lydia and John Osage Ross, another captive, left Brainerd for the Union Mission. When the Osages were reunited with Lydia later that fall, they proclaimed that Lydia "having been raised from the dead" would be permitted to return to Brainerd. Several months later she died of fever and ague, possibly malaria, before reaching the mission.[36]

Despite Lydia's untimely death, Cornelius found her short life a victory and an inspiration as he would extort: "Let it every where be deeply impressed upon the minds of children and youth that the wants of the heathen are great; and it is the duty of all, who have the means to send them the Gospel."[37] And Cornelius would conclude his book by invoking the trope of "perishing heathens" without knowledge of Christ or the promise of the Gospel. He urged support of the missionary spirit: "Millions of others, in Heathen lands, are still ignorant of the Saviour! What numbers of them will die before the news of his salvation can reach them! Who would not labour to save them from their wretchedness, and cheerfully deny himself the gratifications of this life, for the sake of sending them the Gospel."[38]

The Union Mission was not without hope or favorable prospects. Much rested upon the fate of two Osage youths. During September 1824, K and

Stephen Van Renssalaer were selected as qualified students to continue their education in preparation for missionary work at the Cornwall Foreign Mission School of Connecticut. They were chosen according to Vaill "as a probable means of hastening on the reformation of this people, We look forward a few years to the time when the two sons of the forest, so lately rescued from the hunting camp and the war party, shall return laden with the experience of God's mercy."[39]

K and Stephen had attended the Mission School at Union for two years from 1822 until September 1824. The domestic secretary of the UFMS approved the plan to send these two youths to "the Foreign Missionary Seminary at Cornwall, in the state of Connecticut, to finish their education. They left Union on the 23rd. inst. immediately after examination of the school. They had resided in the family almost two years, and had made as good proficiency as could have been expected."[40] After an eight-week journey by canoe, riverboat, and overland stage, they arrived in Cornwall, Litchfield County, Connecticut. K and Stephen matriculated as students in December 1825.[41] The Osage scholars sent letters informing their adopted family at Union of their safe arrival in Connecticut. Vaill recorded on February 26, 1825, "We have just received two good letters from our Sons at Cornwall School, Connecticut which gives us great satisfaction."[42]

An article in the *Religious Intelligencer* in 1825 argued that the conversion of these heathen youth would prevent their declension into paganism and render them useful as teachers, translators, and auxiliary preachers to the Union Mission upon their return:

> The conversion of these young men is the chief of our desire concerning them. . . . Need I suggest the probable amount of good which will result to these youth themselves, to the people, to the tribes around, and to the souls of thousands yet unborn! . . . These youth, if converted to God, will become powerful auxiliaries to the mission, and the salvation of many, may be the glorious result.[43]

The Cornwall School (1817–1826) was another extraordinary experiment of the Second Great Awakening in Connecticut. Founded in 1816 for the purpose of educating heathen youth under the auspices of the ABCFM, the mission school brought these youths to New England "to afford a hospitable asylum for such unevangelized youth, of good promise ... providentially brought to our shores, and cast upon us."[44] The people of Connecticut, guided by the leadership of Yale's president, Reverend Timothy Dwight, and Lyman Beecher of Litchfield championed a mission school based upon the success and example of Henry Obookiah, a Hawaiian youth who fled intertribal warfare and finally reached New Haven in the winter of 1809. His subsequent education and well-publicized conversion narrative symbolized the efficacy of Christianity to redeem him "from that cruel bondage in which millions of heathen, and all who are ignorant of God may be found."[45] Obookiah's untimely death in February 1818 and the publication of his *Memoirs* as an evangelical bestseller increased the fundraising and fame of the Heathen School.[46]

Cornwall represented an idealized New England farming community situated in Litchfield County. Cornwall supported grain mills, small factories, traditional village crafts, two physicians, and one lawyer. "It represented, in short, exactly that ideal society that leaders of the missionary movement wished to see replicated across the American countryside and around the world.... The location of the school would hopefully encourage students to emulate the towns people and their habits."[47]

After eight years of operation, the Cornwall School had achieved national renown. The student body typically housed 30–35 scholars from the Sandwich Islands, tribes of New England and Iroquoia, the tribes referred to as the Five Civilized Tribes in the Southeast, and the Osages.[48] In December 1825, students included representatives of the Tuscaroras, Iroquois, Oneidas, Mohegans, Stockbridges, Narragansetts, Senecas, Cherokees, Choctaws, Chippewas, and Osages as well as Hawaiians, Chinese, a Portuguese Catholic from the Azores, and a British Jew.

The school consisted of a commodious building set aside for instruction in English and religion, a dormitory, a barn, farmland, and eighty acres of woods. Under the supervision of Reverend Herman Daggett, principal, the mission school sought to civilize and Christianize heathen youth and return them to their native lands to effect the civilization of their tribes. As set forth in the Constitution of the Cornwall School, the education in our country, of Heathen Youths, in such a manner, as, with subsequent professional instruction, will qualify them to become useful Missionaries, Physicians, Surgeons, School-Masters, or Interpreters; and to communicate to the Heathen nations such knowledge in agriculture and the arts, as may prove the means of promoting Christianity and civilization.[49]

The school became a cause celebre, attracting generous donations, international correspondents, and funding from the ABCFM and the UFMS. Known colloquially as the "Heathen School," this short-lived experiment exemplified the ideals of the missionary spirit in America: the crusading mentality of American exceptionalism as a redeemer nation and the sublime millennial hopes of converting Native peoples as a requisite step to converting the world.[50] The prime directive of the school envisioned "native scholars, shorn of heathenism and full now of pious intent, returning to their homeland to spread God's Word."[51] Cornwall produced scholars of distinction such as David Brown, a Cherokee who went on to attend Andover Seminary and returned to work as a clerk to congress in Washington.[52]

Although the detailed daily records of the operation of the school, correspondence, and student papers do not survive, the superintendent's reports to the ABCFM detail troubling issues with the Native scholars that included difficulty with English that precluded making intelligible religious testimonies, homesickness, bed-wetting, lapses in discipline, fights among students, runaways, and continuing health issues with infectious diseases like consumption and dysentery that caused the death of seven students.[53] Several students were so maladjusted as to appear insane. The records report a student who "manifest[ed] a suspicious & gloomy disposition, which render[ed] him unhappy and pleasant ... [who at times suffered] a considerable degree of mental derangement."[54]

However, in 1826 the school met with a heated controversy after "the marriage of a promising young Cherokee to a young female of this vicinity ... gave rise to the numerous false reports against the character and authority of the school and the people of the village."[55]

Isaiah Bunce, editor of the *Litchfield American Eagle*, published vicious editorials against the practice of intermarriage after the public announcement of the engagement of yet another couple. Elias Boudinot, a Cherokee scholar of exceptional ability, had received permission to marry Harriet Gold, the daughter of one of the town's leading citizens.

The spirit of the revivals fostered a profound concern for the salvation and enlightenment of mankind with a special regard for the plight of heathens who might perish without benefit of Gospel light. These ideals of salvation, of bringing the world to Christ antecedent to the advent of a millennium, promoted acosmic love and universal brotherhood. However sincerely evangelicals promoted these theological concerns with respect to the idea of saving heathens, this *caritas* did not prevail over the powerful prejudices against *connubium* felt toward flesh and blood Christianized racial Others—"savages" living in their localities. The controversy over racial intermarriage between white women and Indian men spread throughout the town and school. Increasingly, support for the school eroded until the directors abruptly announced the closing of the Cornwall School in the early fall of 1826.

Indeed, the Cornwall School represented the strategy promoting the "gentle extinction" of Indian peoples through forced acculturation.[56] The "metaphysics of Indian hating" even among Godly evangelicals did not prevent them from viewing Indians as inferior and deserving of discrimination. The establishment of the Foreign Mission School had initially attracted favorable publicity and considerable financial support as a "permanent exhibit of 'savable heathen' for New Englander's to marvel at."[57] When Indian scholars fraternized with local women and expected the rights of full inclusion in this community as regenerate Christians, they discovered that Indian birth marked them with a permanent racial inferiority, in the eyes of New Englanders, that civilization and salvation could not expunge.[58] The ABCFM report of 1826 acknowledged these issues:

> This results not merely from the difference in complexion, but from the hereditary feelings of our people in regard to the Indians. These different kinds of treatment, which result from inquisitive curiosity, mixed with Christian benevolence on the one hand, and from established prejudices

on the other, make the young men feel as though they were *mere shows*, a feeling which is too accurate an index of their real situation.[59]

Missionaries succeeded frequently in converting mixed race and socially marginal individuals who faced a double discrimination from both white and Native cultures.

> No matter how pious and exemplary the Indian Christian became, the white population still considered him a savage and an inferior. In most cases, furthermore, the Indian Christian was easily differentiated from his white coreligionists by the retention of native habits or language, which only deepened white discrimination against him. On the other hand, the pagans despised him for his departure from the customs of his forefathers.[60]

In light of these issues of double discrimination, the difficulty in achieving salvation, and the goal of producing educated, Christian Indians, K's residence at Cornwall proved stressful and perplexing. Upon his shoulders rested the future hopes of the Union Mission who needed him to become a Christian Indian and work as an interpreter and missionary. In September 1826, when the Cornwall School failed to reopen, K had attended nearly ten months of classes. He remained in town as a houseguest of Elisha Loomis, a missionary who had recently returned from the Sandwich Islands.[61]

In October of 1826, K exhibited religious excitation and mania that necessitated that Loomis restrain him in chains. K's religious crisis did not resolve in the expected release from suffering and the psychological conviction of regeneration. K had been able to come only to the brink of conversion. Unfortunately, the asylum records and other historical sources do not shed light on K's spiritual crisis and experience of religious melancholy. During his residence at Union and Cornwall, he was continually exhorted to undergo an emotional experience of salvation and conversion, and to renounce an Indian identity in favor of that of a Christian missionary. The predominant desire of these schools was expressed by Reverend Daggett, who wrote, "The conversion of these young men is the chief of our desire concerning them."[62] We also do not know K's reaction to the racism, violence, and intolerance directed against the Cornwall School and the Indian scholars during the months preceding the suspension of classes. It is likely that these events proved traumatic and contributed to his religious melancholy and mania.

K was brought for treatment to an asylum for the insane on January 26, 1827, diagnosed with "mania despondens" caused by pursuing his studies and a sedentary life ("bodily inaction") that were foreign to his former habits. He asked for a gun so that he might end his life. At the hospital, he was provided with a nutritious diet and a regimen of medications that included Spanish Madera wine and conium (hemlock) in quantities designed to tranquilize and treat his agitated state. Moral treatment sought to divert K from ruminating on religious subjects and to focus on the moderate and rational exercise of his faculties that included supervised walks on the asylum grounds and carriage rides.

After one month of treatment, K manifested a calm demeanor and the restoration of bodily and mental health. He was discharged from the asylum as a recovered patient on April 24, 1827, after three months of involuntary treatment. K joined Stephen Van Rensselaer, who had remained in Cornwall as a blacksmith, residing with Mr. Loomis.

John Demos explains in *The Heathen School*,

> Five "Osage Boys," apparently quite recent arrivals, would set out for the West as soon as "a careful, prudent, and economical man" could be found to accompany them. The group would go "on the [Erie] Canal, to Buffalo, thence by water to Cleaveland [sic]"; if all went well, they might be placed at Miami University in Oxford, Ohio.[63]

Reverend Vaill traveled to Cincinnati on March 7 to arrange alternative educational plans for Stephen and K. Reverend Robert Bishop of Miami University provided for one or possibly two Osage youth to matriculate under the tuition-free sponsorship of the university. Vaill communicated this intelligence to Jedidiah Evarts, corresponding secretary of the ABCFM, which had recently incorporated the UFMS. Vaill proposed that

> at least two of the Osage boys, now, or late at Cornwall, be sent to that place for instruction & for tuition & guardianship under the care of

Dr. Bishop. He is indeed a worthy good man—& will be a Father to these as he is indeed to his pupils—I would propose, two instead of the whole, at present for in that case a selection could be made. It would be important, that the first educated be the brightest, especially in the part of the country where prejudice against the missions are many—and need to be removed, and would likely to be by the presence of likely young Indians, I would propose Stephen Van Renssalaer [sic] and Lewis Rogers.[64]

K was chosen instead of Lewis Rogers and traveled to Oxford, Ohio, where he matriculated at Miami University. He spent one year in college before returning to Union in June 1828. He had progressed considerably in his command of English, and he had made a profession of faith. Vaill records this triumph with considerable apprehension as K was also dying of consumption. The mission journal records the following:

> Union Mission, June 12, 1828
> K returned to us last week and his health is poor, but he appears humble & pious, he has made a profession of religion, as also Stephen Van Renssalaer of this you have undoubtedly been apprised—We are concerned about K lest his disorder should terminate in the consumption and in death—But we must submit—there is one trait in K's character which strikes me, he appears very much as John Honaxii did, who is now laboring successfully among the Sandwich Islanders—humble, sincere, and correct in all his manners.[65]

All too frequently Indian students died at an early age from infectious diseases contracted by exposure to mission schools—too soon to repay through service the years of training invested in their education and conversion. K died of consumption, a plague to Indians and whites alike, on June 26, 1828. K's untimely death confirmed the idea of the vanishing American—contact with white civilization destroyed Indians through vice or disease. His obituary states,

> He lived to reach home, and gave us all the comforting evidence that he was a new creation. . . . We looked upon him—as the first friend

of the Osage nation unto God. After his return he appeared humble and sincere and anxious—and expressed a strong desire to be useful as an Interpreter.[66]

Although K had died, Stephen returned to assist the mission family as indicated in a letter of January 1, 1829, from William G. Requa to Jeremiah Evarts:

> Stephen Van Renssalaer, the youth who has been to the East for an education has returned in good health & we have reason to hope is pious. He is an amiable, pleasant young man, and bids fair to be very useful not only as an Interpreter but as a teacher of Righteousness to his benighted kindred according to the flesh. We have much to hope from him as an instrument in the hand of God, but we rejoice with trembling.[67]

Both Osage youths had traversed a spiritual and geographical itinerary as they were taken from their natal village and brought to Union as an offering of diplomacy and friendship by the Osage peace chief Tally. After two years at the Union Mission school, they journeyed to the Heathen School in Cornwall. Despite many adversities, they ultimately completed their education at Miami University and succeeded in fulfilling the principal goal of this failed experiment in Native boarding school education. Both youths returned as literate, new born Christian Indians, prepared to serve as interpreters, exhorters and missionaries to evangelize their people, the Osages.

White Protestant missionary men and women actively chose their religious vocation as adults, as champions of evangelical culture, imbued with the sublime missionary spirit that anticipated a harbinger of the millennium. With a capacity for agency, self-expression, and self-realization, they attempted to forge their religious identity and personhood on the smithy of God-willed activism in the cause of rescuing perishing heathens. Whatever adversity, suffering, religious despondency, and failure prevented them from realizing their goals, these men and women would bear the responsibility and consequences of their decisions.

K was a youth, not an adult, when he became part of a diplomatic gift exchange between his band and the Union Mission. He did not act as an autonomous agent, an individual who chose his own life course. Instead, others made the key decisions in his life. K devoted himself or was chosen to undertake a course of action for the benefit of his people, consistent with collective tribal values. He served as Tally's agent of diplomacy with the Protestant missionaries. K was destined to return as an educated and literate young man who could assist his people. He also served as a model student and exemplar of how mission school education at Union, Cornwall, and Miami University would transform heathen youth into regenerate Christians, indoctrinated into the mission cause, who would return to convert and transform their people. In the end we raise these questions: who was K? He left no documents or statements in his own voice that answer this question. Given his experiences of religious insanity and subsequent conversion, what did Christianity do for this Osage youth? Which cause did he serve? Or was he a double agent mediating between Native and Christian worlds? As with the travails of John Hu, we are left with a compelling story and many unanswered questions.

5

The First Fruits of the Cherokee Nation

Catharine Brown and Sister Margaret Ann

During the first three decades of the nineteenth century, before the Treaty of New Echota in 1835 and the forced removal of the eastern Cherokees to Arkansas and territories west of the Mississippi River, the U.S. government sponsored missionaries and Indian agents to promote a plan of civilization. This plan addressed the devastating losses inflicted on the Cherokees following the Revolutionary War. Allied with the British and Tory loyalists, the Cherokees were reduced to a conquered people at the Treaty of Paris, relinquishing half of their one-hundred-thousand-square-mile homelands. Their population declined from 22,000 in 1770 to 12,295 in 1809. A Chickamauga faction fled inland to the lower Tennessee River Valley and continued their warfare from 1780 to 1794, resulting in the destruction of more than forty towns that were absorbed by encroaching American settlers.[1] By the Treaty of Holston in 1794, the Cherokees acknowledged the destruction of their way of life with the loss of the fur and deer skin trade and hunting grounds and the unending death of their people and destruction of their villages. The plan of civilization served as a blueprint for the revitalization of tribal sovereignty through "conscious acculturation."[2]

Civilization envisioned that Cherokee men would abandon their roles as hunters and warriors in favor of agricultural labor, plowing fields, and herding livestock as yeomen—heads of patrilineal households. Women would renounce matrilineal clans and communal ownership of land and the political influence in selecting chiefs and setting policy in peace and war. No longer cultivating gardens and corn, they would embrace the cult of domesticity, leaving the fields for the kitchen to become mistress of the household where they would spin and weave.[3]

William G. McLoughlin in *Cherokees and Missionaries, 1798–1839* identifies six dimensions of institutional and cultural transformation associated with the plan of civilization. These include the economic transformation of traditional Natives into a slave-holding planter elite who championed the logics of a market economy and built plantations, trading stores, mills, taverns, ferries, and roads. Kinship and personal identity changed the exogamous matrilineal clan system to patriarchal nuclear families that eschewed communal obligations in favor of competitive individualism. The traditional ethics of hospitality, generosity, and reciprocity of gift exchange gave way to the pursuit of private property, patrilineal inheritance, the accumulation of wealth, and the growth of social inequality based on class and educational differences. Political transformations included the centralization of government authority in a bicameral legislature, courts, and the Lighthorse police force to uphold tribal laws against thievery and evict white squatters. A small minority of Cherokees became Christian Indians in response to Moravian, Presbyterian, Methodist, and Baptist schools and missions. They rejected conjuring, traditional ceremonies, and *anetso* (ball play). Finally, the transformation from an oral to a written culture was facilitated by the growth of literacy in English and the introduction of a syllabary by Sequoyah.[4]

The Cherokee mixed-race planter elite adopted these six dimensions of civilization and by 1830 had achieved a "model Christian Indian republic."[5] This faction of the Cherokee Nation built the Lower Town settlements in North Georgia and Alabama while the full-blood traditionalist faction resided in the Upper Towns in the Tennessee River Valley. The mixed-race planter elite modeled a redefinition of personal and collective identity that left many questions unanswered. "Could one be a good Cherokee and speak English, dress as whitemen did, and attend Christian religious services? Was it enough to defend the nation's political independence and territory or did being a good Cherokee also require a Cherokee view of the world—of man's relationship to nature and the supernatural?"[6] The conversion narratives and lives of Catharine and David Brown and the Moravian convert, Sister Margaret Ann Crutchfield, exemplify the personal and collective ideals of this mixed-race planter elite and suggest answers to questions of Cherokee identity for those who chose the spiritual pilgrimage of Christian Indian identity in the decades before removal.

THE EXEMPLARY LIFE OF CATHARINE BROWN,
CHEROKEE AND "AFFECTIONATE SISTER IN CHRIST"

Two years after Catharine Brown's death from consumption at age twenty-three, an anonymous poet published "Inscription: For the Grave of Catharine Brown" in *Zion's Herald* in February 1825. An excerpt from the first stanza reads,

> Here, midst the scenes where once untaught and wild,
> She rov'd neglected, simple nature's child,
> Her ashes rest, whose name, now widely known,
> Asks no memorial from the crumbling stone.
> Sprung from a race, degraded, fierce and rude,
> And nurtur'd midst the forest's solitude.
> Yet o'er her tomb no heathen rites were paid,
> Nor pagan darkness gathere'd all its shade.
> But Christian hands prepar'd her last abode,
> And mingled tears of joy and sorrow flow'd . . .
> Spoke of Immanuel's love, and power, to save
> His saints triumphed o'er the vanquished grave.[7]

Her life and memory now forged a new link in the chain of religious and missionary intelligence where a sentimental and romantic poem depicted her as a simple child of nature, a Cherokee characterized as being from a race "degraded, fierce, and rude." Yet a transformation had occurred bringing her out of pagan darkness and into the light of Christian salvation. Christ's love had redeemed her and vanquished death.

Rufus Anderson, assistant secretary of the ABCFM, edited Catharine Brown's letters and diary and published in 1825 the *Memoir of Catharine Brown, a Christian Indian of the Cherokee Nation* that became an antebellum evangelical bestseller through more than ten editions that reached publics throughout the new nation and the Atlantic world. Theresa Strouth Gaul explains in *Cherokee Sister*, "Widely reviewed and excerpted in periodicals at the time of its publication, *Memoir* sold 2,500 copies within six month of release. The development and growth of an evangelical print culture and readership combined with changes in the publishing industry, which included new printing technologies that allowed for the successive editions of a book."[8]

Catharine recounted her life and spiritual pilgrimage as a story of the triumph of the missionary spirit. She enrolled at Brainerd Mission in Tennessee in 1817 and became the first Cherokee student to experience conversion, baptism, and admission as a communicant in the mission church by March 1818. On May 31, 1820, she left Brainerd to serve as a teacher, exhorter, and missionary to her people at Creek Path, Alabama, until her early death from tuberculosis in 1823. She chronicled her extraordinary life as a Christian Indian woman by writing a series of letters that were published in the evangelical press from 1818 to 1823.

In this religious intelligence, Catharine expressed an abiding, acosmic love for humankind—Christian and heathen, new born children of God and unregenerate alike. She signed her letters "[an] affectionate sister in Christ" and anguished over the conversion of her mother and father and the Cherokee Nation. Writing from Brainerd on July 5, 1819, to her former missionaries and teachers, Catharine expresses a debt of gratitude to them and especially "to that god who sent you here to instruct the poor ignorant Indianss [sic] in the way that leads to everlasting life."[9] As part of a vocabulary of evangelical humiliation and a vocabulary of a racial Other, she cast her people as worthy of charity and pity—poor, ignorant, and unredeemed by the Gospel living and perishing in heathen darkness. This rhetoric of Christian Indian identity characterized previous generations of evangelical Christian Indians in southern New England and was reflected in the writings of Samson Occom, Joseph Johnson, and others who embraced the religious paternalism of Eleazar Wheelock's "Grand Design."[10]

Consistent with the missionary spirit that informed her life, Catharine implores her former teachers and now fellow missionaries to pray for the salvation of her parents, "I hope you will pray for them & also pray, for me, that I may become useful to my dear people—My heart bleeds for their immortal souls. oh that I might be made the means of turning many souls from darkness unto marvelous light."[11] It is important to note that she desired to be useful to her kin and nation as a Christian Indian missionary, teacher, interpreter, and exhorter. She longed to serve as an instrument of the providential will of God in converting her people to Christianity.

Repeatedly and throughout the thirty-eight letters that she wrote to her correspondents, who included missionaries, donors, and her younger brother David Brown, who was attending Cornwall Foreign Mission School and Andover Theological Seminary, Catharine was steadfast as an agent in the cause of missions. She wrote of the central organizing principle of her life in a letter that she signed "your heathen sister in Christ."

> How many of our brethren and sisters are yet in darkness, living without God and without hope in the world. They have become precious and immortal souls to be lost or saved. O, may I then be willing to sacrifice any thing for the sake of bringing the heathen, especially those of my own Nation, to a knowledge of God and the Saviour, whom I have found to be so precious in my heart.[12]

Catharine acknowledged the importance of other women's missionary memoirs in shaping her aspirations and evaluating her spiritual attainments as a missionary. Her published letters in the evangelical press championed the cause of missions while simultaneously crediting previous memoirs that helped solidify her religious vocation. In 1820, in a piece published in two religious magazines about sharing a Sabbath evening reflection called "To a Young Lady in Philadelphia," she wrote, "I have this day been reading the good book, the life of Mrs. Harriet Newell; you have probably read it. O what a good missionary she was. After reading this invaluable book, I cannot help feeling a deep concern for the salvation of the heathen.—She was indeed a professor of the meek and lowly Jesus."[13]

Finally, she endorsed the missionary spirit by voicing the millennial expectations that anticipated the imminent conversion of the world. She pens this sublime vision that "we ought to rejoice that the latter day of Millennial glory is just approaching when a nation shall be born in a day, and when all shall know the Lord from the least to the greatest."[14] In her own voice as a Christian Indian neophyte, with sincerity and without artifice, she dedicated her life to the missionary cause that included publishing these personal documents as additions to the endless chain of religious intelligence that were intended to inspire others to make generous donations and become new recruits.

When Rufus Anderson edited, compiled, and published selected letters, diary entries, and accounts of Catherine's life in the 1825 *Memoir*, he added a new hagiography to the genre of missionary memoir. He imposed a coherent narrative structure by organizing her brief life as the pilgrimage of a Christian Indian heroine who traversed from heathen darkness to the light of conversion, from rude Native lifeways to civilization.[15] This is how evangelical publics throughout America and the Atlantic world would come to know her, as an exemplar of the promise and success of the missionary spirit, and as an extraordinary life devoted to the realization of core religious values.

Anderson recounts that Catharine (*Kat ty*) was born in 1800 in Wills Valley, Alabama. Her father, John (*Yau-nu-gung-yah-ski*, Drowned Bear), and his second wife, Sarah (*Tsa-luh*), "belonged to the more intelligent class of their people."[16] The Brown family resided in a Lower Town near Creek Path, Alabama, in the Chickamauga region. They were part of a propertied, slave-holding political elite who favored a progressive plan of civilization, the education and evangelization of their children, Catharine and David, and the eventual removal to the Arkansas Territory. However, they differed from most Cherokees, who did not send their children to mission schools and did not convert. The seven mission schools established by 1825 (Brainerd, Taloney, Creek Path, Wills Town, Turnip Mountain, Hightower, Candy's Creek) to educate an Indian school-age population that numbered in the thousands recruited only 200–250 enrolled each year, and a total of 882 students attended from 1817 to 1833. Catharine was the first of only 167 converts.[17]

The Brainerd Mission, named after David Brainerd, was built on Chickamauga Creek, under the direction of Reverend Cyrus Kingsbury and assisted by missionaries Moody Hall and Loring S. Williams and their respective wives. Brainerd Mission enjoyed the support of a mixed-race Cherokee elite who included the powerful families of John Ross, Major Ridge, Charles Hicks, and Charles Reece.

The transplanted New England missionaries worked tirelessly to eradicate heathenism, represented by traditional beliefs and practices like conjuring and healing ceremonies, ball play, the Green Corn Dance, and other "heathen frolics."[18] Cherokee scholars needed to embrace evangelical Protestant character and personhood characterized by prayer, piety, and evangelical humility. Christian Indians organized their life by scrupulous adherence to the values of obedience, hard work, and self-discipline.[19]

By 1823, the mission had grown into a model New England village complete with separate schools and boarding arrangements for young men and women, a library, a grist and saw mill, a blacksmith shop, a stable, a barn, a grain storehouse, and a smokehouse. Brainerd operated a large farm with crops under cultivation, vegetable gardens, and herds of livestock.[20]

Catharine arrived in July 1817 during the first year of operation. Anderson describes her as "of the middle stature, erect, of comely features, and blooming complexion; and even at this time she was easy in her manners, and modest and predisposing in her demeanour."[21] She arrived at the mission dressed in fashionable clothing and adorned with jewelry and earrings. She appeared to Reverend Kinsgbury as prideful and ill-suited to the missionary project that stressed modest, unadorned fashion, evangelical humility, and piety.[22] Catharine would succeed as a model scholar and neophyte as she accomplished what Joel Martin terms the double-sided conversion of appearance and piety.

After two months she was literate, read the Bible, and progressed in her spiritual attainments. She attended weekly prayer meetings, prayed alone in the woods, and by January 1818 had experienced conversion and baptism.

In March she received admission to full communion in the mission church. Her tender religious affections alternated between convictions of sin and grieving the Holy Spirit with times of exaltation. Anderson explains one acquaintance described Catharine as having "seasons of exalted joy. When to use her own language, 'she felt as though she was in heaven, and was disappointed, when her thoughts returned to earth, and she found herself here!' She had, also, seasons of deep sorrow of heart, when she mourned the hidings of her Saviour's countenance, and groaned under the pressure of indwelling sin."[23]

Martin argues that the female sphere of the mission family—teachers and wives of missionary workers—created an intense spiritual hothouse of surveillance, spiritual guidance, and correction during Catharine's immersion into schoolwork and religious indoctrination. He explains,

> The tight and charged domestic scene generated intense psychological pressures and emotional tensions. These women saw Brown not just in school but in their homes. They taught European domestic arts to the young Cherokee woman, showed her proper dress and behavior, inquired about her spiritual state, monitored her behavior closely, corrected her manner of expression, supervised her morals, taught her to seek God, and listened to her nightly prayers.[24]

Catharine successfully traversed the spiritual itinerary from unredeemed sinner to a neophyte who surrendered to Jesus and had attained the inward experience of the Holy Spirit, renovating her heart as a new born child of God. The female sphere of the mission family guided, supported, and consoled her through this three-month journey.

The mission journal frequently recorded the intense religious affections of Cherokee scholars and neophytes who openly wept and groaned in agony, falling down in anguish over a newly awakened consciousness of their sin and depravity. While Elias Cornelius was preaching in November 1817 one unnamed Cherokee felt "pricked to the heart. After the meeting he went a few rods from the house & stood against a tree apparently in great agony. This being discovered Br. C[ornelius] & Br. K[ingsly] went to him & gave him some further instructions. His wounds were deepened until (like Saul) he was unable to stand. He fell on the ground & burst into a flood of tears."[25] During her conversion crisis in 1817, Catharine herself experienced such powerful religious affections.

She related a dream to a teacher and missionary sister Isabella Hall, who told her husband and recorded it in his journal. In 1824 he sent an account of the dream to the American Board. Thus, we have a third-hand retelling of the dream, written and revised seven years after the fact. Catharine never wrote about this event in her letters or diary, and the dream does not appear in Anderson's *Memoir*. We do not have her explanation and interpretation of the meaning of the dream.

Catharine's dream as recounted by Moody Hall involved an attempt to climb a steep incline where her feet slipped and she grew weary, never able to reach the top. In great fear of failing, unsure whether to go back or press forward, she saw a bush and a little boy who reached out to her. Grasping his thumb, Catharine climbed to the summit where she was informed that the boy was the savior.

Martin's meticulous research uncovered this document, and he provides an extensive interpretation identifying the Christian and Cherokee elements of the dreamscape. He argues that this was a pivotal moment in Catharine's acceptance of Christian dogma: a "singular dream" that signaled a transition to Christian Indian identity. It is plausible, as Martin argues, that the dream needs to be understood as the story of a traditional Cherokee spirit protector, the boy in the dream identified as the savior by Hall, but who might have symbolized a member of the "Little People." This other-than-human person rescued her in a time of anguish and peril and resolved Catharine's spiritual crisis by protecting her on the ascent, and permitted her to accept Christ in safety. Had Catharine accomplished this dreamwork and provided this account of the meaning of the dream, the interpretation would be a compelling narrative of the hybrid mix of Native and Christian elements.[26]

Theda Perdue argues that Catharine's habit of solitary fasting, prayer, and meditation in the woods and her concern for kin and the Cherokee community were indicative of the preservation and continuity of traditional spirituality and Native-centered concerns. Perdue maintains that Catharine was less concerned with her individual conversion and progressive sanctification as she longed to create a Cherokee Christian community of pious, regenerate, and "civilized" members who might be seen as acceptable to Euro-Americans and be permitted to remain in their homelands.[27] In her brief time at Creek Path from 1819 to 1823, she taught young women at the mission school and organized a weekly prayer circle and female charitable society.

However, there is no evidence that Catharine's solitary woodland retreats involved engaging in traditional rituals and contact with other-than-human persons that were part of Cherokee religiosity. Her letters are unequivocal about her individuated spiritual pilgrimage that does not valorize Cherokee culture or spirituality. She wrote to William and Flora Hoyt Chamberlain after departing from Brainerd in May 1819, "When I think and see the poor thoughtless Cherokee going on in sin I cannot help blessing God that has led me in the right path to serve him."[28]

Catharine forged a new identity as a Christian Indian and embraced a distinctive religious personhood best summarized in Anderson's eulogy. She embraced a Christ-centered life, one surrendered to Jesus and characterized by self-abasing humility. She organized her life through the practice of piety, each day reading scripture and devotional books, engaged in private devotions of prayer and meditation. She employed self-examination to uncover evidence of sin or a heart grown cold and indifferent—a methodical evangelical humiliation that prompted renewed spiritual exertions.

Throughout her writings Catharine relates the discovery of indwelling sin and a cold-hearted indifference to God that represented the fruits of methodical self-examination that served as an impetus for spiritual growth. She wrote on September 3, 1821, "I see nothing to trouble me, but my own wicked heart. It appears to me, that the more I wish to serve God, the more I sin. I seem never to have done any thing good in the sight of God."[29]

Catharine would send this letter to the Halls in November 1819, reiterating the themes of self-examination, evangelical humiliation, and surrender to Christ: "It appears strange to me, that I am not more interested in the cause of Christ, when he has done so much for me. But I will now give myself up entirely to Him. I should be willing to leave everything for

God, and to undergo any suffering, if it would but make me humble, and it would be for his glory."[30]

Catharine embraced the religious personhood as a new born child of God, who regardless of Cherokee Christian Indian identity sought an equal footing with white American coreligionists. She addressed them as sister and brother in a powerful democratic voice where she felt authorized to testify about her religious experiences and spiritual attainments. She held monthly prayer meetings that connected her small congregation at Creek Path to the imagined communities of evangelicals throughout America.

Perdue argues that Catharine, ever pious and subservient, did not abandon her culture. "Catharine's omnipresent spirituality, her women's prayer and philanthropic societies, her fasting and prayer in the forests and mountains helped her link her Cherokee world to that of Christian missionaries. Only in death could missionaries separate those worlds and claim Catharine for their own."[31] However, Catharine's writings offer no evidence of mediation between traditional Cherokee culture and her nascent evangelical identity. Her letters and journal provide the only evidence extant and these writings support her abandonment of traditional lifeways and ceremonies in favor of a new Cherokee Christian Indian identity.

Nancy Ruttenburg argues in *Democratic Personality* that the model of evangelical conversion in the eighteenth-century revival (repeated in the Second Great Awakening) fostered an individuated, democratic personality where the regenerate, open to the illumination of the Holy Spirit, were transformed into instruments of God's will, duty bound to speak in public, to testify about God's glory, and to exhort. This is what evangelical conversion did for Catharine Brown.[32]

Imbued with the missionary spirit, and possessing the agency of a religiously grounded democratic personality, she labored ceaselessly as a teacher, interpreter, and exhorter who witnessed the conversion of her parents and siblings at Creek Path. She wrote to her brother David, who was then a scholar at the Heathen School in Cornwall. Catharine rejoiced in her success in 1821 at forging a Christian Indian community as the fulfillment of her most profound desires: "I am very happy at home since my friends embrace religion. It is truly pleasant for brothers and sisters to live in the fear of God. When their hearts are united in the love of Christ, it is like a little heaven below."³³

Anderson credited the missionary wives and sisters as God's instruments for Catharine's achievements. He wrote, "Such was Catharine Brown, the converted Cherokee. Such too, were the changes wrought in her, through the blessings of the Almighty God on the labours of Missionaries. They [her missionary teachers], and only they, as the instruments of divine grace, had the formation of her Christian character . . . resulted from the nature of their instructions."³⁴ In death Catharine's voice endured to appeal to Christians everywhere to act with benevolence. "Though dead, she speaks: oh, let her voice fall with persuasive and irresistible eloquence upon every ear."³⁵

Catharine Brown's accomplishments need to be seen in the context of the Brainerd Mission, which formed a church community of the ingathered faithful, bound together by a covenant with God and their brothers and sisters in faith. Writing on March 9, 1817, Reverend Kingsbury, who kept the mission journal during the first year, made an entry for Sabbath, consecrating this "little band of Missionaries, who profess to have renounced the world for the sake of Christ. O! that we may be faithful to our covenant vows!"³⁶ They called their community the mission family and addressed one another as brother and sister, speaking directly to one another about the intimate details of piety and the state of each person's heart. Catharine soon embraced her new identity as a new born child of God, literate, acculturated, referring to herself as "an affectionate sister in Christ."

The Brainerd Mission church was established in October 1817, and the mission instituted Wednesday afternoon lectures and evening prayer meetings as integral to the brotherly watch and fraternal correction of missionaries and their families and hired workers who resided in the community. Their church community, united in belief and action, needed to act as a vessel to capture the Holy Spirit, cleansed of sin, and marked by a loving unity that proved difficult to maintain. By 1820, the mission voted to hold all things in common arguing that it was "injurious to hold private property."³⁷ They relied on American Board support and continued shipments of books, clothing, and sundry household items from charitable organizations in New England and throughout the Eastern Seaboard. The mission family viewed themselves as "indigent beggars before God & men." Addressing the charitable groups who supported the mission, Hoyt wrote that they can do nothing to repay this kindness. He asked, "Do they see our tears? Do they hear our groans?" And he continues in self-abasing humility:

> We fear grieving the Holy Spirit, through the depravity of our hearts. We fear erring from the path of duty. . . . We know that through the multiplicity of our care, & the infirmity of our bodies, we are unable to answer their kind & affectionate letters as we would wish, or to give them that information they long for, & have a right to expect. And we are frequently grieved, fearing they will consider us ungrateful.[38]

Beginning in July 1, 1818, the mission family initiated periodic days of fasting, prayer, self-examination, and repentance to prepare for communion or monthly concerts. Ard Hoyt, who kept the journal, wrote, "We had, in truth, great cause to humble ourselves before God, for we had become almost dead with lukewarmness, temporal cares, & other evil affections known only to our God, *& which we are ashamed to enter into our journal*" (emphasis added).[39] As was common in Moravian missions that constituted a *Brüdergemeine* (congregational community of brothers united in faith), Brainerd devoted the Saturday before the communion service as an opportunity for spiritual preparation and to repair any divisions that threatened the unity of the church community.

The celebration of the monthly concert and communion provided an opportunity for spiritual quickening, the resolution of personal differences, repentance, and evangelical humiliation. Hoyt wrote on July 6, "The return of another monthly concert was very refreshing to our languid spirits. . . . We felt this day as if the Lord was hearing the prayers of our brethren for us, unworthy as we are and fondly hoped we should no more be left to so cold & lifeless a state as we sometimes have been."[40]

Communicants of the mission church and members of the Brainerd Mission family apparently made a lifetime vow of service to Brainerd and the missionary cause. This commitment underlies the crisis and turmoil recorded in a curious episode beginning on May 1, 1820, when Brother Talmage—a blacksmith residing at Brainerd with his wife and children, stated they intended to leave. Talmage felt unhappy and argued that he had no duty to remain. The mission family appears to have received this news as a direct threat to church unity and solidarity. Hoyt wrote, "Our distressful feelings respecting the designed departure of Br. Talmage are quite indescribable."[41] Thus began a campaign to pressure the blacksmith and his wife to reconsider, devoting a day of "fasting, humiliation & prayer" the following Sabbath. The church community beseeched Christ's intercession and struggled to understand the mysteries of Providence:

> O dearest Saviour intercede.
> For us in this our time of need
> Thou see'st O Lord each asking heart,
> Which mourns & bleeds with inward smart.
> Thou also see'st thy little band
> All helpless leaning on thy hand,
> To thee we look, to thee we pray
> O help us in this trying day.[42]

Br. Talmage remained adamant in his decision to quit, which prompted the mission officials to exclude him from communion on May 6. The church formally charged him with breaking his vow to engage for life at the mission and they conducted a disciplinary hearing later that month. Talmage stated that he disliked the "common board of course food," the practice of eating communal meals of poor quality. He also opposed collecting firewood and salting meat instead of working in the blacksmith's shop. Attempts to persuade the blacksmith to reconsider or to divide his family and convince his wife to remain true to her vows failed. The family departed by wagon for Augusta on May 25.

The explicit lifetime vow made by communicants and members of the mission family explains the episodes of extreme distress when Catharine's father pressured her to leave the mission and return to Creek Path in 1817 and in response to her final leave-taking on May 20, 1820, when she wrote, "Tomorrow morning I shall leave this School, perhaps never to return. . . .

It is truly painful to me to part with my dear Christian friends; Those with whom I have spent many happy hours in the house of worship. This is the place where I first became acquainted with the Savior. He now calls me to work in his vine yard [sic]."[43]

Ever obedient to her father in 1817 and to the mandates of God's will, Catharine honored her lifetime commitment to the cause of missions and departed Brainerd for Creek Path to go wherever her Savior beckoned. Putting personal interests aside she asks, should she refuse the call in order to remain with her friends and for her own pleasure "while many of [her] poor red brothers and sisters, are perishing for lack of knowledge?"[44]

A trope found throughout Catharine's letters involves pining for absent members of the mission family and her longing for reunion with distant teachers and friends who also left Brainerd for other mission schools. She understood that they would remain apart in this life until their reunion in heaven. Writing to her brother David on February 10, 1823, during her final visit to Brainerd, she explained, "I feel truly attached to Brainerd, where I first found the Saviour; and O how I love the dear sisters, with whom I have spent many happy hours, both in school, and in walking to the house of worship. But those happy hours are past. We must be contented, and look forward to the day when we shall meet to part no more."[45]

The endless chain of religious intelligence depicted Catharine Brown as a Christian Indian who forged a life of self-sacrifice and disinterested benevolence devoted to the salvation of her "poor red brothers and sisters." Her early death evoked a "melancholy sense of noble futility."[46] As Hilary E. Wyss argues, religious intelligence produced a construction of the missionary imagination, a caricature of the "Readerly Indian" who acted with docile acceptance of religious doctrine, appropriated Protestant character, organized his or her life by appropriating a methodical ethos of work and piety, and was represented as a passive convert to evangelical religion. Like the indigenous people depicted in Faber's *The Book of Strange New Things*, Catharine and the mixed-race elite openly welcomed the Christian message. However, Christian Indians like Catharine and her brother David also forged religious personhood as regenerate children of God, with powers of agency and self-determination to speak and advocate for the good of the people. They emerged as "Writerly Indians" who bristled at missionary control and made claims as social equals despite the pernicious racial ideas that divided them from Euro-Americans. Writerly Indians at times cooperated with the evangelical plan of civilization and conversion when these ideas resonated with Cherokee claims of autonomous nationhood that could effectively resist policies of removal and expulsion from their homelands.[47]

No memoir was published adding to the chain of religious intelligence for Catharine's younger brother David, who died at age twenty-nine of tuberculosis. However, he represented an extraordinary example of the success of the Brainerd missionary project dating from his first admission in October 1819 through his conversion, baptism, admission as a communicant in the mission church in the spring of 1820, continued education at the Cornwall Foreign Mission School (1820–1822), and year spent in preparation for the ministry at Andover Theological Seminary. He returned home in 1823 on a speaking tour sponsored and celebrated by the American Board to work as a missionary at the Dwight Mission in Arkansas in 1824. He served as secretary to the Cherokee National Council, married Rachel Lowry (Sequoyah's niece) in 1827, and assisted in the publication of the syllabary before his death in 1829.[48]

The Brainerd Mission journal records David Brown's progress after four months in attendance. He "at times appeared exercised with pungent conviction—Now he thinks he has found the Savior, & we hope he is not deceived."[49] After a six-week sojourn at Creek Path to visit his ailing father, he returned with Catharine. With the consent of his father, and after sessions of private Sabbath prayer with his sister, David stated that he was "anxious to get an education preparatory to becoming a minister of the gospel."[50]

Catharine corresponded with David until her death in 1823. Although his letters have not survived, five of her published letters to him are extant and reveal their mutual concern for family, their support of the cause of missions, and their mutual spiritual encouragement and edification as Christian Indians. Catharine's words, written from Creek Path in February 1822, typify their practice of piety as "children of a glorious and holy God" when she relates the death of their brother John after a long struggle with tuberculosis. She inquires,

> Are you still living as a stranger and pilgrim in the earth? Is the Saviour near your heart, and the object of your chief delight and conversation? I trust that you will continually possess and imitate that meek and lowly spirit, which Jesus possessed in the days of his flesh.... May we be submissive to all the dispensations of his Providence, not only in prosperity, but also in adversity, and say, The Will of the Lord be done.[51]

Time and again Catharine told her brother of her prayers for him, wishing that they could cultivate an abiding love to God and divine mercy, and an expectation that imminent death necessitated that he should devote precious time in God's service. She exhorted him to serve as an instrument of God as a minister to the heathen.[52] And from her deathbed, too weak to write these words that she dictated to her missionary friend Laura Potter, Catharine uttered a final note of pious submission: "I have found that is good for me to be afflicted. The Saviour is very precious to me. I often enjoy his presence, and I long to be where I can enjoy his presence without sin.... You must remember; that this world is not our home, that we all must die soon."[53]

David Brown is best remembered not for his pious letters or memoirs but for his public address delivered repeatedly during the speaking and fundraising tour accompanied by the American Board corresponding secretary Jeremiah Evarts in 1823. Brown addressed church groups and audiences in Hartford, New Haven, New York, Newark, New Brunswick, Princeton, Trenton, Philadelphia, Wilmington, Baltimore, Washington DC, Alexandria, Fredericksburg, and Richmond. Brown, "when not at the podium, pursued his own agenda of generating goodwill and social capital for the Cherokee people. Visiting or dining with prominent citizens such as the President of Yale College, he built a network of important and well-connected white allies with whom he would correspond subsequently to gain support for Cherokee political objectives."[54]

He found his voice as a Writerly Indian, as an advocate for the politics of missionary conversion and the plan of civilization as a strategy to resist removal and permit the Cherokee to claim a sovereign nation-state in their contested homelands in Georgia, Tennessee, and Alabama. During his address, David presented himself as an articulate, educated, accomplished Christian Indian, dressed in fashionable clothing. He did not appear in buckskins and moccasins, speaking halting pidgin English but presented a dramatic contrast with popular stereotypical depictions or sentimentalized noble or vilified ignoble savages and heathens. Here, David proudly proclaimed his Cherokee identity, speaking of his exploits as a warrior seeking Osage scalps, as "one of the sons of the forest. Yes! The image of an Indian is upon me, and aboriginal blood runs in my veins."[55]

Brown paints an idyllic portrait of Native life before European colonization and laments the ravages of settler colonialism, where Cherokees find themselves surrounded by foreigners, the victims of warfare, dispossession of their homelands, and declining numbers bordering on extinction. "What dire catastrophes have darkened the pages of American history!"[56] However, the Cherokees persist as a people and sovereign nation, he thought, in need of missionaries to instruct them in schools, to remedy the deficiencies of Native religions and show them the path of evangelical religion. "When we view them through the gospel of Jesus Christ, we lament their deplorable condition. Like all heathen nations of the earth they are in darkness."[57]

He made a compelling argument for the capacity of the Cherokees to adopt Christianity and "civilized" laws, constitutional governance, agriculture, language and literacy, schooling, and evangelical religion. Arguing against the prevailing attitude that Natives were racially inferior, Brown asserts their "natural capacities for moral cultivations" made them "susceptible to mental as well as religious improvement as much as any people on the Globe."[58]

Although a pious convert, missionary, and advocate for evangelical religion and the plan of civilization, Brown devoted the last years of his life to working with Sequoyah on the syllabary. While embracing the rhetoric of Brainerd, the Heathen School, and Andover, he used this cultural legitimacy to promote Cherokee sovereignty and nationhood and the position that he and others of his tribe could claim equality with Americans and their coreligionists as Christian Indians—cultivated, reborn children of God.[59]

John Arch (Atsi, 1797–1825) was a full-blood Cherokee from North Carolina, the subject of a short biography, *The Memoir of John Arch, a Cherokee Young Man*, published in 1829 and compiled from missionary accounts recorded in the *Brainerd Journal*. He distinguished himself as a translator, interpreter, teacher, and fundraiser. A stalwart champion of the missionary spirit and a cultural mediator, he toured the Cherokee and Choctaw nations after his conversion in 1820 to promote evangelical religion and the plan of civilization. Little remains of his writing, but "Brother" Arch's voice is expressed through the filter of the religious paternalism of Brainerd teachers whom he considered to be his "fathers." The journal records for October 15, 1823,

> Br. John Arch returned from a circuitous tour in which he has been to the eastern extremity of the nation, & visited his relations & many of his former acquaintances. He finds a very pleasing change since he traveled in those dark regions a year ago. Then he found multitudes who had never heard of a Savior, & almost all quietly pursuing the old way—Now in every cabin where he visited, they were inquiring with a seriousness. He says all the Cherokees in these parts are now prepared to receive missionaries.[60]

Arch arrived at Brainerd in January 1819, twenty-one years of age, dressed in filthy rags, melancholy after a poor hunting season, and eager to enroll as a scholar following the advice of tribal leader Hicks to attend Brainerd and learn to read and write. Arch exchanged his rifle for a set of new clothes donated from a Philadelphia charity. "His dress and appearance, when he came to Brainerd, shows at once that he belonged to the most uncultivated portion of his tribe; having spent so many years in savage life, that the missionaries received his application with reluctance."[61]

After thirteen months, John had achieved his goal of English literacy and had progressed in the spiritual itinerary from first conviction of sin through conversion, baptism (November 1819), and admission as a communicant in the mission church (May 7, 1820). Following religious instruction regarding sin, forgiveness, and salvation, he experienced self-loathing and profound distress—a repugnance about accepting grace.

"That repugnance seemed to him more criminal than all other sins, and his distress became almost unsupportable. One night he lay awake, as he said, expecting sudden distraction, such was his terror, that he trembled all the while (to use his own comparison) like one in an ague."[62] The next morning he experienced the selfless rapture of grace that augured rebirth, conversion, and the promise of salvation.

His memoir presents the perfect Christian Indian as a young man who rejected heathen ways in favor of education and conversion, and who would devote his life to assisting missionaries laboring among his people. A classmate of David and Catharine Brown, Arch declined a nomination to attend the Cornwall Foreign Mission School and chose to remain at Brainerd. He enthusiastically agreed to translate school primers and chapters of the Bible, teach school at Creek Path, and interpret and exhort Natives by accompanying Daniel Butrick, William Chamberlin, and Jeremiah Evarts on their respective tours of the Southeast from 1822 until his death in 1825.

THE SPIRITUAL PILGRIMAGE OF SISTER MARGARET ANN

> The blooming flow'r
> Has faded, and the withering matron stem
> Cast its pale blossom in Salvation's path,
> Strewing the steps of Sorrow. Thou hast fall'n,
> Thou mild Moravian Sister! Thou wert deck'd
> With what the giddy, unreflecting world
> Might call accomplishment, but thou didst own
> A pearl it could not purchase. . . .
> Thou hast obtain'd
> Eternal gain, from sublunary loss,
> And tribulation; for thy robes are white
> In atoning blood. Say, shall we shed
> The tear for thee, blest Sister! when thy lot
> Is better far than ours?

Lydia H. Sigourney published this memorial in 1822 to the "first fruit of the Cherokee nation." The Moravian missionaries who evangelized her referred to Margaret Scott Vann as "our Peggy" and conferred upon her the baptismal name of Sister Margaret Ann.[63] As the poet noted, this blooming flower would forsake the gentility and accomplishment of a mixed-race Cherokee planter elite to seek salvation as a Moravian Pietist, a Christian Indian.

She was born in August 1783 to Sarah Hicks (Cherokee, Wolf clan) and Walter Scott, an English agent to the Cherokee Nation. Peggy came of age in the Upper Town settlements in north Georgia and embraced the contradiction of Native cultural identity and the emerging American individualist orientation of patriarchal kinship and households suited to a commercial and business elite. In 1797 at age fourteen she became the fifth wife of James Vann, a mixed-race Cherokee who embraced aspects of traditional Cherokee culture by taking multiple wives while simultaneously pursing aspects of the plan of civilization. Vann had previously married her sister Betsy Scott. Peggy brought a dowry worth seven hundred dollars in cattle and African slaves that her husband appropriated, adding to his considerable holdings on the plantation at Diamond Hill.[64]

James Vann was born in the 1760s, the son of a Cherokee mother and Scottish trader. Approximately 15 percent of the population of Cherokee women in this era married white traders, and their children identified as Cherokee. This mixed-race elite were proficient in English, and through their allegiance to American values of the market economy they enjoyed success as merchants and slave holders.[65]

Diamond Hill covered eight hundred acres of farmlands and woods bordering the Conasauga River. Vann established a trading post, tavern and inn, campgrounds, and ferry service. He owned more than eighty slaves, who built this plantation that included two large houses, slave cabins, storehouses, a workshop, a blacksmith's shop, a stable and barns, and a home for Mother Wali Vann. He traded deerskins, cash crops, and manufactured goods and managed the federal post and mail service. An ambitious man, he became wealthy and politically influential, lobbying for the construction of the Federal Road through his property, holding office in the Cherokee National Council, leading the Lighthorse brigade.

A grandee and champion of Cherokee sovereignty, a sponsor of the

Moravian mission on his property at Springplace, and an advocate for education and the plan of civilization, Vann was a complex and conflicted person. He became infamous for his violent and tyrannical conduct. By 1805 only Peggy remained, as his other wives had left him. In marriage she had lost control of her property and remained isolated from family and friends, as James prohibited visitors during his absences. Peggy would turn to the Moravians for support, seeking respite and protection from this domestic terror.

He frequently hosted slaves and Cherokee and Euro-American guests for all-night drinking parties that ended in drunken melees. Executing summary justice by burning men alive, he put to death two slaves who stood accused of stealing a large sum of cash. Vann repeatedly beat his wife, Mother Wali Vann, and other family members and killed his brother-in-law in a duel before Vann was himself murdered in 1809 while pursuing horse thieves with the Lighthorse Brigade. And as a widow, Peggy looked to Moravians for spiritual direction and friendship.

Sister Margaret Ann's spiritual pilgrimage is inextricably tied to her association with the Springplace Mission that was founded in 1801 on thirty-five acres on loan from James Vann's plantation at Diamond Hill. Vann and leaders of the Cherokee Nation desired a school to educate Native youth in English literacy. The Moravian missionary couple, Brother Gottlieb and Sister Dorothea Byhan, who founded the mission, resisted opening a school and instead intended to create a new congregational community of Christian Indians modeled after the experiment in Fairfield in Canada. The National Council issued an ultimatum: open a school by 1804 or face expulsion. The missionaries complied, and in 1805 Brother and Sister John and Anna Rosina Gambold arrived to assist in these efforts and to build Springplace into a model farm.[66] The mission allowed scholars to board on the Vann plantation, as they had limited resources with which to offer food and clothes and could house no more than four scholars in the beginning. They frequently turned away pupils. The table below presents an overview of the mission school from 1804 to 1821.

In the period from 1804 through 1821, the school admitted sixty-nine Indian students ages 5–15, comprising fifty boys and nineteen girls, in

Table 2. Number of students enrolled at the Springplace Mission school

YEAR	MALE	FEMALE	TOTAL
1804	3	0	3
1805	7	1	8
1806	9	1	10
1807	8	1	9
1808	8	1	9
1809	9	3	12
1810	8	3	11
1811	10	5	15
1812	7	5	12
1813	9	4	13
1814	9	4	13
1815	10	3	13
1816	10	1	11
1817	9	1	10
1818	10	0	10
1819	10	0	10
1820	12	1	13
1821	16	3	19

Source: McClinton, *The Moravian Springplace Mission to the Cherokees*, vol. 2, "Catalog of Scholars," 445–54.

addition to nineteen children of white settlers. The predominately male scholars were the children of the next generation of the ascendant planter elite from the Upper Town settlements and the Cherokee National Council. The Moravians baptized only one student in this period.

In 1818 Springplace sent five students to the Cornwall Foreign Mission

School (CFMS) with the expectation that they would complete their education and return home as converted missionaries and Christian Indian leaders. The Moravians anticipated that Buck Watie (Elias Boudinot), Leonard Hicks, John Ridge, Dawzizi, and John Vann would fulfill the missionaries' highest aspirations and become literate and Christianized Indians.[67]

Buck Watie entered Springplace at age ten in 1810 and remained for eight years before attending the CFMS as a scholar until 1822. His sister Dawnee arrived at age nine in 1811. However, she died during her first year of residence. Stand Watie came to Springplace at age thirteen in 1815 and remained for six years until 1821. Buck would accept the sponsored name Elias Boudinot and achieve notoriety after the controversial interracial marriage with Harriet Gold. Although he converted to Christianity and was accepted to train for the ministry at Andover Theological Seminar, he rejected the idea of evangelizing his people in favor of a political career as an editor of the *Cherokee Phoenix*. He would write in October 1821 in a letter published in the *Religious Remembrancer*, "There is a great leanness in my soul. Many are called, few are chosen. Perhaps my profession is unsound for evidences of true do not consist in the outward performances of the duties required."[68] He attained a democratic personality as a Writerly Indian to advocate against removal to Indian Territory (present-day Oklahoma) in the 1820s, but later accepted the provisions of removal in the 1830s.

Dawzizi, son of The Tyger and Oodeisaski Smith, entered in 1810 and remained for seven years. After returning from CFMS, he requested baptism but was repeatedly refused after unsuccessful drawings of the Lot. In frustration, he joined the Brainerd Mission, who baptized him as David Steiner and where he served as an interpreter.[69]

The school at Springplace instituted a methodically organized daily round of work, prayer, and study as girls assisted carrying water, washing clothes, milking cows, feeding the hogs, and working in the gardens. Girls learned the new gendered division of labor of domestic duties: weaving, spinning, cooking, and sewing. Boys worked clearing fields, plowing, harvesting crops, and undertaking other hard labor. Both girls and boys were instructed in reading, writing, arithmetic, and grammar. Religious instruction included the catechism, hymns, Bible stories, and important prayers in the liturgy.

The mission school attempted to forge a new type of religious personhood founded on an ascetic ethos of work, piety, obedience to a Moravian code of conduct, and surrender to Jesus. David Zeisberger had created a model for Christian Indian community and religious personhood for both children and adults based on the following religious regimen and ethos: "belief in one God; respect for elders, including parents; examination by and absolute obedience to teachers; rest on Sundays; exclusion of thieves, murderers, whoremongers, adulterers, or drunkards, prohibition of dances, sacrifices, 'heathenish' festivals or games, monogamy; abstinence from intoxicating liquors."[70]

From 1805 until her death in 1821, Anna Rosina worked as the school's principal, kept the mission journal, supervised the kitchen and food preparation, and tended vegetable and medicinal herb gardens. John served as religious leader and interpreter of the Word, cooper, mason, carpenter, tailor, and farmer. Like other Moravian missions, Springplace was organized as a community of goods, without private ownership, and eschewed the accumulation of wealth and emphasized building a church community. The missionaries planted orchards, established fenced pastures for livestock, and planted gardens and fields of corn, oat, hay, wheat, and flax. They built two mission houses, barns, stables, a springhouse for dairy products, a brick kiln, a bake oven, and a smokehouse.[71]

Rowena McClinton explains that the Moravian pilgrims intended to build a self-sufficient and self-contained model farm. However, their journal records continued participation in a local bartering and market economy.[72] Located near the frequently traveled Federal Road and the Conasauga River, Springplace hosted a seemingly endless stream of Native and non-Native travelers and visitors. The missionaries suffered from continued shortages of fresh meat and food and they embraced the hospitality proffered by James Vann and other Cherokee who brought game (venison, fish, turkey) and beef and pork in exchange for corn, clothing, tailoring, spinning, and weaving or sharpening of axes and knives.

The mixed-race planter elite who concentrated economic and political power in the new towns and their associated households sponsored and supported the Springplace Mission. Here children could receive an education to succeed in the new market economy. Here Cherokees would demonstrate their accomplishments in the plan of civilization as Christian Indians. In this manner, they could claim the right to sovereignty and control over their homelands and resist removal. As McClinton explains, "pragmatic and resourceful, the Cherokee people permitted the Moravian missionaries to live with them on a prolonged basis because they provided the tools necessary to preserve the Cherokee's homelands."[73]

The United Brethren or Unitas Fratrum were known as Moravians from their country of origin. Under the patronage of Count Nikolaus Ludwig von Zinzendorf, they established the community of Herrnhutt in Saxony in 1722 and opened foreign mission communities in Georgia in 1730–39, in Bethlehem, Pennsylvania, in 1741 and in Salem, North Carolina, in 1799. These enclaves supported the formation of mission communities to Native peoples in Connecticut (Pachgatgoch, 1746), New York (Shekomeko, 1741), western Pennsylvania (Gnadenhütten, 1749), Nain and Wechquetank (1761), and Fairfield on the Thames River, Ontario, Canada (1792). These Christian Indian communities were a multitribal, polyglot collection of refugees who joined together in new church communities united by faith and under the protection and supervision of Moravian religious paternalism. Here brothers and sisters in the faith—Moravian missionaries and their Native converts—needed to maintain a unity in belief, thought, and action to foster a *Brüdergemeine* (congregational church community) as a vessel to capture the Holy Spirit. Missionary brothers and sisters and their Indian neophytes viewed themselves as children of God, open to fraternal correction and mutual edification. They pledged to make a life united in love for Jesus, a Christ-centered fusion of souls who submitted to the leadings of the Holy Spirit as mediated to the faithful by Moravian elders and by the random dictates of decision by the Lot.

As I have argued in *Tears of Repentance*,

> Moravian evangelical piety encouraged meditation, prayer, and forms of communal worship with a loving and compassionate God and a

savior-prophet who had redeemed humanity by his suffering and sacrifice. The United Brethren practiced a public and communal auricular confession of sin that cleansed communicants of sin, healed social divisions, and unified the congregation before they celebrated Communion. In addition, rites of baptism, foot washing, and love feasts—ceremonial and celebratory meals—created joyful and vital religious exercises that characterized this new Christian tribalism.[74]

Springplace differed from this Christian tribalism. They established a mission within the Cherokee nation that did not admit adults and had a limited capacity to educate children in their boarding school. Where previous Moravian missions gathered together multiethnic refugee and detribalized peoples suffering from powerlessness and cultural anomie, only the planter elite minority of the Cherokees valued Springplace's mission school and education, as a strategy in the plan of civilization. Initially, they showed little interest in Moravian teachings or conversion. From 1804 to 1819, none of the mission students had converted. The missionaries had turned inward to foster their own personal spiritual development but seemed resigned to a limited role of educating Native and white students while forgoing the sublime expectation of converting the Cherokees from heathen darkness. However, the conversion of Peggy Scott Vann in 1810 brought new hope to the Springplace missionaries.

At age twenty-seven, after more than a decade of marriage to a violent, abusive man, she grieved his murder. Peggy faced the unsettling conflicts arising from her husband's estate, and proved receptive to Moravian efforts at pastoral care, mutual aid, and assistance in these legal and kinship controversies. The missionaries consoled Peggy with what Max Weber terms a "rational theodicy of misfortune." All forms of adversity and misfortune that characterize the human condition challenged individuals and groups with the threat of having to endure meaningless suffering. A rational theodicy of misfortune gave meaning to sickness and death, natural disasters like drought, floods, and earthquakes, and the painful changes and dislocations associated with colonization and the plan of civilization. All of these events needed to be understood as the unfolding of divine Providence. The faithful endured suffering by placing their complete trust in the goodness of the savior and the promise of salvation from adversity in this world and the vision of paradise in the world to come. These religious ideas rendered the events and suffering associated with human existence—the transitions in the passage of one's life, and the transformations in community and the world—into a rational, comprehensive, and compelling narrative. Those afflicted by adversity no longer viewed their travail as senseless or meaningless suffering. A Christian religious ethos prescribed that the faithful embrace a penitential stance toward the world, and through acts of self-mortification and humiliation transform their hedonistic avoidance of pain into ethically mandated action that fostered redemptive suffering as an opportunity for spiritual growth. As Weber explains, "this rational view of the world has often furnished suffering with a 'plus' sign which was originally quite foreign to it."[75]

The marrow of Moravian divinity that the Gambolds mediated to Peggy through private heart-to-heart talks in these months of grief and anguish emphasized the methodical obedience to God's law, the wages of sin for disobedience, and the need for sincere repentance as evidenced by weeping and contrition. The neophyte would adopt a distinctive religious stance toward self and world—the childlike believer who through a penitential sorrow for one's sin could prepare the heart for the experience of the inner-worldly mystical contemplation of Christ—shedding joyful tears, flooding with religious affections of acosmic love that brought believers into a new congregational community of faith that superseded bonds of blood, marriage, and tribal affinity. The faith community, constituted by *agape* and through repeated ritual and ceremony, expressed gratitude for the blood of the Lamb and the crucifixion and redeeming suffering of the savior.[76]

On June 10, 1810, Peggy attended Sunday service at the start of Pentecost where Brother Gambold preached about the striving of the Holy Spirit in convincing men and women of their sinfulness and the possibility of redemption through Christ's blood. She was invited to remain for a conversation about the state of her heart but was summoned to return home, thus preventing this exhortation. Brother Gambold visited her later that evening, but any conversation proved impossible given the presence of

Mother Vann, who objected to the visit by white missionaries at Diamond Hill. The mission journal records their sense of wonderment and surrender to divine will as the Moravians expressed their frustration: "We then commended her to the dead Savior and laid our urgent request to speak with her today at His feet, full of childlike confidence that if it were His holy will, He Himself would soon find an opportunity. And behold!"[77]

After nearly a decade of missionary travail, the Gambolds marveled when Peggy returned to Springplace early the next day and reported about her travail having spent a sleepless night reading scripture, meditating on the suffering of Jesus, and weeping over the possibility of baptism. She grasped Sister Gambold's hand, crying out in the affirmation of her faith. In response to a series of questions Peggy affirmed that "she was prepared to set aside all other considerations, to subscribe completely to Him who bought her with His precious blood."[78]

Despite the opposition of the Vann family and others among the mixed-race Cherokee planter elite who ridiculed Peggy for her nascent spiritual concerns about the salvation of her soul, she affirmed her newfound experience of grace by forsaking all for her Savior and asked to be accepted as a baptismal candidate. The mission conference later met in private and granted her request. Brother Gambold gave her the *Idea Fidei Fratrum*, the guide to Moravian doctrine, instructing her to study the chapters about faith and baptism. He scheduled her baptism for August 13.

On the appointed day Peggy Scott Vann arrived in the early morning, dressed completely in white. She requested the opportunity for private prayer and reflection, the *Anbeten*, or ritual of ordination before the Lord. Prostrated on the floor with her face down and her arms folded, she prepared for baptism.[79] The service began with the hymn "Come Holy Ghost, Come Our Lord Our God" as the candidate was brought into the congregation. The mission journal describes this momentous event as the "first fruit of the Cherokee Nation" turned to God in conversion, and she received the Christian name Sister Margaret Ann. Those in attendance openly wept. "It was really as if the place moved, yes, as if Jesus Christ, the crucified Son of God, stood there in the flesh and overflowed the souls thirsting for His Blood. All those present were moved by grace. Shame and humiliation at such divine condescension filled each heart, and each one of us could do nothing more than cry and sigh."⁸⁰

Joyful together, the small mission congregation, who addressed one another with the fictive kinship as brothers and sisters in Jesus, experienced a unity that for them constituted the prerequisite to form a vessel to capture the Holy Spirit and to experience the presence and inner mystical possession of Jesus. Sister Margaret Ann appeared "happy, [and] like quite a blessed holy child, she talked with us for a while about the great love and goodness of the dear Savior, especially for her, who herself had proved to be completely unworthy. We accompanied her on her way home all the way into the thicket and once again wished her a thousand blessings from the fullness of Jesus in her new life."⁸¹

During the six months between her baptism in July 1810 and admission as a communicant to the mission church in January 1811, Peggy attended liturgies, love feasts, and holiday celebrations. She manifested a demeanor of humility and docile submission to the religious paternalism of Brother and Sister Gambold, who routinely examined her in *Das Sprechen*—pastoral care and spiritual direction proffered in private, heart-to-heart conversations designed to probe the neophyte's sincerity. They inquired seeking to ascertain: had Peggy rejected traditional Cherokee lifeways and turned her back on frolics, ball play, dances, ceremonies, and traditional healing practices? Did she forsake her extended kin for the new congregational church community of faith? Did she embrace daily prayer, meditation, and reading devotional books? Did she manifest a childlike spirit and resign herself to the leadings of the Holy Spirit as mediated to her by the Moravian missionaries?

This benevolent religious paternalism replaced the conjugal paternalism and patriarchal domination that James Vann exercised over his powerless and dependent wife. The missionaries directed her attendance at worship and her reading and advised her about mundane affairs in managing her household. During the months of probation, surveillance, and close examination, she frequently shared in private conversations with Brother Gambold the concerns of her heart, her insecurities, and her feelings of unworthiness. Peggy exhorted her older sister Betsy and others and translated for the children at the mission school. She reminded them,

Oh, you dear children, may it indeed be very important to you that you have come to a place where you hear so much about the Savior. Oh, if you had stayed home, you might never have heard such things. Oh, we are a poor, needy nation. Our countrymen go around in ignorance! How highly *we* should esteem our fortune that we received the opportunity to hear what the dear Savior suffered and did for us out of love! Oh, what would have become of *me*?[82]

At the service when Peggy joined the church as a communicant, she expressed the religious emotions of a true believer—effusive tears of joy, tears of repentance, and tears that flowed freely as she admitted a profound humility and unworthiness to receive this sacrament. Sister Gambold reported, "Our confirmand was completely transformed and cried unceasingly."[83]

True to her newly forged religious personhood as an evangelical Pietist, Peggy experienced a direct, personal relationship with her savior, an inner mystical presence and possession of the Holy Spirit. "She said that it had seemed to her as if she saw the dear Savior in flesh and blood standing in our midst."[84] Repeatedly throughout her life as a Moravian sister in this congregational brotherhood, Peggy experienced ecstatic and rapturous mystical encounters with her redeemer. The mission journal records her words in April 1811 during Passion Week following rituals of foot-washing, religious services, and Holy Communion. After this ceremony, she exclaimed, "Oh, something indescribable happened to me! I am overcome with shivering so that I could hardly stand, and yet I felt as well in my heart as if I were already with the dear Savior in heaven. Oh, how good He is! Oh, if only all people knew how good he is!"[85]

Tears of repentance and public performances of weeping structured Sister's Margaret's religious emotions as she methodically exercised a spiritual discipline of self-imposed humiliation. During this practice of piety, after self-examination and auricular confession, "Tears flowed from our Peggy's eyes."[86] She also wept tears of joy during communion; having confessed her sins and unworthiness, she enjoyed the presence of the savior. Through public religious performances, openly weeping, she exclaimed,

"I am the greatest sinner. How could even I come to see such great grace? How indescribably great is the love of our Savior indeed! Oh, I do love Him, but oh! not nearly enough."[87]

As a young woman, Peggy Scott Vann had appropriated the secular idea of personhood as a lady of refinement and accomplishment, the highest ideal of mixed-race planter elite. She came of age in the recently settled new town of Hiwasse that was founded after the Revolution, where Cherokees rejected traditional communal villages and matrilineal clan affiliations to form individuated patriarchal households organized by an ethic of competitive individualism suited to a market economy. These "progressive" Cherokees imposed a gender revolution that stripped women of collective property ownership, ending their agricultural contributions from tending gardens and cornfields and undermining their political influence in the development of male-dominated centralized government. For Peggy the many accomplishments of her elite status included proficiency in English and Cherokee, sewing and needlework, and the domestic arts of managing a household of servants and slaves. She adopted the pose of a refined, educated, and cultivated lady, marked by luxurious couture.[88] She lived a life of enforced leisure, confined to the Diamond Hill plantation under the family governance of her tyrannical husband.

When reborn as Sister Margaret Ann, she embraced an evangelical Pietist religious personhood that simultaneously rejected traditional Cherokee lifeways and identity and the role of plantation mistress and lady that valorized the secular accomplishments of the mixed-race elite. As a Moravian sister and communicant in the *Brüdergemeine*, she organized her life according to an ascetic religious ethos of hard work by laboring in the fields and the household in the manner of a common worker, toiling alongside slaves and servants. Sister Margaret rejected the style of life of a grandee that prohibited her from performing productive labor. In addition, she rejected worldliness, disposed of her Indian jewelry, and wore simple, less fashionable clothing as she eschewed ostentation and the enjoyment of luxury. Abstaining from alcohol and rejecting Cherokee celebrations and ceremonial life, this neophyte toiled in a sober, methodical fashion, devoting her time unceasingly as a tool of divine will. When she labored clearing the lands of her Mountjoy farm and tended to the cornfield and gardens, slaughtering pigs and tending to livestock, her actions were prescribed by the ethos of ascetic religious personhood and not by the dictates of traditional Cherokee womanhood.

Peggy adopted a new ethic of *caritas* and Christian charity in her relations with others. During the month of her baptism in April 1811 a man, the Trunk, and his impoverished family, consisting of his wife, Naki, and their six children, who were from the new town of Oostanaula, were camped in the woods of the Vann estate. Starving, they pleaded for something to eat, "otherwise they would all have to die."[89]

Traditional Cherokee practices of hospitality, generosity, and reciprocal gift exchange enveloped each person in a web of social affiliations and obligations organized by corporate kinship bonds. When someone related by blood, marriage, or tribal-cultural identity appeared at the door, hungry, tired, and in need of assistance, the host was obligated to feed, clothe, and shelter the guest. Even in time of scarcity and hunger, the host needed to offer hospitality without calculating the cost.

Peggy consulted with Brother Gambold about her obligations to this family. Given the scarcity of corn, how could she take on this burden? What did she owe this Cherokee family who appeared at her door? Gambold instructed her about the rational and economic dimensions of charity and the spiritual meaning of *caritas*.

The prudential act of charity stipulated that in exchange for food, the Trunk promised to work at Mountjoy. Peggy calculated how she might secure additional supplies of corn from her uncle. The religious rationale for *caritas* interpreted the appearance of the starving family as a providential event that required obedience and submission to her savior. She explained, "Is it not as if my dear Savior led this poor family, who otherwise would starve to death to me? I cannot turn them away.... My dear Savior, who has so often miraculously helped me out of great distress, will know how to help me in this."[90] Charity provided an opportunity for spiritual maturation as an act of faithful surrender and trust in the savior. The missionaries concluded, "We encouraged her in this trust and told her also that we would help her. She went home very satisfied."[91]

Acts of *caritas*, indeed her emerging Christian Indian identity, required a Christ-centered, childlike spirit of submission and surrender to divine will as ascertained by prayer, meditation, and the leadings of the Holy Spirit as mediated to Peggy by Moravian religious elders and missionaries. Submission motivated by the dictates of her religious vocation would shape her life.

As a widow and for the first time in her life, Peggy enjoyed relative autonomy to live on her own terms, managing Mountjoy and pursuing a religious vocation as a Christian Indian without undue interference from family, or as a dependent in a patriarchal household. Attractive, propertied, and young, she fended off advances from Cherokee suitors. She also rejected the marriage proposal of Joseph Crutchfield, a white man and former overseer of slaves on the Vann plantation. On July 4, 1812, he appealed to Brother Gambold for assistance. The missionaries expressed concern that Peggy needed a respectable husband to manage her household and felt that she needed again to submit to the bonds of a patriarchal marriage. The mission journal records their consideration of Crutchfield as the best candidate from a field of eager suitors. "Mr. Crutchfield is not only known as an honest, diligent, and sober man, but also had clear signed that he is serious about salvation, so we believed we would have to grant this matter further consideration."[92]

When the Gambolds spoke with "our Peggy" in confidence, she resisted the idea of marriage but agreed to submit to the guidance of the savior as determined by the missionaries and the religious elders of the Salem Helper's Conference for the Entire Congregation. Several days later the missionaries received approval from the Helper's Conference, and the couple married on July 9 at Mountjoy in the presence of Peggy's sister, Mother Vann and extended kindred, and Joseph's kin. In less than a week Sister Margaret had accepted the dictates of Moravian spiritual guidance, and motivated by the dictates of her religious vocation, she had married a man that she did not love. As a new born child of God, she submitted to the leadings of the Holy Spirit and the religious paternalism of the missionaries, who acted in loco parentis for their first fruit who remained in perpetual tutelage. It was decided for her that she needed to wed and whom she needed to marry.

Sister Margaret's religious vocation required that she voluntarily submit to frequent private conversations (*Das Sprechen*) where the Brother Gambold examined her heart to ascertain a deepening piety as reflected by evidence of humility, repentance of sin, and a childlike acceptance of this brotherly watch and fraternal correction for wayward thoughts or actions. The brotherly watch and church discipline guaranteed that the *Brüdergemeine* collectively maintained a congregational purity, avoidance of sin, and unity of thought and action requisite to capturing the Holy Spirit during religious services and communion.

In November 1817 Peggy opened an informal Sunday school to instruct slaves and their children at Mountjoy. She wanted to offer them moral instruction to foster godly living and encourage literacy through reading the Bible and other religious literature. This work, however laudable from the perspective of the Moravian missionaries, prevented her from attending services at Springplace and represented a course of action that challenged the logic of religious paternalism. Peggy had withdrawn from participation in the congregational community without first seeking approval from her spiritual advisors. Could she take this initiative and still remain a humble, childlike believer who surrendered to the leadings of the Holy Spirit?

Brother Gambold examined Peggy on Sunday, July 9 to answer this question and to ascertain whether she could participate in communion. With copious tears she wept, affirming her unworthiness, giving evidence of her sincerity. The mission journal recounts,

> After evening prayer, we held one more painstaking conversation with our poor Pleasant. We confronted her in a vigorous manner right before her eyes about her previous behavior and how the great impulse to accept invitation from Negroes in our neighborhood had often prevented her from attending our church services.... She was warned that she might die, and that her end might be close at hand, as she believes, and she might not have the opportunity any longer to hear the Word of God.[93]

They explained that her life might end at any time and that she must avail herself of every opportunity to attend worship so that her heart would be prepared should death find her. Touting the fear of death and the precariousness of human existence, the Moravians insisted that "our Peggy," the first fruit of the "Brown Brethren," needed to engage in continual spiritual examination according to the dictates of religious paternalism by accepting Moravian spiritual direction. And Peggy needed to express gratitude that this fraternal correction reaffirmed their love and concern for her.

She returned to Springplace two days later, bearing the gift of a bowl of butter and some onions. She submitted to another heart-to-heart conversation and thanked the missionaries for this fraternal correction. She remarked, "If I do not often discuss *especially* the condition of my heart, I am sorry, and I think that you do not love me anymore, and if I have deserved it then you should scold me; do not try to protect me. Oh, I really feel thankful every time when I am reminded of this."[94]

Brother and Sister Crutchfield owned slaves and enjoyed the economic benefits of chattel and expropriated unfree labor without any self-conscious consideration of abolitionism or the controversies associated with slavery. Peggy, with the encouragement of the Moravians, increasingly concerned herself with the moral education of slave children on her farm. She attempted to impose on adult slaves a religious ethos that regulated their sexuality and prevented them from partaking in frolics and dances. When the Crutchfields visited the ABCFM Chickamauga Mission in Tennessee in January 1817 and learned about a Sunday school for black slaves, they returned to build a school that taught twenty adults and children literacy and attempted to evangelize slaves with little success. "Like the majority of Cherokees whom the missionaries tried to reach, most enslaved blacks on Diamond Hill did not seek spiritual transformation."[95]

Like Catharine and David Brown, Peggy Crutchfield was a Writerly Indian whose voice and published letters contested the politics of land dispossession and removal to Arkansas and the trans-Mississippi West. Moravian Pietist religious personhood and literacy in English permitted her to speak and write with moral authority as a distinctly democratic personality. Between 1817 and 1821, Peggy joined a group of Cherokee women who petitioned the Cherokee Council against removal. The petition of June 30, 1818, maintained that the nation had successfully completed the agenda of the plan of civilization and would degenerate into savagery if they removed to the West. The petition states, "Some of our children have become Christians. We have missionary schools among us. We have hard [sic] the gospel in our nation. We have become civilized & enlightened, & are in hope that in a few years our nation will be prepared for instruction in other branches of sciences & arts, which are both useful & necessary in civilized society." Removal would undo this acculturation as the emigrants would be "brought to a savage state again."[96] With the assistance of Anna Rosina Gambold, Peggy's letters were published in the *Religious Intelligencer* and the *Missionary Herald* in 1819, and her appeal for Cherokee sovereignty as a civilized nation reached evangelical publics throughout America. Tiya Miles observes, "The very same Christian faith that posed a challenge to longstanding Cherokee beliefs created a platform for Peggy Scott, who boldly challenged U.S. mistreatment of the Cherokee Nation using writing skills and publicity channels derived from Christian missionary networks."[97]

Consistent with Moravian religious personhood, Sister Margaret Ann adopted an aggressively conversionist stance by working tirelessly to promote the salvation of others.[98] She assisted the missionaries by interpreting sermons and religious conversations from English to Cherokee. She exhorted the children at Springplace and most importantly labored to convert her husband, family, and friends. By the time of her death in 1820, Peggy could note with gratitude the conversion of fourteen mixed-race persons, a harvest of souls unequaled in the previous two decades of Moravian outreach. These converts included her husband, Joseph, Mother Wali Vann and her husband Clement, and many kindred. In addition, key political elites from the Cherokee National Council, including her uncle Charles Hicks and her friend Susanna Ridge, wife of Major Ridge, joined the Moravian congregational church community. As Miles explains, "beginning with her own mother and sisters, and then reaching out to aunts, in-laws, and other women in nearby towns, Peggy spread the gospel to which she was so devoted. By 1819–20, she had gathered around her a circle of Cherokee women who turned to her to translate the missionaries' words, to read the Bible as a group, and to interpret the meanings of Christianity."[99] For Peggy, the formation of a Christian Indian *Brüdergemeine* founded on extended kinship bonds of sisters and brothers united in faith meant the promise of a newly constituted Indian identity and community that might effectively contest the politics of removal and racial inequality.

Table 3 reveals the fruits of Sister Crutchfield's evangelism.

Table 3. Christian Indian converts

NAME	RELATION TO SISTER MARGARET ANN	DATE OF CONVERSION
Charles (Renatus) Hicks	uncle	1814
Joseph Crutchfield	husband	1814
Sally McDonald	sister	1818
Mother Wali Vann (Mary Christina)	mother-in-law	1819
Clement Vann	father-in-law	1819
Sally Hicks	niece	1819
Delilah Amelia Van McNair	stepdaughter and niece	1820
Nancy (Ann Dorothia)	great-granddaughter	1820
Betsy (Ann Elizabeth)	sister	1820
Nancy Van (Amelia) Tally	sister-in-law	1820
Elizabeth Scott	sister	1820
Susanna (Catharina) Ridge	aunt	1820
William (Abram) Hicks	nephew	1820
Sally (Sarah Bethniah) Hicks	niece	1820

Note: A name in parentheses indicates the baptismal name.

Source: McClinton, *The Moravian Springplace Mission to the Cherokees*, vol. 2, "Biographical List," 455–502.

In 1820 Sister Margaret Ann and her husband relocated to Oothcaloga, thirty miles from Springplace, near the home of Susanna and Major Ridge. This new town became the site of an emerging Cherokee Christian Indian community.[100] Although in failing health and near the end of her life, Peggy conducted weekly female prayer circles. Anna Rosina Gambold notes, "When our Sisters are together like this, it is exceptionally instructive to hear their childlike and yet solid expressions. Thus they spoke to each other about their baptismal names and each one's was important to her. Those who had forgotten what theirs meant in their language had it repeated through Sister Crutchfield."[101]

Peggy made frequent visits to Springplace for religious services, spiritual direction, and pastoral care. The mission journal records how Peggy and Susanna Ridge had returned to celebrate communion in March: "Sister Susanna Catherina [Ridge] spoke with Sister Crutchfield almost all night long, and among other things, she said with great respect, 'You have eaten the dear Savior's flesh and drunk His Blood!'"[102]

Without a formally organized church and a minister, the Cherokee Christian Indians did not form a *Brüdergemeine* in their new settlement and remained dependent on Springplace for missionary instruction and leadership.[103] Unlike the Christian Indian community of Brothertown New York, they did not seek religious autonomy and attempt to break free from religious paternalism. Peggy, in perpetual tutelage, confided to Sister Anna Rosina her spiritual and personal dependence that she interpreted as love (*agape*): "I am very happy when I am with you. Since I love God, I also love you very much!"[104]

During a visit on April 12, she beseeched the Gambolds to relocate to Oothcaloga and establish a *Brüdergemeine* under Moravian religious paternalism:

> Will you not move to our place at Oothcaloga? Oh, what a joy that would be to see you climb out of the wagon in front of our house! Oh, if you lived at our place, no grass would grow on the road to our house! We neighbors would meet *together* very often in your house though we now see each other seldom. On Sundays we always comfort ourselves

that you remember us here in your services and Brother Gambold prays for us.[105]

The Gambolds replied with pious resignation by reiterating that important decisions were determined by powers outside of their control—by the Lot and the leadings of the Holy Spirit: "If the *dear Savior* sends us, we would gladly move! If it is His will, however, that we stay here, then He will certainly send other teachers who will love you as we do and be concerned about your welfare."[106]

On September 10 Peggy removed to Springplace to spend the last month of her life under the care of the Moravian brotherhood. The mission journal referred to her as "the patient" and recorded her exemplary dying as a model for all to emulate, as evidence of her spiritual attainments. The Gambolds rescheduled communion a week earlier than planned on Sunday, October 15, to ensure that Sister Crutchfield might enjoy this last sacrament: "Thus after the sermon, we gathered around her bed and let our hearts, hungry for grace eat and drink His own body and precious blood for eternal life. Oh what happened to us there?" Assembled family and friends felt overwhelmed with emotions of joy at the presence of the Holy Spirit, "which made such an impression on us under these circumstances that no one will easily forget it."[107]

The next day, anticipating her imminent death, the missionaries went out to select a site for her burial in the consecrated ground of God's Acre cemetery. After supper the congregation bestowed on her a special blessing, openly weeping in joy for her election to grace, celebrating a life well-lived in surrender to Jesus. On October 18, lying on her deathbed, surrounded by her coreligionists and family, Peggy suffered great pain. The congregation assembled at her bedside to sing and comfort her as she made this reply: "Oh, my dear Savior, help me; oh my dearest Jesus come, come soon and take your poor child." She died peacefully while others sang hymns, "her released soul passed into the arms of the One Whom she loved and Who had bound her to Himself."[108]

The mission journal recorded on the evening of October 19 as a sign of the significance of the death of the first fruit of the Cherokee Nation that a meteor streaked across the sky, crashing to earth nearby: "A bright light, in the form of a very great fireball moved slowly from the northeast to the southwest, and was accompanied by a muffled noise like distant thunder. Here the place designated for the burial was cleared, and a gravesite for the first body from the faithful of the Cherokee Nation was prepared."[109]

Sister Margaret Ann Crutchfield died at age thirty-seven, having completed a spiritual pilgrimage from mixed-race acculturated elite to a child of God, a participant in a *Brüdergemeine* devoted to an ascetic religious ethos surrendered to Jesus. Bound by the strictures of religious paternalism, she continually purged her heart of sin, shedding copious penitential tears of repentance to prepare for the joyful and ecstatic presence of the Holy Spirit. This distinctive religious personhood equipped her with the moral authority to serve as a Writerly Indian and democratic personality, to educate slaves, advocate for the political sovereignty of her people by resisting removal to Arkansas, and proselytize her kin and fellow Cherokee. Under the cope of Moravian religious paternalism, she began a Cherokee Christian Indian community with the sublime hope that together they would build a church community that might endure. Sister Margaret Ann Crutchfield's life added another link in the endless chain of missionary intelligence as a victory for those who devoted their lives to the project of redeeming perishing heathens.

Catharine Brown was a product of the Brainerd Mission and her widely read *Memoir* provided a compelling account of the success of Brainerd's model of inner piety as the foundation for religious personhood and a missionary career. Unlike other elite Cherokee women, Catharine did not marry, submit to the patriarchal authority of her husband, or pursue the cultural, social, and economic initiatives of her social standing. Instead, she elected to live her life by emulating Brainerd, Harriet Newell, and her white missionary teachers whom she referred to as sisters and later as equals in piety and religious vocation.

However, the mixed-race elite Christian Indians who advocated the plan of civilization and the importance of missions and evangelization as a strategy to champion national sovereignty did not stop the seemingly inexorable momentum of removal and the loss of their homelands. As Joel

Martin concludes, "in a nation with Andrew Jackson as its president, male and female Cherokees could change their clothes and quote the Bible all they wanted and more, but this conversion would not prevent the forced removal of most of their nation or the theft of most of their lands."[110]

The exemplars in the evangelical literature that extolled the lives of Cherokee converts in this continuing chain of religious intelligence as triumphal victories were indeed an extraordinary few. Missionaries had very limited success in converting large numbers of Cherokee, especially the full-blood residents on the Lower Towns, who proved reluctant to abandon their lifeways and ceremonies. By 1830 Presbyterians could claim 200 converts while Moravians converted fewer than 50. Methodist circuit riders and Baptist missions established Native congregations that reached another 800 Cherokees, although many drifted away from the new religion as backsliders. Of a population of 18,000, fewer than 1,100 became Cherokee Christian Indians.[111] Perdue explained that Cherokee cosmology offered a coherent cultural worldview and identity after the restabilization of their settlements following the anomic dislocations of war, loss of homelands, and the revolution of gender roles. She writes,

> Cherokee religion promoted cosmic balance, not sacred hierarchy, and community welfare, not individual salvation. It promised to heal the sick and make corn grow, and it connected Cherokees to a particular place in this world rather than a nebulous existence in the next. Male and female spirits inhabited the Cherokee world, and religion gave both men and women access to them. The role of women as presenters of the new crop in the Green Corn ceremony, the Cherokee's most important annual religious rite, recognized and confirmed their centrality in Cherokee society as farmers and mothers.[112]

Throughout this period Cherokee visionaries and prophets provided an "ethnotheology" of resistance to Protestant missions. Lee Irwin defines ethnotheology as "a creative synthesis of indigenous religious beliefs (and practices) with a variety of Christian theological ideas, particularly sin, salvation, reward, punishment after death, and moral teachings of kindness, nonviolence and the preservation of family and communal values."[113] The

Cherokee visionary resistance to missions never achieved the coherence of an intertribal military uprising, a spirited resistance in the manner of Tenkswatawa and Tecumseh or Hillis Hadjo of the Red Stick Creeks and the Muskogee Prophets.

In 1815 Cherokee elder Elk articulated an alternative creation story depicting racial polygenesis where Selu's twin sons, one red and one white, allowed the people the choice of American values and the plan of civilization—the white sand of atomistic individualism—or the cohesive red clay of clan-based communitarian values. In 1812 Big Bear reported a vision to Moravians that the earthquake in 1811 and other natural disasters resulted from the loss of lands and the failure to perform traditional ceremonies. Finally, in 1827–28 White Path (Nunnatsunega) organized a religious and political resistance to the Cherokee National Council, objecting to an evangelical Christian oath of allegiance for officeholders and forcing a political compromise.[114]

In conclusion, the receptivity of the first fruits of the Cherokee Nation to missionary outreach was extraordinary and remarkable. Like so many Christian Indians in earlier colonial praying towns and mission communities, these Cherokee neophytes enunciated sublime hope that their spiritual attainments and worldly accomplishments in Euro-American civilization would ensure both their individual salvation and the collective preservation of their tribal nation on ancestral homelands. However, the few Christian Indians, the "first fruits," stand in marked contrast with the many who embraced the ethnotheology of resistance and with the majority of Cherokees, who were indifferent or hostile to Protestant missions in the 1820s at the onset of the era of forced removal.

6

Métis Christian Indian Lives
Jane Johnston Schoolcraft and Mackinaw Mission Converts

During the first decades of the nineteenth century, an estimated fifty village communities and cities in the Great Lakes region emerged as centers of commerce in the fur trade and later in the growing markets for lumber and mineral ore. Market towns like Detroit, Mackinaw, and Prairie du Chien flourished as burgeoning and stratified communities of Native households and a multiethnic mixture of French, English, and American settlers who married Native women to create a métis subculture. In the decades following the War of 1812 and continuing with the Black Hawk War in 1832, American settler colonialism would transform the region, displacing and dispossessing Native peoples and imposing the hegemony of American laws, courts, language, commercial culture, and Protestant missions. Creoles—those populations already in place when the Americans arrived—included an elite group of households comprising French Canadian husbands and Native wives who served as interpreters and cultural mediators who mobilized their extended kin networks to assist their husbands in business. The mixed-ancestry children in these elite Creole families, and Native children from humbler circumstances, were sent to Protestant mission schools to ensure their success as literate neophytes who might reap the benefits of the Americanization of their communities.[1] This chapter explores the religious experiences of Indian neophytes from the Mackinaw Mission, the life of Jane Johnston Schoolcraft, a gifted Métis poet, and the trials of Reverend Edmund F. Ely as they variously encountered and pursued the missionary spirit.

A generation after Reverend David Bacon had failed in 1802 to build a mission to evangelize the Anishinaabe and Métis peoples of the Great Lakes, Sarah Tuttle published a triumphal account of the American Board's mission in Mackinaw Island begun by Reverend William Ferry in 1823. Tuttle's *Conversations on the Mackinaw and Green-Bay Missions* added to the growing chain of missionary intelligence and introduced evangelicals to this mission and the remarkable conversion narratives of Native young women during a revival that appropriated Charles Grandison Finney's New Measures of protracted meetings, public prayer for the souls of the unconverted, and anxious benches for the awakened to struggle with prospect of damnation and explore the depths of religious melancholy. This revival burned over Mackinaw with the white heat of the Holy Spirit between 1828 and 1829. Most notably, the life and conversion of Me-sai-ainse, a Chippewa-Métis, who was baptized as Caroline William Rodgers and sponsored by the Ladies Fragment Society of Glenn Falls, New York, served as one focal point of Tuttle's short book.[2] Caroline succeeded as a literate Christian Indian who would devote her life to the cause of missions, and in 1830 she joined Frederick Ayer in a mission school at La Pointe to serve as an interpreter.

Tuttle published eight books between 1830 and 1838 under the imprimatur of the Massachusetts Sabbath School Union covering American Board missions to the eastern Cherokees, the Arkansas Cherokees, Iroquois groups in New York and Ohio, Pawnees, Chickasaws and Osages, and Choctaws. These works and her studies of the American Colonization Society and foreign missions championed the missionary spirit with uncritical religious intelligence, urging her readers to join these efforts by offering material and emotional support to the conversion of perishing heathens among indigenous peoples throughout the world. Caroline's story offers an idealized example of the purported success of missions to Native Americans. In an era of Indian removal of groups from the Southeast to the trans-Mississippi West and from the Upper Midwest to the western plains, the unending chain of missionary intelligence depicted Natives through the lens of romantic primitivism as vanishing and benevolent reformism in the salvationist ideal of conversion and civilization.[3]

Me-sai-ainse arrived at the Mackinaw Mission school in 1826 at age fifteen, sent by her aunt from their home in Lac Court Oreilles. Apparently an orphan, marginal to her Chippewa-Métis band, discouraged from joining a Midewiwin society, and without supportive kin, Me-sai-ainse suffered hunger in the winter. The Mackinaw mission promised food, clothing, shelter, and secular and religious education.

Reverend Ferry sent an extended account to American Board secretary Jeremiah Evarts in 1828 detailing Me-sai-ainse's missionary encounter and a translation of her religious testimony and experience during her recent conversion. This correspondence provides an account of her spiritual journey, noting that a pious missionary, Mary Holiday, openly prayed for the conversion of poor, ignorant, and wicked Indians. Me-sai-ainse began a self-examination as this prayer had pricked her conscience: was she wicked and ignorant?

To relieve her distress, she invoked Catholic prayers. However, Mary discounted such piety as "prayers of the mouth" that were not acceptable to God. With the realization that she was indeed a sinful and wicked creature prevented from enjoying communion or the promise of salvation, Me-sai-ainse began months of unrelenting anxiety, sleeplessness, and religious melancholy as one forsaken by God.[4] The continued pastoral care by missionaries, Bible-reading, and solitary prayer exacerbated her religious despair. She lamented, "My heart was so hard, I could not weep—could not shed a tear.—It seemed a *perfect combat*."[5]

In a final episode of religious despondency during an evening prayer meeting, fearing that she might become deranged and acknowledging the prospect of Hell and eternal damnation, Me-sai-ainse experienced the selfless agony of her inability to influence God's will. "Neither prayer nor anguish do any good.—They led to no relief—It's right—It's just in God to destroy me.—I ought to perish. If He sends me to Hell, let Him do it. And if He shows me mercy—Well.—Let Him do just as He wishes with me."[6]

As she ended her meditation and stood up, no longer kneeling in supplication, she reported feeling serenity, a possession of the love and mercy of her savior, "A fullness of joy beyond expression," and the redemptive promise of Christ's sacrifice in the words of a familiar hymn: "Alas! And did my Saviour bleed!"[7]

Me-sai-ainse had traversed the familiar guideposts of the evangelical morphology of conversion that was prescribed for New Measure Presbyterians in the context of a local revival of religion. Possibly, Reverend Ferry reconstructed her narrative to authenticate Native conversions during a season of revival and to demonstrate that the conversion narratives conformed to a normative model of the soul's journey from sin to grace, a conversion or turning toward God.

The path to conversion included the awakened conscience and the awareness of the enormity of one's sin and depravity. Each awakened sinner came to the painful realization after a protracted period of attempting prayer, meditation, hymn-singing, spiritual direction, and attendance at religious meetings of his or her helplessness—the inability to find God's grace and the dependency on divine will. In a moment of selflessness, in the depths of despair, the candidate for grace espouses a willingness to accept God's judgment. Me-sai-ainse stated, "I am willing and ready to die for Christ."[8] Next, the religious seeker experienced a peace that passeth all natural understanding, an interlude of serenity, of ecstatic joyful surrender to God that represented the irradiation of God's grace that renewed the sinner's heart. And finally, the neophyte began a lifelong journey of progressive sanctification, continued self-examination, the daily practice of piety, and frequent interludes of renewed religious melancholy. At times, the new born Christian uncovered indwelling and secret sins and accused himself or herself of hypocrisy. Ferry would write about Me-sai-ainse's religious experiences after conversion, "She said she had seasons; when, conscious of no *sensible* spirituality of feeling that she has been much distressed for fear she was deceived, because it was not with her as in days past."[9]

While Me-sai-ainse's spiritual journey joined the growing literature of religious intelligence, William Ferry recounted the conversion narratives of several other Métis scholars during the revivals in 1828–29. He sent David

Green, corresponding secretary of the American Board, these stories in 1830. Two of these stories merit consideration.

Julia Beaulieu came to the mission in 1826 at age thirteen and left in 1831 at age eighteen to marry a prosperous American fur trader, Charles H. Oaks. The mission served as a finishing school to instruct this young woman, the daughter of a French Canadian father and a Chippewa mother, in etiquette and Protestant moralism and piety. Julia experienced almost four years of unrelenting religious anxiety bordering on despair. She states that she could not eat or drink but desired only to pray. Ferry wrote a separate commentary and indicated that before her experience of grace and conversion, Julia confessed to having committed the unpardonable sin of blasphemy for grieving the Holy Spirit and "that God was just in her ruin."[10]

Mary Ann Willard was the daughter of a Chippewa mother and French father who abandoned her as a child. Mary was sponsored and named in honor of John Willard of Albany, New York. She came to the mission in 1826 as a young mother with her daughter after being abandoned by her British husband. Having come of age as a Roman Catholic, impoverished and marginal, she was coerced by the Indian agent at Drummond Island to remove to Mackinaw. Ferry explained her initial resistance and unhappiness:

> She looked upon every thing of religious instructions & movement as wrong; & would be displeased at any thing said to her on the subject—was very self righteous in her own religion—would often kneel among a room full of girls & say her prayers—& sometimes several times a day.—If any thing was said to her implying pity for her blindness, she would be quite indignant—And, as she now says, she thought herself the only Christian in the house.[11]

During the revival in 1828 before she joined the church as a professor of religion, Mary suffered the familiar signposts of the evangelical morphology of conversion. During the stage of religious doubt and despair, she reports bodily experiences of being unable to move and falling to the floor. In a moment of grace, meditating on the redemptive sacrifice of the savior, Mary enjoyed an ecstatic transport: "On rising from my knees I thought of my burden, but it was all gone—I felt in a new world—Can *this* be that change of which they have told me?"[12]

Were the experiences of Caroline, Julia, and Mary representative of the nearly two hundred young men and women who attended the mission school? Keith R. Widder explains in *Battle for the Soul* that in this period the mission school admitted 175 Native scholars, mostly mixed-race children who were sent to the mission to learn the skills necessary to succeed in an increasingly Americanized society. One hundred-thirty of the students had French Canadian or French-Métis fathers. Thirty-one had American fathers. Eighty-five had Chippewa or French-Chippewa mothers. The remaining students came from Odawa, Sioux, Cree, and Assiniboine groups. Only fourteen students were full-blood. Ironically, despite the program of Protestant evangelism, approximately 95 percent of these students returned to their natal communities to participate in a revitalization of Catholicism and an enhanced participation in the fur trade that was increasingly under the control of the American Fur Company.[13] As with the Cherokee missions in this period, only a small minority of mixed-race children entered missions, and few who did were converted. Most students attended school to acquire literacy in English and thus facilitate their individual advancement or act on behalf of the collective good of their people.

The Anishinaabe peoples inhabited local village communities organized by matrilineal kin and clan affiliations, enmeshed in a social nexus of gift exchange, creating trade alliances through marriage to other Native groups and, after the War of 1812, to Americans. Previously, Natives hybridized the Catholicism of the Jesuit fathers with Chippewa Midewiwin societies that fostered ceremonies, shamanism, dream interpretation, visions, and sweats to promote health and prosperity for the people. Métis young men became multilingual, speaking French and English to prepare for careers in the fur trade as clerks, runners, and boatmen, and as small farmers who adopted European forms of agriculture and animal husbandry. In this manner they would forsake traditional roles as hunters and warriors and traditional lifeways that relied on game, fishing, gathering wild rice in the autumn and maple sugaring in the early spring.[14] Increasingly Métis constituted an ethnically distinct group whose ethnogenesis in the eighteenth century was formalized in the nineteenth century by treaty, law, and culture. They were denied the status of First Peoples in Canada.[15]

The Métis youth who entered the Mackinaw Mission came from detribalized families organized as patriarchal nuclear households. They ate a European diet, practiced a syncretized spirituality, and simultaneously incorporated traditional Chippewa and other tribal cultural practices and embraced the values of competitive individualism and private property consistent with the plan of civilization. Some came from elite families of wealth and prestige, and others came from the middling classes seeking advantages for their sons in commerce and for their daughters in marriage. They wanted to ensure every advantage for their sons and daughters in a social order increasingly differentiated by association with American political and economic hegemony, national origin (French, British, and American), and social class distinctions. Widder argues that the missionaries and teachers "often perceived them to be Indians instead of Métis. These children have more in common with New Englanders than first meets the eye, and both these commonalities and the missionaries' failure to perceive this reality did much to shape the experience of the students and the teachers at the mission."[16]

The American Board mission to Mackinaw shared much in common with the Union Mission to the Osages and the Cherokee missions at Brainerd and Dwight. Forty fervent true believers from New England and New York wrote testimonials to the American Board's Prudential Committee in their applications attesting to a heart regenerated in the religious ferment of revivals. Each man and woman chose the path of duty on the frontier to bring salvation to perishing heathens, humbly accepting the providential will of God in directing their lives and fortunes. In a letter to her sister, Amanda Ferry spoke of her vocation and utter dependency on God, tropes that characterized an exemplary missionary vocation: "I believe the Lord has called me to this work. How can I ever distrust his providence for our future! He who hears the young ravens when they cry, will not be unmindful of the daily supplications ascending for the prosperity of the Mackinaw Mission."[17]

The school attempted to inculcate what amounted to a gender revolution for Native students—the appropriation of true womanhood for young women and the values and skills of the yeoman ideal for young men. Above all, through the integration of a carefully regimented daily round of work, prayer, and vocational and academic education, the missionaries sought to instill an ethic of sober, rational asceticism. Hard work, a refusal to surrender to sensuous pleasures, and a rejection of Native dances and ceremonial life characterized the new ethos of Protestant life regulation for all scholars, the many who remained unconverted and the new born alike.

This transformation of self and identity appropriated a Protestant ethic of self-control, moderation, and asceticism for those who would surrender as instruments of divine will that stands in sharp contrast to Métis existence as characterized by many outside observers. George Nelson's memoir, *My First Years in the Fur Trade* (1802–1804), describes autumn trading meetings and Ojibwe divination ceremonies to locate game or Midewiwin initiations that involved eat-all feasts, alcohol binges fueled by barrels of whiskey, gambling, dancing, and fighting.[18] He describes many nightmarish encounters with Natives who were intoxicated, crying, singing, and laughing that frequently devolved into bloody fights and extremes of domestic violence. He offers an account of an incident where a husband beat his wife, tore off sections of her hair, and rolled her in a blanket.[19]

Reverend William Ferry established a Presbyterian congregation in Mackinaw in 1829 that included prominent members of the local community that grew through the New Measure revivals from 1827 to 1829 to eighteen Métis and seven full-blood Native scholars and adults. The church prescribed strict Sabbath-keeping, religious worship, Sunday school attendance, and the enforcement of the Protestant ethos of disciplined life regulation in concordance with Americanization and the commercial culture of the fur trade.[20] Thus, the vision for the mission included a school and church community to transform this strategic site of the fur trade and military and political administration into a community tempered by Protestant moralism and piety.

Henry Rowe Schoolcraft (1793–1864) was a prominent member of Ferry's congregation, having joined in 1833 after he relocated to Mackinaw as United States Indian agent for the Lake Superior Region, and later, in 1836, he served as the superintendent of Indian Affairs for the Michigan Territory. He relocated from Sault Ste. Marie with his family, which included his wife, Jane Johnston (a Métis translator, poet, and Ojibwe keeper of the oral tradition) and their two young children. Schoolcraft received a commission from Lewis Cass, governor of the Michigan Territory, to serve as Indian agent, a position he held from 1822 to 1841. Schoolcraft published numerous books, including travelogues of the upper Midwest and the West and in the fields of geology, history, biography, ethnology, and Native American folklore and culture. He is renowned for his 1839 work investigating the "Indian mind," *Algic Researches*.

From his first contact with Native peoples, Schoolcraft embraced the prevailing idea of the vanishing American, destined to extinction as a racial Other, incapable of benefiting from the improvements of religion or civilization. Maureen Konkle explains that Schoolcraft considered Natives "childlike, incapable of reason, improvident, and unable to form true governments."[21] He wrote in *Personal Memoirs of Thirty Years with the Indians* a journal entry for 1822:

> What my eyes have seen and my ears have heard, I must believe; and what is their testimony respecting the condition of the Indian on the frontiers. He is not like Falstaff's men, "food for powder," but he is food for whisky. Whisky is the great means of drawing from him his furs and skins. To obtain it, he makes a beast of himself, and allows his family to go hungry and half naked.[22]

Embracing the ideology of Indian removal in the face of advancing American settlement during Andrew Jackson's presidency, Schoolcraft supported mission schools after his conversion in 1833. He had previously doubted the efficacy of the missions of John Eliot or David Brainerd, stating that it was an error to believe "that some extraordinary effort is thought to be necessary, that their sons must be cooped up in boarding-schools and colleges, where they are taught many things wholly unsuited to their condition and wants, while the mass of the tribes is left at home in the forests, in their ignorance and vices, untaught and neglected."[23]

Schoolcraft began his career in 1821 as "Indian agent and wilderness scholar," as his biographer Richard G. Bremer characterizes him, by boarding in the home of John Johnston, an Irish trader and notable in the small Métis community in Sault Ste. Marie. Johnston successfully navigated the transition from French to British and American hegemony in the Upper Peninsula Michigan Territory and grew prosperous and politically influential through marriage with an important Ojibwe woman, Ozhaguscodaywayquay (Susan). Her extensive kin relations brought him trading partners. Their daughter Jane was named Obabaamwewe-giizhigokwe, translated as the Sound the Stars Make Rushing through the Sky. The eldest of eight children, she came of age in a household distinguished by French, English, and Ojibwe languages and a hybrid Native culture combined with the emerging commercial ethos of the American market economy.[24]

Jane was an accomplished young woman whom Schoolcraft courted when he boarded in the Johnston household. With only a brief formal education during a childhood visit to England and Ireland, she was accomplished in English literature, history, and other subjects in a common school curriculum. She also learned Ojibwe folklore and oral tradition from her mother and served her father as a translator during his diplomacy and trade with Natives. Schoolcraft married Jane Johnston on October 12, 1823. In addition to her considerable linguistic skills and ethnological knowledge, she brought a dowry of ten thousand dollars. The couple resided in a new wing added to Johnston's home in 1824, and Jane gave birth to their first child, William Henry (Willy), that year.[25]

Both John Johnston and Henry Schoolcraft benefited from marriage to skilled and influential women, who were in large part responsible for their husbands' respective success. These wives served as the "makers of self-made men" in this era characterized by de Tocqueville by the unbridled personal ambition of the "go-ahead spirit."[26] Jane transcribed Ojibwe stories, songs, and folklore into English that her husband appropriated (without crediting her) into his prodigious publications and ethnographies. Jane never published her poetry and ethnological writings during her lifetime. Although she was a pioneering Native voice, her writings were published and preserved by Henry Schoolcraft.

In the spring of 1827 as Jane anticipated the birth of her second child, Willy died suddenly after falling ill with scarlet fever. Jane wrote to her husband on March 14 seeking comfort that Willy had escaped the "numberless evils of this ungrateful world." "Hast thy life been prolonged, thy tender heart might have received *wound* upon *wound*, malice, envy, hatred, & all the evil passions combine, thy innocence to destroy—But sweet Babe, from all these evils thou are free, entirely free."[27]

Later that month, suffering paroxysms of grief, she composed a sentimental poem in ten stanzas written in English. She idealizes "Sweet Willy" and concludes by longing for reunion in death. Stanzas eight through ten capture this doleful resignation to divine will:

My Son! Thy coral lips are pale
Can I believe the heart sick tale,
That I thy loss may ever wail
    My Willy!

The clouds in darkness seemed to low
The Storm has passed with awful power
And swept my tender beauteous flower!
    Sweet Willy!

But soon my spirit will be free
And I my son shall see,
For God I know did this decree
    My Willy![28]

After a year Jane's grief continued unabated and her suffering was compounded by William's frequent absences. She wrote the Elmwood Diary (April–May 1828) from her home in Sault Ste. Marie as an imaginary conversation with Henry. At the end of each day she provided an account of managing their household, planting a garden, describing the visitations of family and friends, childcare duties, and spiritual matters. In the "stillness of [her] lonely evenings" she recounted her ill health and dejection. Jane wrote on April 30, "Visited the grave of my *ever lamented* angel Son I trust I am always spiritually benefited after having contemplated the place that contained *One* who was once so lovely & dear & who will ever continue precious to my poor aching heart.—Oh my dearest Son! My blessed sweet Willy!"[29]

Jane mailed the Elmwood Diary to Henry, who was visiting Detroit. He replied to Jane in three letters in June, noting the stains of her tears on the diary. He cautions Jane not to neglect her new baby in her ceaseless grief. "His death has created a wound that which nothing earthly can heal; and were it not a profanation, I would kiss the very ground which is permitted to hold his remains. Mysterious are the works of God; look to the Book of Job, Christian society, and to God for sustenance."[30]

The traumatic loss of Willy began the alienation in their marriage as grieving brought marital conflict. Henry interpreted Willy's death as the providential chastisement of an angry God. Although he had embraced evangelical pietism in 1824 with Reverend Robert Laird and subsequently kept the Sabbath and refused to meet with intoxicated Natives, he had not yet experienced conversion.

During a visit to Mackinaw in November 22, 1830, under the pastoral care of Reverend Ferry and American Fur Company director Robert Stuart, he fell to his knees in prayer and supplication. The rational theodicy of misfortune of evangelical pietism provided a comprehensive explanation of his prolonged grieving and sense of affliction. He had put worldly concerns and "idolatry" of his intense love for his son ahead of his obedience and duty to God. God justly punished him for his sin and disobedience. To placate an angry God who chastised him, he would risk alienating his wife. Henry wrote to Jane and explained his understanding that, in conformity with the teachings of Paul, she must submit to him as her "guide, philosopher & friend." He exhorted, "Let me entreat you to institute an examination into your own heart and see whether there is nothing there adverse to Christian principles—whether there are not opinions which are improper, weaknesses which ought to be strengthened, & hopes which ought to be abandoned."[31]

Henry continues in his letter and understood Jane's lack of evangelical fervor by impeaching her family and upbringing in a remote village without the benefit of a formal education and, by implication, without the formative influences of Christian institutions. He criticizes Jane's family as contributing to her pride and self-deceit. Implying that she lacked the benefit of a Christian mother, he wrote, "Without a mother, in many things, to direct & with an over kind father, who saw everything in the fairest light, & made even your brothers & sisters & all about you bow to you as their superior in every mental & worldly thing."[32]

Henry prescribed a daily piety that included scripture-reading and personal prayer with meditations of the closet informed by methodical self-examination for indwelling sin and self-abnegation and humiliation before God. He experienced conversion and accepted the church covenant in February 1831, redoubling his evangelical fervor with fasting and the practice of piety. He read Calvin's *Institutes* and imposed upon himself and his family a rigid adherence to dogma and moralism. This religious quickening coincided with his conviction of his impending death that began in 1828 with a paralysis of his right arm and leg and severe headaches in 1831–32. Acute death anxiety occasioned by the death of his son and his health concerns informed this concern for salvation.[33]

Schoolcraft speaks of his conversion and owing the church covenant as "one of the most *important, &* to myself, most *satisfactory* duties of my life, the effects of which will give a *colouring to all my future acts.*"[34] During this time of evangelical fervor and acute death anxiety, he experienced a vocation crisis and briefly considered training for the ministry and devoting his life as a missionary to Native peoples.

Our understanding of Schoolcraft's religious experiences and emotions is aided by a brief discussion of the organization of Protestant temperament and religious personhood in this period. Richard Rabinowitz's *The Spiritual Self in Everyday Life* identifies three types of Protestant identity: the doctrinalist, the moralist, and the devotionalist. Doctrinalists like Schoolcraft were orthodox, consistent Calvinists who emphasized the intellect in seeking to understand their place in the divine order, accepting their innate depravity and inability, and longing for stillness in submission to God. Their conversion narratives eschewed extremes of religious affections. Moralists emphasized the self-determining will to choose for God and salvation and the active ascetic mastery of self and world through obedience to God's laws and acts of benevolence. Devotionalists made the inner-worldly mysticism of evangelical Pietism the distinguishing mark of religious experience by promoting an intensely emotional, loving, sentimental relationship with God personified as Jesus.[35] As I have argued in *Religious Melancholy and Protestant Experience in America*,

> in the lives of evangelicals in the first half of the nineteenth century, men and women mixed and balanced these various streams of religious experience, shaping the praxis of religion that juxtaposed the seemingly contradictory elements of doctrine, asceticism, and mysticism. In the same conversion narrative one finds the torturous, emotionally harrowing struggle to submit to a sovereign deity (Doctrinalism), the risky venture of making the behavioral self solely responsible to choose holiness, conversion, and Christian activism (Moralism), and the inner search for intimacy and communion with a personal God as the warrant of grace in the heart (Devotionalism).[36]

Jane's religiosity centered on devotionalism that differed greatly from the muscular and fervent evangelical pietism of her husband, who blended doctrinalist and moralist elements. Her father, John, maintained an extensive library of Protestant theology and devotional tracts and Jane selected Jonathan Edwards's evangelical classic, *The Life of David Brainerd*, as her favorite. She also admired the work of the English evangelical writer Hannah Moore and wrote a poem extolling Moore's guides to daily piety and godly living, "On Reading Miss Hannah Moore's Christian Morals and Practical Piety. 1816," written in four stanzas, prizing these two works as templates for "all womankind" to seek bliss by surrender to the savior's love and obedience to God's will. The poem concludes,

> Then may I still what's good pursue,
>   And strive to conquer what is ill,
> Keep truth forever in my view,
>   And God's supreme commands fulfill.[37]

Both Brainerd and Moore prescribed a religion of the heart—an inward, introspective piety where the believer embraced a regimen of self-abnegation. By methodical self-examination and humiliation, each person would seek to love God above all else and by attempting to empty the self of pride and worldliness strive for what Moore describes in *Practical Piety* as "a settled, calm conviction that God and eternal things have the predominance in his heart."[38] Without recourse to enthusiasm, visions, or perceived excesses of religious emotions, Moore defines evangelical devotionalism: "To all who love Him unfeignedly, to all who with deep self-abasement, yet with filial confidence, prostrate themselves at the feet of His Throne, saying, Lord, lift up the light of thy countenance upon us and we shall be safe."[39]

Jane expressed her devotionalism and emulation of Brainerd's evangelical piety throughout her correspondence with her absent husband. Writing from Elmwood, Sault Ste. Marie, in September 1832, after having been spared from the cholera epidemic that summer, Jane recounts her sense of dutiful submission to her husband and her inner piety and evangelical humility as she celebrated communion. "I shall not be truly happy in my mind until you return to forgive & bless me. Last Sabbath was a solemn day and a good one I believe. . . . And though I felt unworthy to go to the table of our blessed & adorable Redeemer, yet it would be wrong to stay away."[40] She asked for and received a fleeting sense of remission from her insurmountable sins by seeking refuge through Christ.

Christian Indian identity for Jane permitted a hybridity steeped in Ojibwe oral tradition, storytelling, and ceremonial life and an abiding love for Ojibewemenin—the Ojibwe language. She frequently wrote in her Native language and provided accompanying translations in English.[41] "A Psalm, or Supplication for Mercy, and Confession of Sin, Addressed to the Author of Life, in the Odjibway-Algonquin Tongue," published posthumously by her husband, exemplifies these dimensions of Christian Indian identity and religiosity. In an appeal to the Author of Life, an Indianized Great Spirit that resembles the transcendental Christian deity, creator of the universe, the poet pleads for mercy. The creator has given humanity a soul, a rational mind, and the power of willful action. With these faculties, men and women have sinned and deserve eternal punishment in hell. Unlike the angry punishing God that Henry wished to placate with doctrinal and moralistic piety, Jane's devotionalism envisioned God as benevolent, loving, and merciful. Her poem concludes with a supplication for mercy:

> Have mercy upon us, Merciful spirit, have mercy upon us!
> Have mercy upon us, Jesus Christ!
> Renovate our wicked hearts, and give us new hearts.
> May we love thee with our whole hearts, and keep thy commandments, and give us hearts to take a delight in prayer.
> Show mercy upon all our kindred and people.
> Show mercy to the whole world.[42]

Pain, sickness, invalidism, and loss characterized the final decade of Jane's life. She suffered from pertussis in 1838 and during the prolonged recovery she developed an addiction to laudanum, an opiate dependency that continued until her death in 1842. She mourned the separation from her children John and Jane, who attended eastern boarding schools. Her husband was frequently absent on business, research, and speaking tours, compounding her sense of loneliness and loss.

In "Lines Written under Severe Pain and Sickness" she speaks of submission to divine will with the assurance of mercy in the face of "death's deform'd embrace." The poem concludes with an abiding faith that assuages all death anxiety:

> Teach me each duty always to fulfill.
> And grant me resignation to Thy will,
> And when Thy goodness wills that I should die,
> This dream of life I'll leave without a sigh.[43]

At the end of her life, Jane was marginalized from American society and her Native world and increasingly isolated, separated from her husband and children and extended kin. In her life as a solitary individual, did the practice of Brainerd's inner piety and her submission to God's will as an instrument of divine purpose effectively sustain, console, and guide Jane? Did her religiosity defend her from feelings of failure or alienation? When death found her, did she experience the spiritual fulfillment of the saints' everlasting rest that devotionalism promised, or did death offer only the release from meaningless suffering in this world?

Jane Johnston Schoolcraft, like many other mixed-race and Creole people, encountered evangelical America through marriage, revival and conversion, commerce, culture, and society. Many attempted to secure a place in a society that was increasingly stratified by social class divisions and racial exclusions. For many, religious melancholy and marginalization characterized their embrace of the missionary spirit. We conclude with an account of the rejection of the Great Commission by one Ojibwe group.

Under the auspices of the ABCFM, Reverend Edmund Franklin Ely (1809–1882) in 1833 at the age of twenty-four established a mission school in Fond du Lac on the southern shores of Lake Superior and a mission station among the Ojibwes at Sandy Shore. His journals and correspondence record his early devotionalism, following in the spirit of David Brainerd and his ultimate failure to evangelize the Ojibwes.

Ely grew up in Wilburham, Massachusetts, the eldest of four sons. He briefly relocated with his family to an Ohio homestead in 1824, but in 1825 at age sixteen Ely traveled east to Rome, New York, where he encountered Charles Finney's revival and converted in January 1826. For the next seven years, Ely supported himself by teaching voice and directing church choirs while he continued his theological education at the Oneida Institute in Whitesboro, New York. In 1833 the American Board received and accepted his application to become a domestic missionary. He began his journey to Minnesota in July and reached the shores of Lake Superior in September of that year.

Ely's journal at times resembled a daybook that recorded the weather, encounters with Natives, traders, soldiers, and other visitors—the mundane events of making a life in frontier conditions. His diary from 1833 until his marriage in 1835 also provided a spiritual accounting of a pilgrim's progress as he engaged in a ceaseless inner warfare against sin, pride, a coldhearted indifference to piety, and a perceived alienation from Christ and the Holy Spirit. Ely devoted himself to the daily practice of piety: scripture-reading, meditation on *The Life of Brainerd* and other devotional works, private prayer, and self-examination of his sinfulness. An entry for

Saturday evening, November 16, 1833, exemplifies this inward journey. Despite these exercises in piety, he lapsed into an evangelical humiliation: "I find myself far from God & the humble spirit which a missionary should possess, an amazing insensibility & hardness of heart. I hardly know what to do to approach God."[44] Noting that he alone for 150 miles had assumed the responsibility to evangelize, he wrote, "In this light I stand, a poor, mean, vile worm spared by the long suffering & mercy of the Lord. O! did I feel that the abominations of my heart were in reality spread open to the continual view of God, I should sink to the earth with shame."[45] Later that month, on Sabbath eve, Ely would lament, "O, I want much of humility, a sense of my meanness, filthiness, unfitness to put my hand to God's work. If such a man as Brainerd was so unseemly & vile, what am I?"[46] These inward reflections and the burdensome inward pilgrimage that emulated Brainerd's piety abruptly ended once he married and faced the daily confrontations with recalcitrant Native scholars and their parents.

Ely met Catherine Goulais in 1835, a graduate and convert from the Mackinaw Mission, and the Métis daughter of a French voyageur and Ojibwe woman. The ABCFM sent Catherine to assist him in providing translation and evangelizing the local population. They married later that year and she bore him thirteen children, of whom seven survived. Together they reached out to children and adults, teaching them important skills of reading and writing English.

Ely at first charmed his students with Bible stories and his talent for hymns and songs that mirrored the Ojibwe oral tradition of storytelling and song. With the ascendency of American political administration and the dominance of the American Fur Company after 1816, Natives understood that English literacy and proficiency were essential skills in a market-based society that exchanged manufactured goods for Native resources—the declining fur trade and the emerging markets for land, lumber, and copper and iron ore. In addition, the idea of the Christian God resonated with the Ojibwes who communicated with the Great Spirit (*Gichi-Manidou*) through ceremonies, visions, and dream interpretation. However, the evangelical Protestant concepts of sin, brokenhearted repentance, anxiety about otherworldly salvation, and the focus on praying religion (*annmiewin*) were unwelcome.[47]

The Ojibwes resisted conversion, the Protestant "praying religion," and saw no need for salvation or the existential reordering of their spiritual identity. They recoiled at the prescriptions of Protestant moralism that included temperance and avoidance of alcohol, keeping the Sabbath, and abandoning Native lifeways and ceremonies in favor of the plan of civilization and Christianity.[48] Although an astute ethnographer who observed and recorded Ojibwe ceremonies, Ely openly ridiculed their practices of shamanism and their acceptance of Catholic ritual. He preached against the Midewiwin and characterized the "Welcoming Dance" conducted in his honor as a "ridiculous farce."[49] As Theresa M. Schenck explains,

> the powers Ely brought to the Ojibwe did not make their lives better, although he did assist in burying the dead and healing or caring for the sick.... The word of God that the missionaries brought had little meaning or relevance in their lives. It was not long before the Ojibwe were telling Ely that they would let their children learn to read and write, but there was to be no praying.... Parents wanted their children to go to the Indian afterlife.[50]

In addition, Ely violated the cultural expectations of gift exchange and hospitality, refusing to feed and clothe Natives who demanded reciprocity for the land given to establish the mission station and the access they permitted to timber, fish, game, and other resources. Having failed to convert the local bandleader, Maangozid, Ely encountered escalating hostility and resistance. Angry Natives shot and butchered his oxen, pilfered items from the school and gardens, and rebuffed him when he visited their villages to evangelize. Shortly before he closed the school and mission in 1839, he made this journal entry, in fear for his safety: "Scarce a day passes but the Indians show their hatred or opposition to us in words concerning our residence here—the land, woods, grass, fish that we use—& from all that we can judge it is evident they intend to take some offensive course with us."[51]

Unlike métis peoples, who openly embraced much of the plan of civilization and recognized the benefits of schooling and evangelical religion for themselves and their children, more traditional Ojibwe villages who remained on their homelands and practiced their indigenous lifeways saw only the threat of settler colonialism: invasion, dispossession, forced removal, and the threat of intertribal warfare. The spirit of missions held no value for them, and they responded with anger and hostility, hoping to expel missionaries from their land.

Jane Johnston Schoolcraft and Reverend Edmund Ely modeled their lives on Brainerd's piety and afflicted themselves with self-torture through methodical self-examination, seeking evidence of indwelling sin to stave off seasons of coldhearted indifference to religion. In this state of self-abasement and repentance, the believer welcomed an inner illumination and renewed assurance of God's love and grace. Only then could the penitent move from inward meditation to active engagement in the world through his or her religious vocation. However, the events in Jane's life—the death of her son, her marginalization, loneliness, and ill health—overwhelmed her; pastoral care failed to sustain her. Like Alice Bacon a generation earlier and the American Board missionary women in Hawaii and in missions to Native Americans, Jane spent decades grappling with the question of how to live according to Brainerd's model of piety when confronted with life's predicaments.

Reverend Ely, like Reverends David Bacon and Gideon Hawley and many other missionary men, quickly abandoned Brainerd's cycle of self-examination, repentance, and assurance—the meditative retreat from the world. Once they married, became householders, and encountered the pressing mundane duties in their respective missions, each minister assumed the stance of instrumental activism by confronting conflicts and attempting to solve problems. They abandoned recording their piety in spiritual diaries and the devotionalism of the inward journey that characterized Brainerd's life. Instead they kept secular day-books and account books and wrote necessary correspondence.

The burdens of Brainerd's model of piety and making a Christian life fell most heavily upon the shoulders of missionary women, who toiled as wives, mothers, teachers, and homemakers while cultivating an inward piety. Men, although fully committed to their public religious vocations as missionaries, seemed to shed this model of inner piety like an inconvenient cloak once they found themselves engaged in the business of running a mission station and tending to their responsibilities as husbands and householders. The religious vocations of missionaries were differentiated by gender as women clung more tenaciously to devotionalism and Brainerd's inward piety and men more easily abandoned it.

Conclusion

Bradford Alden's "A Discourse Delivered before the Society for Propagating the Gospel among the Indians and Others, in North America, November 4, 1830" did not repeat the boundless optimism of Abiel Holmes's address that we encountered at the beginning of our study. Writing in 1808, Holmes concluded "that at the knee of Jesus every knee may bend ... every tongue may confess, that Jesus Christ is Lord, to the glory of God the Father."[1] Nearly a generation later, the conflation of religious and political ideals represented by the plan of civilization, an ideology that served as an antecedent for Manifest Destiny in the 1840s, championed missions as an agency to promote nationalism, expansionism, and the Redeemer's Kingdom in America. By 1830, however, enthusiasm for these initiatives was tempered by frustrations and failures in the realization of such sublime and utopian ideals. After two decades in pursuit of the spirit of missions, Alden speaks in more prosaic terms proposing a pragmatic strategy of denominational cooperation advanced in the era of grand revivals where missionaries eschewed doctrinal controversies and emphasized the immutable timeless truths of true religion derived by the Bible, the Sermon on the Mount, and the possibility of salvation through Christ. Instead of the promise of propagating the Gospel to perishing heathens throughout the world, Alden recalls the pessimistic account of colonial New England missions to the Indians in the praying town of Natick, Massachusetts. He quotes Reverend Steven Badger's assessment of the fate of this experiment begun in the 1640s by John Eliot, "Apostle to the Indians." Predicting the inevitable extinction of the Natick Indians, Badger, in a letter in 1797, opined, "The success of missions among the Indians has been very small.... They have generally returned to their habits of indolence, intemperance, and vice. This has been the case with individuals and often, I believe, with whole tribes." There is a "strong natural aversion in the American savage" to Christianity.[2] Badger quotes a Natick Indian leader who states that "ducks will be ducks," implying that Indians will return to their true nature despite the efforts of missionaries.[3] After decades of prosecuting the Great Commission, some commentators like Alden expressed weariness and pessimism tinged with a growing racial consciousness that Indians adopted the white vices of intemperance and indolence, and not the virtues of civilization and religion. Despite missionary outreach, Indians were destined for extinction.

White missionaries and Native neophytes organized their lives in full measure according to the dictates of evangelical religious personhood: conversion, progressive sanctification, devotional piety, and the strictures of asceticism and Protestant morality as a guide to daily conduct. Both missionaries and neophytes joined church communities and participated in the imagined community of the faithful throughout American and the Atlantic world, anticipating that each soul brought to Christ hastened the day of the Redeemer's Kingdom.

Evangelicals everywhere participated in the democratization of religion and society. James H. Moorhead argues, "By the 1820s that ferment had largely succeeded in producing a new set of cultural ideals identified with the Republic and to a considerable extent embodied in its polity: egalitarianism, individual freedom, repudiation of arbitrary authority, diffusion of power, and translocal unity based on shared ideology."[4] Did not Christian Indians hope to claim, as did Samson Occom and Joseph Johnson of Brothertown in the 1770s, legitimacy as children of God, eligible for inclusion in America or deserving of a separate Canaan—sovereign communities on the borderlands or within the American Republic?

The Great Commission and the pursuit of the missionary spirit represented familiar culturally constructed illusions of the final redemption of humankind from history through the creation of a religious utopia characterized by perfect integration and a harmony of interests. The mission families and communities at Brainerd, the Moravian *Brüdergemeinde* at Springplace, and the model village of Talmadge, Ohio, as a community of regenerate evangelicals, each exemplified the cultural illusion of a community forged in total unity by those who adhered to a common belief system. This idea of millennial futurism and the creation of religious communities of total integration proved illusory.

Also, the religious identities of the members of these communities were constituted by evangelical piety and personhood that imagined an unattainable absolute individualism (solipsistic and narcissistic)—an "I" that formed the ultimate reality. Thus, believers forged their identities in the inward practice of Brainerd's model of piety that rotated from despondency to repentance to the blissful possession of the Holy Spirit in a mystical-illuminism. These absolute individuals hoped to participate in communities that were devoid of conflict, in perfect integration. However, the contradictions between religious individualism and the obligation for complete surrender and submission of the believer to a religious community could never be reconciled. The illusions of millennial futurism and the pursuit of religious individualism were destined to fail. As Benjamin Nelson argues in "The Future of Illusions," "mankind must cease to dream of building a utopian society which will transcend the bonds of time, the taint of place, and the limits of political society. It must learn to accept the fact that there never has been and never will be an undivided, wholly consecrated community."[5]

The stories of the missionaries in this study did not end well. David Bacon ventured forth as an agent of the Connecticut Missionary Society, inspired by the example of David Brainerd. We retraced his peripatetic journeys into Seneca homelands, his encounter and rebuff by Red Jacket at Buffalo Creek, and the subsequent rejection by Miami leader Little Turtle. He was unable to complete a mission to the Ojibwes in Mackinaw and at L'Arbre Croche. Undeterred by repeated failures in the pursuit of impossible millenarian projects, he redoubled his efforts to create a holy commonwealth of new born white homesteaders from Connecticut who relocated to Tallmadge, Ohio. When this utopian venture ended in financial ruin, he returned to New England and spent the reminder of his life as an itinerant preacher and traveling Bible salesman. Alice Bacon experienced heroic suffering and deprivation, cultivating Brainerd's inner piety but failing to attain illuminations of the Holy Spirit with the assurance of grace. Alice wrote of, instead, suffering the spiritual afflictions of Job that mirrored her worldly adversities of poverty, ill health, and widowhood. The burdens of religious vocation fell most heavily upon Alice and other missionary women.

The endless chain of religious intelligence and the biographies that we have reconstructed reveal a now-familiar trope: literate young men and women from the middling classes in New England, caught up in the evangelical fervor of an age of revivals, found new birth and eagerly dedicated their lives to the missionary spirit. Their tales recounted recruitment, travel, hardships encountered, and the frustrations they endured in educating and evangelizing Natives given the language barriers. Many women experienced maternal depletion through childbearing and domestic labor in addition to keeping the mission school. They frequently succumbed to infectious diseases like malaria and tuberculosis resulting in invalidism and early death. Others expressed their despair and religious melancholy in their own voices, consistent with the spirit of David Brainerd. As is driven home by the story of Alice Bacon, few attained religious ecstasy and the abiding assurance of grace.

In my study of Anabaptist religiosity, *The Other Side of Joy*, I identified the injunctive for believers who were called upon to appropriate a religious vocation and personhood based on the submission and surrender to Jesus known as *Gelassenheit*—self-abandonment to the will of God. "Self-denial and surrender to the will of God also demanded the willingness to suffer martyrdom, persecution, and profound inner struggle as the way of the cross and a radical discipleship of Christ."[6] Self-abandonment to the will of God, whether the *Gelassenheit* demanded of Anabaptists or the devotionalism and evangelical piety in the spirit of David Brainerd, proved a more onerous burden and an unanticipated benefit for missionary women than their male counterparts.

Mary A. Renda argues that women acting on behalf of the cause of missions in antebellum America could effectively challenge and expand the gender role allocation prescribed by the American Board—"the limits, which a sense of propriety has imposed on female exertion." She explains, "Protestant women seized the gendered structure of obligation—the injunction to live out a tightly prescribed model of womanhood, one in which religious piety, maternal care, and domestic industry defined the main contours of acceptable female behavior—to authorize and enlarge their scope of action, from fundraising efforts to work as missionaries and educators to temperance and moral reform activism."[7]

Perhaps surprisingly, women who selflessly surrendered to God's will and Providence as they pursued their missionary vocation were able to eschew the limitations of conventional lives in the domestic sphere, and they enjoyed an expanded sense of self and enhanced moral authority in their public identities as missionary sisters and teachers. Nancy Ruttenburg argues that in the religious awakening of the 1740s in New England and through the Second Great Awakening, evangelicals achieved an enlargement of the self[8]—an epochal self: "From the depths of suffering, religious melancholy, and self-abasement came the path to self-enlargement—the new creation in communion with the Holy Spirit—and the duty of public speech."[9] As we have seen, Hannah Moore's continual protest and contestation of missionary policy and male authority regarding pedagogy, slaveholding, and other matters is a case in point of her new powers of agency derived from a vocation of submission and surrender. This enlargement of the self proved true for Christian Indian women like Catharine Brown and Sister Margaret Ann, the first fruits of Brainerd and Springplace Missions.

The sublime vision of converting perishing heathens and toiling in God's vineyard, of advancing the cause of American empire and nationalism, could not be sustained in the field. As Christian soldiers, missionary women tenaciously held on to each another, seeking mutual aid, friendship, and support within the female sphere in their mission families. Here women missionaries guided and sustained one another in the face of hostile and recalcitrant Natives and ungodly white settlers, longing for home, feelings of isolation, and the unending drudgery of work in the mission. They especially understood the burdens of self-abandonment to the will of God.

Native converts like Catharine and David Brown and others began their spiritual pilgrimage with such fervor and optimism only to succumb to tuberculosis before they could effectively missionize their people. They entered missions as students and became neophytes who were intended by their teachers to serve as deployable agents in the missionary cause. Like many of their white missionary women counterparts, Christian Indians women and men assumed Writerly identities speaking with authoritative voices, not as passive instruments of the Great Commission. These mixed-race Christian Indians found new powers of agency to advocate for their people in a time of intratribal factionalism and conflict and public controversies surrounding removal and the plan of civilization.

Sister Margaret Ann, the first fruit of the Moravian Springplace Mission, died before she could establish an enduring Cherokee Christian Indian community as a testament to how Christian and "civilized" Cherokees might effectively contest the politics of removal and settler colonialism. Métis Christian Indians like Jane Johnston Schoolcraft lived conflicted, marginalized lives stamped by the iron of religious melancholy.[10] Her distinctive voice and the testimonies of her spirituality and lived experience are found in her unpublished poems, letters, and Ojibwe folklore. We are left with the unanswered question, did the devotionalism and dictates of Brainerd's piety sustain and console her given the adversity that she faced in the death of her son Willy, the separation from her children, the increasing alienation from her husband, and her marginalization from kindred, natal community, and white society?

K's life was given over by his tribe to the missionary cause. He traveled to the Heathen School in Cornwall, succumbed to religious mania and melancholy, and recovered at a New England asylum before completing his education and conversion at Miami University. He too died of tuberculosis shortly after returning to his Osage village as a missionary.

This study has retold the stories and recounted the lives of a small sample of Congregationalist, Presbyterian, and Moravian missionaries and Cherokee, Osage, and Ojibwe Christian Indians, drawn largely from a mixed-race elite group. Accounts of Baptist and Methodist missions to these and others Native peoples, not considered in our study, would offer a more comprehensive and complete consideration of perishing heathens and the rise of the missionary spirit in this era. These stories remain for another time and another telling.

The Christian Indians in this study reshaped their identities with the anticipation that as champions of the plan of civilization and evangelical culture, they might enjoy the benefits of evangelical personhood and the democratization of religion and society for themselves, their families, and tribal communities. Caught in the crushing realities of settler colonialism, swept up in the social and religious movements of their age, neophytes in their own voices enunciated a selfless and altruistic commitment to doing good for their people. However, Christian Indian identity among mixed-race individuals could assume a darker personage as that of double agent or confidence man. Eleazer Williams (1788–1858) is a case in point.[11]

Williams was a descendant of Eunice Williams, the unredeemed Puritan captive taken in a 1704 raid on Deerfield, Massachusetts. He was born into the Mohawk community of Kahnawake near Sault Ste. Louis in Lower Canada. As an adult, Williams always identified himself as a Christian Indian missionary to the Oneida in New York and Wisconsin, and the St. Regis Reservation in New York (Akwesasne). He also served as an advocate of removal, as an agent for white land speculators, and as an interpreter and mediator of Indian affairs in Albany, New York City, and Washington DC.

Williams needs to be seen as a mixed-race individual, a double agent who appealed to white interests and to Iroquois concerns but who ultimately served his own interests, "getting by and making do," marginal to both Native and white worlds. Michael Leroy Oberg characterizes him as a "professional Indian" given the identity choices Williams made by advocating what he thought to be in the best interests of Indians—a progressive agenda of evangelical religion, civilization, and removal. While working as a missionary and community leader for the Oneidas, he also served various private and government patrons. Oberg argues, "Williams was a professional Indian, a role that required that he keep both Native people and white people happy. A man-in-between, in this sense, he appealed to audiences that expected different things, and whose interests inherently clashed."[12]

As one of thirteen children coming of age in an ethnically diverse Mohawk village that incorporated Abenakis, Catawbas, Chickasaws, Hurons, Mahicans, Susquehannocks, and many other remnant groups into Iroquoian culture, speaking French and influenced by British administration and Jesuit religiosity, Williams was brought to Longmeadow Massachusetts at age eleven in 1800. Deracinated from his natal community, he reunited with his New England kin and was placed under the care of Reverend Nathaniel Ely, who taught him English and struggled to rid him of the dangers of "Paganism and Romanism."[13]

As a teenager immersed in awakenings and Protestant evangelical culture, he felt a call go into the world and preach the Gospel. By age nineteen, Williams recalls that he "began to have a desire to become a messenger of the Prince of Peace and manifested a great anxiety for the Salvation of the red men of the forest."[14] He traveled to New York City at age twenty-two in 1810 and joined the Episcopal Church under the patronage of Bishop John Henry Hobart. After soldiering in the War of 1812 under the command of General Dearborn of Southern New York, Hobart sent him on mission to the St. Regis Reservation, on a fundraising tour of the East, and in 1816 at the age of twenty-six he became a lay reader, catechist, and schoolteacher to the Oneidas.

Williams entered a tribal community divided into pagan and Christian factions. He succeeded in converting many traditional Indians through his talents as a preacher, in providing effective pastoral care, in challenging drunkards and promoting temperance and Protestant moralism, and in opening a school for fifty children. Ultimately, many in the Oneida community who opposed removal disavowed him for promoting this policy and facilitating land sales in New York, accusing him of misappropriating funds for church construction for personal gain in securing fifteen hundred dollars in Oneida lands. Representatives of the Ogden Land Company and government patrons no longer employed him to mediate with Indian affairs. By 1823, he had removed to Green Bay, Wisconsin, and married an Indian woman, Madeleine Jourdain, age seventeen, who owned forty-eight hundred acres of land. After Hobart's death in 1833 Williams was recalled as a missionary.[15]

Mired in debt, alienated in his marriage and from Oneida communities in Wisconsin and New York, and unable to secure employment from patrons, Williams lived a peripatetic existence and attempted to reinvent a fictional biography and identity. In an unsuccessful bid to secure a congressional pension for his service during the War of 1812, Williams claimed to have been an intelligence officer as superintendent-general of the Northern Indian Department and commander of the Corps of Observation. He embarked on speaking tours, seeking money to support a mission to the St. Regis Mohawks while pocketing the small sums that he raised. Here he denied his Mohawk-Williams lineage by suggesting through questionable evidence that he may be the dauphin, the lost prince and heir to the throne of France as the child of Louis XVI and Marie Antoinette.[16] He portrayed himself as a noble missionary who would forsake his royal birthright to devote himself to the salvation of perishing heathens.

As a double agent and confidence man, Williams developed a protean self, appealing to different audiences with compelling stories and convincing presentations of identity. Oberg concludes,

> He learned much about what these audiences wanted to hear, and he gave it to them. He needed the approval of whites, because he needed to make a living. He played the role of catechist, a missionary, a leader, and an advocate for native peoples. He saw himself as a man wronged by many who had not appreciated all that he had attempted to do for them. He played that role, too, the victim. His critics—and there were many—would have accepted these labels for him at times, but they would have added to this list a dishonest man, a faithless guardian, a charlatan, and a bad debt.[17]

The lives and stories of Christian Indians in antebellum America deserve to be retold and restored to our historical imagination and collective memory. The perishing heathens who were redeemed by Protestant missions and went on to champion the missionary spirit in sincerity and selfless altruism and those who played the role of professional Indian with tongue-in-cheek cynicism, together with the white missionary men and women enthralled by the utopianism of the Great Commission, continue to instruct us about our American identity, past and present. For who among us today, pursuing our lives in an increasingly secularized civil society, are sustained by such illusions and live with such clarity of purpose, devoted to the pursuit of our individual salvation and a vision of national redemption?

NOTES

PREFACE

1. This tribal affiliation is suggested by a publication of the Middlesex County Historical Society. See "Wangunks, Their Stories: Voices from Middletown's Melting Pot," http://www.middlesexhistory.org/exhibits/wangunks.htm.
2. See entry for Wangunk at the Yale Indian Papers Project, http://www.yipp.yale.edu. Paul Costa-Grant, director and executive editor, suggests that Ann Cornelius was a Tunxis-Farmington Indian. But he could not find any records to substantiate this hunch. See Ives, "Reconstructing the Wangunk Reservation Land System." In response to a research inquiry, Ives checked land records and surnames but found no evidence of a Cornelius among the Wangunk.
3. Research, namely "Connecticut Gravestones" by Caulfield (*Connecticut Historical Society Bulletin*, vols. 10–28) and *Graven Images* by Ludwig, did not reveal who carved the Cornelius stone and who paid for this grave marker. Diane McCain, head of the Connecticut Historical Society Research Center and herself a resident of Durham, suggested in 2013 that nothing is known about Ann Cornelius except for the information found on her grave marker. McCain suggested a search of the Newton Family Papers, but this research yielded no evidence of Ann Cornelius.
4. Research inquiries about Ann Cornelius and the Cornelius family surname were sent to Jason Mancini, director, Mashantucket Pequot Museum and Research Center; Ned Smith, Suffolk County Historical Society; and John Strong, a noted expert on Long Island tribal groups. Each respondent found no evidence of Ann Cornelius or her family.

5. See "Freemen, Rev. Mr. Chauncey's Records, Rev. Dr. Goodrich Record and Proprietors' Record," in Fowler, *History of Durham, Connecticut*, 229–443.
6. Hoady, *Colonial Records of Connecticut, 1772–1775*, vol. 14, appendix 10, 486.
7. Goodrich, "Account Books, 1759–1783," Connecticut Historical Society Library.
8. Newell, "Indian Slavery in Colonial New England," 51–60; Newell, *Brethren by Nature*, 211. Professor Newell suggested in our correspondence that Ann Cornelius might be listed as a Native indentured servant in Brown, *Black Roots in Southeastern Connecticut, 1650–1900*. No record exists for Ann Cornelius in this genealogy.
9. No indenture could be found for Ann Cornelius in the records of the Middlesex County Historical Society, where indentures were recorded for Durham proprietors and servants by the court in Middletown.
10. Clonassey and Cornell, Middletown Probate District Estate Papers, 1752–1880, microfilm 732, record 1000.
11. Fenn, *Pox Americana*, 266, 62–108.
12. Fowler, *History of Durham, Connecticut*, 98–99.
13. Dippie, *The Vanishing American*, 12; Rubin, *Tears of Repentance*, 3.
14. Boyd and Thrush, "Introduction," in *Phantom Past, Indigenous Presence*, viii.
15. Tiro, *The People of the Standing Stone*, 16–17.
16. Kellaway, *The New England Company*, 266; Halsey, *The Old New York Frontier*, 53.
17. Halsey, *The Old New York Frontier*, 55.
18. Halsey, *Journal of Richard Smith*, 67–68.
19. Andrews, *Native Apostles*, 4.
20. Glatthaar and Martin, *Forgotten Allies*, 52.
21. Hauptman, "The Oneida Nation, A Composite Portrait, 1784–1816," 19–21.
22. Andrews, *Native Apostles*, 5.
23. Ronda, "Reverend Samuel Kirkland and the Oneida Indians," 24–26.
24. Pilkington, *Journals of Samuel Kirkland*, 62.
25. Pilkington, *Journals of Samuel Kirkland*, 62.
26. Pilkington, *Journals of Samuel Kirkland*, December 30, 1767, 65.
27. Strong, *Unkechaug Indians of Eastern Long Island*, 64, 105.
28. Strong, *Unkechaug Indians of Eastern Long Island*, 130.
29. Willis, *A Short Account of the Religious Exercise and Experience of Betty*, 4–5.
30. Willis, *A Short Account of the Religious Exercise and Experience of Betty*, 6.
31. Willis, *A Short Account of the Religious Exercise and Experience of Betty*, 7.

INTRODUCTION

1. Bloom, "Religious Meditations," Harvey Harris Bloom Papers.
2. Carey, *An Inquiry*, 62.
3. Miller, *The Life of the Mind in America*, 49; Gundlach, "Early American Missions," 68–71. See also Hutchison, *Errand to the World*, 5, for a discussion of the "Great Commission" to create foreign missions.
4. Hutchison, *Errand to the World*, 2, 8.
5. Holmes, *Discourse*, 33.
6. Holmes, *Discourse*, 35.
7. Sprague, *Lectures on Revivals of Religion*, 272–73.
8. Elsbree, *The Rise of the Missionary Spirit in America, 1790–1815*, 56–58; Berkhofer, *Salvation and the Savage*, 16–18.
9. Hutchison, *Errand to the World*, 47.
10. Woods, "A Sermon Occasioned by the Death of Samuel Worcester," 19.
11. Tracy, *History of the American Board of Commissioners for Foreign Missions*, 85–87.
12. Bowden, *American Indians and Christian Missions*, 121.
13. Kling, *A Field of Divine Wonders*, 127–43, 43. This discussion is excerpted from my essay "The Deferred Ministry of James Lockwood Wright," 1–3.
14. De Jong, *As the Waters Cover the Sea*, 207.
15. Kling, "The New Divinity," 799–810.
16. De Jong, *As the Waters Cover the Sea*, 214.
17. Conforti, *Jonathan Edwards*, 36–77.
18. Hall, *Contested Boundaries*, 84.
19. For an introduction to the historiography of American Protestantism in the antebellum period, please see Ahlstrom, *A Religious History of the American People*; Hatch, *The Democratization of American Christianity*; Noll, *America's God*; Butler, *Awash in a Sea of Faith*; and Stout and Hart, *New Directions in American Religious History*.
20. Rohrer, *Keepers of the Covenant*, 22–29, 115.
21. Rohrer, *Keepers of the Covenant*, 22, 31.
22. Rohrer, *Keepers of the Covenant*, 10.
23. Rohrer, *Keepers of the Covenant*, 11–12.
24. Rohrer, *Keepers of the Covenant*, 108–9.
25. Conforti, *Jonathan Edwards*, 76.
26. Kling, *A Field of Divine Wonders*, 201.
27. Tyler, *Memoir of the Life and Character of Rev. Asahel Nettleton*, 35.
28. Tyler, *Memoir of the Life and Character of Rev. Asahel Nettleton*, 39.
29. Tyler, *Memoir of the Life and Character of Rev. Asahel Nettleton*, 40.

30. Yalom, *Staring at the Sun*, 149–50.
31. Yalom, *Staring at the Sun*, 92.
32. Pettit, "Introduction" to Jonathan Edwards, *The Life of David Brainerd*, 1, 20.
33. Rubin, *Tears of Repentance*, 161, 183–86.
34. Edwards, *Life of David Brainerd*, 101.
35. Edwards, *Life of David Brainerd*, 177.
36. Edwards, *Life of David Brainerd*, 139.
37. Edwards, *Life of David Brainerd*, 148.
38. Rubin, *Tears of Repentance*, 60.
39. Edwards, *Life of David Brainerd*, 154–55.
40. Conforti, *Jonathan Edwards*, 190–92.
41. Rohrer, *Keepers of the Covenant*, 109.
42. Kling, "The New Divinity," 812.
43. Weber, "Social Psychology of the World Religions," 289–90.
44. Rubin, *Tears of Repentance*, 110.
45. Taylor, *Sources of the Self*, 285–302.
46. Rubin, *Religious Melancholy and Protestant Experience in America*, 30.
47. Faber, *The Book of Strange New Things*, 321.
48. Faber, *The Book of Strange New Things*, 371.
49. Faber, *The Book of Strange New Things*, 328.
50. Faber, *The Book of Strange New Things*, 598.
51. Weber, "Social Psychology of the World Religions," 278, 280.

1. THE TRAVAILS OF DAVID BACON

1. Bacon, *Sketch of the Rev. David Bacon*, 3.
2. David Bacon to Nathan Strong, August 5, 1803, *Missionary Society of Connecticut Papers, 1759–1948* (hereafter MSC Papers).
3. David Bacon to Nathan Strong, August 5, 1803, MSC Papers.
4. David Bacon to Nathan Strong, July 17, 1804, MSC Papers.
5. Leonard Bacon to David Bacon, September 10, 1804, Bacon Family Papers, 1800–1933, series 1, box 1, Yale University Library Manuscript and Archives.
6. Bacon, *Sketch of the Rev. David Bacon*, 4.
7. Bacon, *Sketch of the Rev. David Bacon*, 6–7.
8. Bacon, *Sketch of the Rev. David Bacon*, 9.
9. Bacon, *Sketch of the Rev. David Bacon*, 10.
10. *Pastor's New Year's Greeting*, 13.
11. *Pastor's New Year's Greeting*, 14.
12. Bacon, *Sketch of the Rev. David Bacon*, 14.
13. *Pastor's New Year's Greeting*, 15.

14. Nichols, *Red Gentlemen and White Savages*, 39.
15. Wallace, *Death and Rebirth of the Seneca*, 206.
16. Wilson, *The Earth Shall Weep*, 129.
17. Wallace, *Death and Rebirth of the Seneca*, 194. Only 2,628 Seneca were enumerated in 1779.
18. Densmore, *Red Jacket*, 46.
19. Wallace, *Death and Rebirth of the Seneca*, 46.
20. Wallace, *Death and Rebirth of the Seneca*, 199–200.
21. Ganter, *The Collected Speeches of Sagoyewatha*, 102–3.
22. Ganter, *The Collected Speeches of Sagoyewatha*, 104.
23. Ganter, *The Collected Speeches of Sagoyewatha*, 105.
24. Richter, *Facing East from Indian Country*, 229–36.
25. Ganter, *The Collected Speeches of Sagoyewatha*, 141.
26. Ganter, *The Collected Speeches of Sagoyewatha*, 141.
27. Ganter, *The Collected Speeches of Sagoyewatha*, 141.
28. Bacon, *Sketch of Rev. David Bacon*, 15.
29. Sabathy-Judd, *Moravians in Upper Canada*, xiii–xxix.
30. Rubin, *Tears of Repentance*, 210–11.
31. Bacon, *Sketch of Rev. David Bacon*, 19.
32. Bacon, *Sketch of Rev. David Bacon*, 19.
33. *Connecticut Evangelical Magazine*, vol. 1, July 1800, 33.
34. *Connecticut Evangelical Magazine*, vol. 1, July 1800, 34.
35. Cott, *The Bonds of Womanhood*, 140.
36. Cott, *The Bonds of Womanhood*, 139.
37. Bacon, *Sketch of Rev. David Bacon*, 24.
38. Bacon, *Sketch of Rev. David Bacon*, 27.
39. Bacon, *Sketch of Rev. David Bacon*, 32.
40. Bacon, *Sketch of Rev. David Bacon*, 36.
41. Nichols, *Red Gentlemen and White Savages*, 191–96.
42. Bacon, *Sketch of Rev. David Bacon*, 40.
43. Bacon, *Sketch of Rev. David Bacon*, 40.
44. Bacon, *Sketch of Rev. David Bacon*, 41.
45. Bacon, *Sketch of Rev. David Bacon*, 41.
46. Bacon, *Sketch of Rev. David Bacon*, 43.
47. Bacon, *Sketch of Rev. David Bacon*, 45.
48. David Bacon to CMS, February 10, 1803, CMS Papers.
49. Alice Bacon to Miss Jerusha Bayley, February 3, 1803, Bacon Family Papers.
50. Alice Bacon to Miss Jerusha Bayley, February 3, 1803.
51. Bacon, *Sketch of Rev. David Bacon*, 55.

52. Bacon, *Sketch of Rev. David Bacon*, 55.
53. Bacon, *Sketch of the Rev. David Bacon*, 57.
54. Bacon, *Sketch of the Rev. David Bacon*, 61–62.
55. Bacon, *Sketch of the Rev. David Bacon*, 71–72.
56. Bacon, *Sketch of the Rev. David Bacon*, 73.
57. Bacon, *Sketch of the Rev. David Bacon*, 75.
58. David Bacon to David Brown, July 22, 1805, CMS Papers.
59. DeRogatis, *Moral Geography*, 4, 16.
60. DeRogatis, *Moral Geography*, 58–59.
61. DeRogatis, *Moral Geography*, 111, quoted from Hudson, "Some Accounts of the Religious Exercises of David Hudson," *Western Missionary Magazine* 1, 166.
62. DeRogatis, *Moral Geography*, 112.
63. Sill and Bacon, *Proceedings in Commemoration of the Fiftieth Anniversary of the Settlement of Tallmadge*, 14.
64. Bacon, *Sketch of Rev. David Bacon*, 82.
65. Bacon, *Sketch of Rev. David Bacon*, 83.
66. Alice Bacon to David Bacon, May 29, 1811, Bacon Family Papers.
67. Alice Bacon to David Bacon, May 29, 1811, Bacon Family Papers.
68. Bacon, *Sketch of Rev. David Bacon*, 91.
69. Leonard Bacon to Benjamin Tallmadge, January 8, 1812, Bacon Family Papers.
70. Bacon, *Sketch of Rev. David Bacon*, 99–101.
71. de Tocqueville, *Democracy in America, Part the Second*, 137.
72. Alice Bacon to David Bacon, November 17, 1816, Bacon Family Papers.

2. THE MISSIONARY VOCATION OF MISS D

1. Goodheart, in *Mad Yankees*, 82, briefly presents the case of Miss D. Chapter 2 is based on "Crises of Conscience among Missionaries to the Indians during the Second Great Awakening," in Rubin, "Mental Illness," 147–73.
2. Pearce, *Savagism and Civilization*, 10.
3. Bryant, *Miscellaneous Poems Selected from the United States Literary Gazette*, quoted in Dippie, *The Vanishing American*, 13.
4. Lewis, *Letter to a Member of Congress in Relation to Indian Civilization*, 14–15.
5. Prucha, *American Indian Policy in the Formative Years*, 48–50.
6. Pearce, *Savagism and Civilization*, 68.
7. Morse, "Report to the Secretary of War," 79.
8. Schultz, *An Indian Canaan*, 61–63.
9. Andrew, "Educating the Heathen," 333.

10. Morse, *First Annual Report of the American Society for Promoting Civilization and General Improvement of the Indian Tribes in the United States*, 16.
11. *American Missionary Register* 1, July 1820, 23–24.
12. Foreman, *Pioneer Days in the Early Southwest*, 315–16. See also Graves, *The First Protestant Osage Missions, 1820–1837*.
13. *Litchfield, Connecticut Town Records*, vol. 2, 48.
14. This information was developed from the genealogical file for the D family in Litchfield County Historical Society, Ingraham Memorial Library, Litchfield, Connecticut.
15. White, *The History of the Town of Litchfield, 1720–1926*, 83.
16. Keller, *The Second Great Awakening in Connecticut*, 42.
17. Beecher, *Autobiography, Correspondence, etc.*, vol. 1, 213.
18. Beecher, *Autobiography, Correspondence, etc.*, vol. 1, 217.
19. The population of Litchfield, Connecticut, as recorded in the *State of Connecticut Register and Manual*, 1972, 616, was

    1800   4,285
    1810   4,639
    1820   4,610
    1830   4,456
20. Keller, *The Second Great Awakening in Connecticut*, 42; Parmelee, *Discourse*, 39.
21. Beecher, *Autobiography, Correspondence, etc.*, vol. 1, 213.
22. Miss D was from birth associated with the First Ecclesiastical Society of Litchfield, a Congregational church. While the records of this church do not indicate the exact date of her conversion and her entering into the church covenant, the information left by Reverend Laurens P. Hickok ("Alphabetical Lists of Deaths and Marriages," Ingraham Memorial Library, Litchfield Historical Society) does indicate that Miss D was a member and most probably joined between the revivals of 1812 and 1816.
23. Vanderpoel and Buel, *Chronicles of a Pioneer School from 1792 to 1833*, vol. 1, 399; vol. 2, 15, 33, 400, 422.
24. Manager's Minutes of the United Foreign Missionary Society, ABC: 24, vol. 1, 110, American Board of Commissioners for Foreign Missions Archives, 1810–1961, Houghton Library, Harvard University (hereafter ABCFMA), used by permission.
25. Manager's Minutes of the United Foreign Missionary Society, ABC: 24, vol. 1, 152, ABCFMA, used by permission.
26. *American Missionary Register* 1, September 1829, 97.
27. *American Missionary Register* 1, September 1829, 100.
28. *American Missionary Register* 1, July 1820, 23.

29. *Christian Spectator* 2, no. 4, 213.
30. Manager's Minutes of the United Foreign Missionary Society, ABC: 24, vol. 1, 125, ABCFMA, used by permission.
31. Lewis, *Letter to a Member of Congress in Relation to Indian Civilization*, 3–4.
32. Keller, *The Second Great Awakening in Connecticut*, 99–100.
33. *Religious Intelligencer* 5, no. 31, 514.
34. Conforti, *Jonathan Edwards*, 71–72, 78.
35. Emmons, *Works*, vol. 3, 213.
36. Hopkins, *Works*, vol. 1, 376.
37. Hopkins, *Works*, vol. 1, 398.
38. Conforti, *Jonathan Edwards*, 78.
39. Journal of the Union Mission to the Osages, 1820–1826, April 24, 1820, Oklahoma Historical Society (hereafter referred to as Union Mission journal).
40. *American Missionary Register* 1, September 1820, 88–93.
41. *American Missionary Register* 1, September 1820, 92.
42. *American Missionary Register* 2, June 1822, 409.
43. Union Mission journal, August 6, 1820, 23.
44. Billings, *The National Medical Dictionary*, 162–63, 409; Ackerknecht, *Malaria in the Upper Mississippi Valley*, 4, 7. Here Ackerknecht states, "Striking examples of the confusion between malaria and other fevers are plentiful all through the nineteenth century."
45. *American Missionary Register* 2, June 1822, 409.
46. Drake, *A Systematic Treatise*, vol. 1, 56.
47. Drake, *A Systematic Treatise*, vol. 1, 74. See also Johnson, *The Influence of Tropical Climates on European Constitutions*; and Miner and Tully, *Essays on Fevers*.
48. Macculloch, *An Essay on the Remittent and Intermittent Diseases*; Ackerknecht, *Malaria in the Upper Mississippi Valley*, 16.
49. Nuttall, *A Journal of Travels into the Arkansa Territory*, 213.
50. Union Mission journal, January 1, 1821, 35.
51. Duffy, *Epidemics in Colonial America*, 205–14.
52. *Religious Intelligencer* 5, no. 26, 344.
53. Union Mission to the Osages, ABC: 18.4.8, vol. 1, 128–33, ABCFMA, used by permission.
54. Correspondence from Stephen Fuller, Union Mission to the Osages, to Jeremiah Evarts, corresponding secretary, Union Mission, September 11, 1826, ABC: 18, no. 158, ABCFMA, used by permission.
55. Correspondence from William Vaill to Jeremiah Evarts, ABC: 24, vol. 2, 19, ABCFMA, used by permission.
56. Union Mission journal, November 4, 1821, 88–89.

57. *Religious Intelligencer* 6, no. 43, 677.
58. Union Mission journal, November 15, 1823, 150.
59. *American Missionary Register*, vol. 2, August 1822, 409.
60. Graves, *The First Protestant Osage Missions, 1820–1837*, 58.
61. Correspondence from William Vaill to Jeremiah Evarts, ABC: 24, vol. 2, 130–31, ABCFMA, used by permission.
62. Holmes, *Dissertation on Intermittent Fever in New England*, 46.
63. Holmes, *Dissertation on Intermittent Fever in New England*, 53.
64. Rubin, "Mental Illness," 169.
65. Rubin, "Mental Illness," 170.
66. Degler, *At Odds*, 14.
67. Chronic patients, incurables, and violent and unmanageable lunatics were housed in basements, sheds, and other more remote sections of the asylum.
68. Forrest, "Malaria and the Union Mission to the Osage Indians, 1820–1837," *Journal of the Oklahoma State Historical Society* 69, July 1976, 326.
69. White, "Counting the Cost of Faith," 19.
70. Hoyle, "Missionary Women among the American Indians, 1815–1865," 5–6.
71. Hoyle, "Missionary Women among the American Indians, 1815–1865," 33–34.

3. THE CHAIN OF RELIGIOUS INTELLIGENCE

1. Nord, *Faith in Reading*, 5–9.
2. Nord, *Faith in Reading*, 86.
3. Nord, *Faith in Reading*, 114.
4. Welter, "She Hath Done What She Could," 112–17.
5. Pierson, *American Missionary Memorial*, 282.
6. Edwards, *The Life of David Brainerd*, 95–101; Weddle, "The Melancholy Saint," 298–99.
7. Jensen, "Introduction," *The Pawnee Mission Letters*, xxv–xxvi.
8. Samuel Allis to Reverend David Green, July 14, 1836, in Jensen, *The Pawnee Mission Letters*, 176.
9. Kling, "The New Divinity," 799–810.
10. Rogers, "'A Bright and New Constellation,'" 50–60.
11. Clemmons, *Conflicted Mission*, 24.
12. Clemmons, *Conflicted Mission*, 26–28.
13. Letter to the Honourable East India Company, in Sargent, *Life and Letters of the Rev. Henry Martyn*, 25.
14. Sargent, *Life and Letters of the Rev. Henry Martyn*, 140.
15. Kling, "The New Divinity," 792.
16. Gillespie, "'The Clear Leadings of Providence,'" 197.

17. Hooker, *Memoir of Mrs. Sarah L. Huntington*; Knowles, *Memoir of Mrs. Ann H. Judson*; Wisner, *Memoirs of Mrs. Susan Huntington*.
18. Wisner, *Memoirs of Mrs. Susan Huntington*, 124.
19. Jones, *Memoir of Mrs. Sarah Louis Taylor*, 146.
20. Jones, *Memoir of Mrs. Sarah Louis Taylor*, 111.
21. Jones, *Memoir of Mrs. Sarah Louis Taylor*, 82–83.
22. Pruitt, *A Looking Glass for Ladies*, 3.
23. Pruitt, *A Looking Glass for Ladies*, 7–8.
24. Westerkamp, *Women and Religion in the Early America, 1600–1850*, 142–48.
25. Cayton, "Canonizing Harriet Newell," 70.
26. Cayton, "Canonizing Harriet Newell," 85–87.
27. Newell and Woods, *Memoir of Mrs. Harriet Newell*, 44–45.
28. Newell and Woods, *Memoir of Mrs. Harriet Newell*, 12.
29. Newell and Woods, *Memoir of Mrs. Harriet Newell*, 34.
30. Newell and Woods, *Memoir of Mrs. Harriet Newell*, 45–46.
31. Newell and Woods, *Memoir of Mrs. Harriet Newell*, 70.
32. Newell and Woods, *Memoir of Mrs. Harriet Newell*, 74.
33. Newell and Woods, *Memoir of Mrs. Harriet Newell*, 121.
34. Grimshaw, *Paths of Duty*, 49.
35. Hoyt, *Memoirs*, 47.
36. Winslow, *Memoir of Mrs. Harriet L. Winslow*, 34–35.
37. Brumberg, *Mission for Life*, 40–42.
38. Brumberg, *Mission for Life*, 40–41.
39. Judson, *The Kathayan Slave*, 50.
40. Judson, *The Kathayan Slave*, 36.
41. Judson, *The Kathayan Slave*, 54.
42. McCoy, *History of Baptist Indian Missions*, 484.
43. Bliss, *The Encyclopedia of Missions*, vol. 2, 185–86.
44. Mills and Smith, "Report of a Missionary Tour," 47.
45. Bliss, *The Encyclopedia of Missions*, vol. 2, 108.
46. Spring, *Memoirs of Rev. Samuel John Mills*, 154.
47. Spring, *Memoirs of Rev. Samuel John Mills*, 239–45.
48. Pierson, *American Missionary Memorial*, 230.
49. Bliss, *The Encyclopedia of Missions*, vol. 1, 416.
50. Griffin, "Preface," in Hervey, *The Spirit of Missions*, 4.
51. Hervey, *The Spirit of Missions*, 24.
52. Hervey, *The Spirit of Missions*, 12.
53. Champion and Champion, *Rev. George Champion*. See also Champion and Booth, *Journal of the Reverend George Champion*.

54. Correspondence of Susana Champion, Ginani Mission, October 3, 1837 to H. Hill, treasurer, ABCFM, Edwards Family Papers, 1805–1874, Sterling Memorial Library Manuscripts and Archives, Yale University, MSS# 191.
55. Correspondence of Reverend George Champion to Jonathan Edwards, March 8, 1838, Edwards Family Papers, 1805–1874, Sterling Memorial Library Manuscripts and Archives, Yale University, MSS# 191. See also Dinnerstein, *The American Board Missions to the Zulu, 1835–1900*, 17–32; Correspondence of Reverend George Champion to Jonathan Edwards, Port Elizabeth, September 19, 1838, 150: "God has afflicted me on a tender point & my wife and child. The bodily afflictions of one & bodily & mental afflictions of the other—If you have not been much conversant with nervous folks, I shall tell you in vain what I mean here."
56. Correspondence of Rev. George Champion to Aldin Grout, March 8, 1838, in Kotze, *Letters from the American Missionaries, 1835–1838*, 225.
57. Weigold, *Hannah Moore*, 1–8.
58. Weigold, *Hannah Moore*, 13.
59. Weigold, *Hannah Moore*, 15.
60. Weigold, *Hannah Moore*, 26.
61. Weigold, *Hannah Moore*, 26.
62. Weigold, *Hannah Moore*, 25.
63. Grimshaw, *Paths of Duty*, 5–6.
64. Grimshaw, *Paths of Duty*, 49.
65. Grimshaw, *Paths of Duty*, 75.
66. Grimshaw, *Paths of Duty*, 122.
67. Grimshaw, *Paths of Duty*, 151.
68. Grimshaw, *Paths of Duty*, 139–40.
69. Grimshaw, *Paths of Duty*, 150.
70. Grimshaw, *Paths of Duty*, 140.
71. Grimshaw, *Paths of Duty*, 147–48.
72. Grimshaw, *Paths of Duty*, 149.
73. Beck, "Missions and Mental Health," 13.
74. Stouffer et al., *Studies in Social Psychology in World War II*, 110–25.
75. Sexton and Maddock, "The Missionary Syndrome," 59–60.

4. THE QUESTION OF K

1. *Religious Intelligencer* 9, no. 34, 538; 9, no. 35, 548.
2. Spence, *The Question of Hu*. I am indebted to Ann Marie Plane for suggesting the comparison of John Hu and the Osage youth K.
3. Spence, *The Question of Hu*, 6–25.

4. Mathews, *The Osages*; Baird, *The Osage People*; Chapman, *The Origin of the Osage Indian Tribe*, vol. 3, 7.
5. DuVal, *The Native Ground*, 180.
6. DuVal, *The Native Ground*, 5.
7. Rollings, *Unaffected by the Gospel*, 3.
8. Wilson, *Bibliography of the Osage*, 3.
9. DuVal, *The Native Ground*, 197; Rollings, *Unaffected by the Gospel*, 4.
10. DuVal, *The Native Ground*, 224.
11. Durkheim and Mauss, *Primitive Classification*, 81–84.
12. Chapman, *The Origin of the Osage Indian Tribe*, 33.
13. Chapman, *The Origin of the Osage Indian Tribe*, 49–50.
14. Chapman, *The Origin of the Osage Indian Tribe*, 58.
15. Foreman, *Indians & Pioneers*, 47.
16. Foreman, *Indians & Pioneers*, ch. 9.
17. *Religious Intelligencer* 6, no. 46, 728.
18. *Religious Intelligencer* 6, no. 19, 299.
19. Union Mission journal, June 29, 1822, 126.
20. *American Missionary Register*, vol. 3, October 1822, 142.
21. *Religious Intelligencer* 6, no. 15, 234.
22. The mission journal records that during this initial period of the school many Osage parents objected to placing their children into the mission and gave any number of excuses to retrieve them.
23. Berkhofer, *Salvation and the Savage*, 35.
24. Union Mission to the Osages, ABC: 18.4.8., vol. 1, 128–33, ABCFMA, used by permission.
25. Correspondence from Abraham Redfield, Union Mission to the Osages to Jeremiah Evarts, corresponding secretary, August 21, 1827, ABC: 18.4.8. vol. 1, no. 61, ABCFMA, used by permission.
26. Union Mission to the Osages, ABC: 18.4.8. vol. 1, 128, ABCFMA, used by permission.
27. Union Mission to the Osages, ABC: 18.4.8., vol. 1, 128, ABCFMA, used by permission.
28. Union Mission to the Osages, ABC: 18.4.8 vol. 1, 128, ABCFMA, used by permission.
29. Union Mission to the Osages, ABC: 18.4.8., vol. 1, 128, ABCFMA, used by permission.
30. Berkhofer, *Salvation and the Savage*, 69.
31. Correspondence from Dr. Marcus Palmer, Union Mission to the Osages,

to Jeremiah Evarts, July 23, 1827, ABC: 18.4.8. vol. 1, no. 61, ABCFMA, used by permission.
32. Rollings, *Unaffected by the Gospel*, 113.
33. Cornelius, *The Little Osage Captive*, 146–47.
34. Edwards, *Memoir of Rev. Elias Cornelius*, 27–60.
35. Cornelius, *The Little Osage Captive*, 83–108.
36. Cornelius, *The Little Osage Captive*, 131.
37. Cornelius, *The Little Osage Captive*, 9.
38. Cornelius, *The Little Osage Captive*, 137.
39. *Religious Intelligencer* 9, no. 37, 554. See also "Fund for the Education of Heathen Youth," *Religious Intelligencer* 5, no. 46, 748, a letter from the UFMS to the Cornwall School.
40. *Religious Intelligencer* 9, no. 35, 548; *Religious Intelligencer* 10, no. 1, 12.
41. *Religious Intelligencer* 9, no. 34, 530.
42. Union Mission journal, February 26, 1825, 304.
43. *Religious Intelligencer* 9, no. 37, 554.
44. Gabriel, *Elias Boudinot*, 50.
45. Keller, *The Second Great Awakening in Connecticut*, 135.
46. Demos, *The Heathen School*, 77.
47. Andrew, *Rebuilding the Christian Commonwealth*, 322–23.
48. Demos, *The Heathen School*, 98.
49. Foreman, "The Foreign Mission School at Cornwall, Connecticut," 245; Wardell, "Protestant Missions among the Osage, 1820–1838," 285–97.
50. Demos, *The Heathen School*, 4–5.
51. Demos, *The Heathen School*, 93.
52. Starr, *A History of Cornwall, Connecticut*, 147.
53. Demos, *The Heathen School*, 115.
54. Demos, *The Heathen School*, 115–16.
55. *Religious Intelligencer* 9, no. 34, 539.
56. Andrew, *Rebuilding the Christian Commonwealth*, 333.
57. Fredrickson, *White Supremacy*, 40–49, 150–61.
58. Andrew, *Rebuilding the Christian Commonwealth*, 91.
59. Andrew, *Rebuilding the Christian Commonwealth*, 341.
60. Berkhofer, *Salvation and the Savage*, 123.
61. Starr, *A History of Cornwall, Connecticut*, 150, 328.
62. *Religious Intelligencer* 9, no. 37, 554.
63. Demos, *The Heathen School*, 225.
64. ABCFMA. Houghton Library, Harvard University, ABC: 18.4.8., vol. 1, no. 94,

Correspondence of Reverend William F. Vaill, Union Mission to the Osages, to Jeremiah Evarts, Cincinnati, Ohio, March 7, 1827, used by permission.
65. ABCFMA. Houghton Library, Harvard University ABC:18.4.8., vol. 1, no. 99, Correspondence of Reverend William F. Vaill, Union Mission to the Osages, to Jeremiah Evarts, June 12, 1828, used by permission.
66. ABCFMA. Houghton Library, Harvard University ABC:18.4.8., vol. 1, no. 101, Correspondence of Reverend William F. Vaill, Union Mission to the Osages, to Jeremiah Evarts, Union Mission, June 27, 1828, used by permission.
67. ABCFMA. Houghton Library, Harvard University, ABC:18.4.8., vol. 1, no. 103, Correspondence of William G. Requa, Union Mission to the Osages, to Jeremiah Evarts, January 1, 1829, used by permission.

5. FIRST FRUITS OF THE CHEROKEE NATION

1. McLoughlin, "Cherokee Anomie, 1794–1810," 456–57.
2. McLoughlin, *Cherokees and Missionaries, 1798–1839*, 6–7; Fogelson and Kutsche used the term "conscious acculturation" in "Cherokee Economic Cooperatives," 98.
3. Young, "The Cherokee Nation," 504; Perdue, "Cherokee Women and the Trail of Tears," 15–18.
4. McLoughlin, *Cherokees and Missionaries, 1798–1839*, 8–9.
5. Young, "The Cherokee Nation," 520.
6. McLoughlin, *Cherokees and Missionaries, 1798–1839*, 9.
7. "Inscription," in Brown, *Cherokee Sister*, 159.
8. Brown, *Cherokee Sister*, 4.
9. Catharine Brown to Loring S. Williams and Matilda Loomis Williams, July 5, 1819, in Brown, *Cherokee Sister*, 66.
10. Rubin, *Tears of Repentance*, 140–48.
11. Catharine Brown to Loring S. Williams and Matilda Loomis Williams, July 5, 1819, in Brown, *Cherokee Sister*, 67.
12. Catharine Brown to Mrs. A. H., April 17, 1820, in Brown, *Cherokee Sister*, 77.
13. "To a Young Lady in Philadelphia," January 28, 1820 in Brown, *Cherokee Sister*, 73.
14. "Catharine Brown to Matilda Williams," May 1822, in Brown, *Cherokee Sister*, 103.
15. Brown, *Cherokee Sister*, 45–47.
16. Anderson, *Memoir of Catharine Brown*, 12.
17. Brown, *Cherokee Sister*, 7–15.
18. Satz, "Cherokee Traditionalism," 381.
19. Wyss, *English Letters and Indian Literacies*, 111–14.
20. Philips and Phillips, "Introduction," *Brainerd Journal*, 16.

21. Anderson, *Memoir of Catharine Brown*, 20.
22. Martin, "Almost White," 43–46.
23. Anderson, *Memoir of Catharine Brown*, 164.
24. Martin, "Visions of Revitalization in the Eastern Woodlands," 75.
25. Phillips and Phillips, *Brainerd Journal*, 39.
26. Martin, "Visions of Revitalization in the Eastern Woodlands," 75–81.
27. Perdue, "Catherine Brown," in *Sifters*, 80–83.
28. Catharine Brown to William and Flora Hoyt Chamberlin, May 8, 1819, in Brown, *Cherokee Sister*, 65.
29. Anderson, *Memoir of Catharine Brown*, 92.
30. Anderson, *Memoir of Catharine Brown*, 54.
31. Perdue, "Catharine Brown," 89.
32. Rubin, *Tears of Repentance*, 126.
33. Catharine Brown to David Brown, August 10, 1821, in Brown, *Cherokee Sister*, 94.
34. Anderson, *Memoir of Catharine Brown*, in Brown, *Cherokee Sister*, 253.
35. Anderson, *Memoir of Catharine Brown*, in Brown, *Cherokee Sister*, 257.
36. Phillips and Phillips, *Brainerd Journal*, 32.
37. Phillips and Phillips, *Brainerd Journal*, June 20, 1820, 180.
38. Phillips and Phillips, *Brainerd Journal*, February 9, 1821, 208.
39. Phillips and Phillips, *Brainerd Journal*, 67.
40. Phillips and Phillips, *Brainerd Journal*, 68–69.
41. Phillips and Phillips, *Brainerd Journal*, 169.
42. Phillips and Phillips, *Brainerd Journal*, 169.
43. Brown, *Cherokee Sister*, diary, May 20, 1820, 115.
44. Brown, *Cherokee Sister*, diary, May 20, 1820, 115.
45. Brown, *Cherokee Sister*, diary, February 10, 1823, 111.
46. Wyss, *English Letters and Indian Literacies*, 111.
47. Wyss, *English Letters and Indian Literacies*, 6–14.
48. Martin, "Crisscrossing Projects of Sovereignty and Conversion," 67–81.
49. Phillips and Phillips, *Brainerd Journal*, January 23, 1820, 152.
50. Phillips and Phillips, *Brainerd Journal*, March 3, 1820, 156.
51. Catharine Brown to David Brown, February 16, 1822, in Brown, *Cherokee Sister*, 97.
52. Catharine Brown to David Brown, October 21, 1821, in Brown, *Cherokee Sister*, 90–91.
53. Catherine Brown to David Brown, June 13, 1823, in Brown, *Cherokee Sister*, 113.
54. Martin, "Crisscrossing Projects of Sovereignty and Conversion," 69.
55. Brown, "Address of Dewi Brown," 30.
56. Brown, "Address of Dewi Brown," 31.

57. Brown, "Address of Dewi Brown," 33.
58. Brown, "Address of Dewi Brown," 36.
59. Wyss, *English Letters and Indian Literacies*, 189.
60. Phillips and Phillips, *Brainerd Journal*, October 15, 1832, 382.
61. *Memoir of John Arch*, 8; Phillips and Phillips, *Brainerd Journal*, January 26, 1819, 104.
62. *Memoir of John Arch*, 11.
63. Sigourney, *Traits of the Aborigines of America*, 168. Several lines of this verse are quoted in Miles, *The House on Diamond Hill*, 184.
64. Miles, *The House on Diamond Hill*, 50–55.
65. Miles, *The House on Diamond Hill*, 51.
66. Crews, *Faith and Tears*, 45.
67. Crews, *Faith and Tears*, 45.
68. Perdue, *Cherokee Editor*, 44–45.
69. McClinton, "Catalog of Scholars," in *The Moravian Springplace Mission to the Cherokees*, vol. 2., 448.
70. McClinton, "Introduction," *The Moravian Springplace Mission to the Cherokees*, vol. 1, 16.
71. McClinton, "Introduction," 22–23.
72. McClinton, "Introduction," 23.
73. McClinton, "Introduction," 60.
74. Rubin, *Tears of Repentance*, 200.
75. Weber, "Social Psychology of the World Religions," 274.
76. Rubin, *Tears of Repentance*, 197.
77. McClinton, *The Moravian Springplace Mission to the Cherokees*, vol. 1, 364.
78. McClinton, *The Moravian Springplace Mission to the Cherokees*, vol. 1, 364.
79. McClinton, "Introduction," 30.
80. McClinton, *The Moravian Springplace Mission to the Cherokees*, vol. 1, 375.
81. McClinton, *The Moravian Springplace Mission to the Cherokees*, vol. 1, 376.
82. McClinton, *The Moravian Springplace Mission to the Cherokees*, vol. 1, 378.
83. McClinton, *The Moravian Springplace Mission to the Cherokees*, vol. 1, 421.
84. McClinton, *The Moravian Springplace Mission to the Cherokees*, vol. 1, 409.
85. McClinton, *The Moravian Springplace Mission to the Cherokees*, vol. 1, 425.
86. McClinton, *The Moravian Springplace Mission to the Cherokees*, vol. 1, 467.
87. McClinton, *The Moravian Springplace Mission to the Cherokees*, vol. 1, 490.
88. Gaul, *To Marry an Indian*, 5.
89. McClinton, *The Moravian Springplace Mission to the Cherokees*, vol. 1, 424.
90. McClinton, *The Moravian Springplace Mission to the Cherokees*, vol. 1, 424.
91. McClinton, *The Moravian Springplace Mission to the Cherokees*, vol. 1, 424.

92. McClinton, *The Moravian Springplace Mission to the Cherokees*, vol. 1, 495.
93. McClinton, *The Moravian Springplace Mission to the Cherokees*, vol. 2, 185–86.
94. McClinton, *The Moravian Springplace Mission to the Cherokees*, vol. 2, 186.
95. Miles, *The House on Diamond Hill*, 159.
96. Perdue and Green, *The Cherokee Removal*, 125.
97. Miles, *The House on Diamond Hill*, 160.
98. I borrow the term "aggressively conversionist" from Peyer, *The Tutor'd Mind*.
99. Miles, *The House on Diamond Hill*, 160.
100. Miles, *The House on Diamond Hill*, 184.
101. Miles, *The House on Diamond Hill*, 170–71.
102. McClinton, *The Moravian Springplace Mission to the Cherokees*, vol. 2, 346.
103. Sister Margaret Ann did not appear to understand the problems associated with fulfilling her desire for a new community.
104. McClinton, *The Moravian Springplace Mission to the Cherokees*, vol. 2, 349.
105. McClinton, *The Moravian Springplace Mission to the Cherokees*, vol. 2, 348.
106. McClinton, *The Moravian Springplace Mission to the Cherokees*, vol. 2, 348.
107. McClinton, *The Moravian Springplace Mission to the Cherokees*, vol. 2, 388.
108. McClinton, *The Moravian Springplace Mission to the Cherokees*, vol. 2, 389.
109. McClinton, *The Moravian Springplace Mission to the Cherokees*, vol. 2, 389.
110. Martin, "Almost White," 60.
111. Young, "The Cherokee Nation," 520.
112. Perdue, "Catharine Brown," 89.
113. Irwin, *Coming Down from Above*, 7.
114. Irwin, *Coming Down from Above*, 202–10.

6. MÉTIS CHRISTIAN INDIAN LIVES

1. Murphy, *Great Lakes Creoles*, 2–17.
2. Tuttle, *Conversations on the Mackinaw and Green-Bay Indian Missions*, 42–48; Widder, *Battle for the Soul*, 158.
3. Peyer, *The Tutor'd Mind*, 243.
4. Widder, *Battle for the Soul*, 159–60.
5. Widder, *Battle for the Soul*, 162.
6. Widder, *Battle for the Soul*, 163.
7. Widder, *Battle for the Soul*, 163.
8. Tuttle, *Conversations on the Mackinaw and Green-Bay Indian Missions*, 48.
9. Widder, *Battle for the Soul*, 164.
10. Widder, *Battle for the Soul*, 157, 154–55.
11. Widder, *Battle for the Soul*, 166.
12. Widder, *Battle for the Soul*, 168.

13. Widder, *Battle for the Soul*, xiii–24.
14. Widder, *Battle for the Soul*, 14–15.
15. Fiola, *Rekindling the Sacred Fire*, 37–39.
16. Widder, *Battle for the Soul*, 25.
17. Widder, *Battle for the Soul*, 35.
18. Peters and Schenck, *My First Years in the Fur Trade*, 13–15, 42.
19. Nelson, "The Future of Illusions," 976.
20. Widder, *Battle for the Soul*, 70–75.
21. Konkle, *Writing Indian Nations*, 167.
22. Schoolcraft, *Personal Memoirs*, vol. 1, location 1730.
23. Schoolcraft, *Personal Memoirs*, vol. 1, location 3202.
24. Parker, *The Sound the Stars Make Rushing through the Sky*, 9.
25. Bremer, *Indian Agent and Wilderness Scholar*, 96–97.
26. Johnson, *A Shopkeeper's Millennium*, 15–36, finds that enterprising New England emigrants to Rochester, New York, during the era of the Finneyite revivals converted, joined churches, and married the daughters of established merchants and businessmen. These wives were the makers of self-made men.
27. General Correspondence, Henry Row Schoolcraft Papers, box 60, reel 4.
28. Unpublished poems, Jane Johnson Schoolcraft, Henry Row Schoolcraft Papers, box 60, reel 4, March 17, 1827.
29. General correspondence, Henry Row Schoolcraft Papers, box 60, reel 4, April 30, 1828.
30. General correspondence, Henry Row Schoolcraft Papers, box 60, reel 4, June 27, 1828.
31. Bremer, *Indian Agent and Wilderness Scholar*, 111.
32. Bremer, *Indian Agent and Wilderness Scholar*, 111.
33. Bremer, *Indian Agent and Wilderness Scholar*, 114–15.
34. Bremer, *Indian Agent and Wilderness Scholar*, 113.
35. Rabinowitz, *The Spiritual Self in Everyday Life*, 49–50, 94, 184.
36. Rubin, *Religious Melancholy and Protestant Experience in America*, 127.
37. Parker, *The Sound the Stars Make Rushing through the Sky*, 153.
38. Moore, *Practical Piety*, vol. 1, 30.
39. Moore, *Practical Piety*, vol. 1, 33.
40. Elmwood Diaries, Henry Row Schoolcraft Papers, box 60, reel 5, September 18, 1832.
41. Konkle, "Recovering Jane Schoolcraft's Cultural Activism," 86–87.
42. Parker, *The Sound the Stars Make Rushing through the Sky*, 151.
43. Parker, *The Sound the Stars Make Rushing through the Sky*, 140.

44. Schenck, *The Ojibwe Journals of Edmund F. Ely*, 51.
45. Schenck, *The Ojibwe Journals of Edmund F. Ely*, 51.
46. Schenck, *The Ojibwe Journals of Edmund F. Ely*, 54.
47. Schenck, "Introduction," in *The Ojibwe Journals of Edmund F. Ely*, xii–xvii.
48. Schenck, "Introduction," xvii–xviii.
49. Schenck, *The Ojibwe Journals of Edmund F. Ely*, 22.
50. Schenck, "Introduction," xviii.
51. Schenck, *The Ojibwe Journals of Edmund F. Ely*, 292.

CONCLUSION

1. Holmes, *Discourse*, 37.
2. Bradford, *A Discourse*, 5–6.
3. Simmons, *Spirit of the New England Tribes*, 281.
4. Moorhead, "Between Progress and Apocalypse," 531.
5. Nelson, "The Future of Illusions," 978.
6. Rubin, *The Other Side of Joy*, 156–57.
7. Renda, "Religion, Race, and Empire in the U.S.," 371.
8. Ruttenburg, *Democratic Personality*, 114.
9. Rubin, *Tears of Repentance*, 126.
10. King, *The Iron of Melancholy*, 5.
11. See also the invented autobiography of George Copway: Copway, *Life, Letters, and Speeches*.
12. Oberg, *Professional Indian*, ix, 138.
13. Oberg, *Professional Indian*, 17–22.
14. Oberg, *Professional Indian*, 33.
15. Oberg, *Professional Indian*, 34–76.
16. Oberg, *Professional Indian*, 164–65.
17. Oberg, *Professional Indian*, 206.

BIBLIOGRAPHY

UNPUBLISHED WORKS

American Board of Commissioners for Foreign Missions Archives, 1810–1961. Houghton Library, Harvard University, Cambridge MA.

Bacon Family Papers, 1800–1933. Manuscripts and Archives Collection, Sterling Memorial Library, Yale University, New Haven CT.

Clonassey, Thomas, and Cornell, Andrew. Middletown Probate District Estate Papers, 1752–1880. Connecticut State Library, Hartford.

Curtis, Philo Nichols. "Dissertation on Intermittent Fever." MD thesis, Yale University, 1842.

Edwards Family Papers, 1805–1874. Sterling Memorial Library Manuscripts, Yale University, New Haven CT.

Goodrich, Elizur. Account Books, 1759–1783. Connecticut Historical Society Library, Hartford CT.

Harvey Harris Bloom Papers. Manuscripts and Archives, Yale University Library, New Haven CT.

Hoyle, Lydia Huntington. "Missionary Women among the American Indians, 1815–1865." Ph.D. diss., University of North Carolina at Chapel Hill, 1992.

Journal of the Union Mission to the Osage, 1820–1826. Oklahoma Historical Society, Norman.

Litchfield, Connecticut, Town Records. Ingraham Library, Litchfield Historical Society, Litchfield CT.

Missionary Society of Connecticut Papers, 1759–1948. Sterling Memorial Library, Manuscripts and Archives Collection, Yale University, New Haven CT.

Schoolcraft, Henry Rowe. 1822–1833, General Correspondence. Henry Rowe Schoolcraft Papers. Library of Congress, Washington DC.

PUBLISHED WORKS

Ackerknecht, Erwin Heinz. *Malaria in the Upper Mississippi Valley, 1760–1900*. Baltimore: Johns Hopkins University Press, 1945.

Ahlstrom, Sydney E. *A Religious History of the American People*. New Haven CT: Yale University Press, 1972.

Anderson, Rufus. *Memoir of Catharine Brown: A Christian Indian of the Cherokee Nation*. 3rd ed. New York: Crocker and Brewster, 1828.

Andrew, John A. "Educating the Heathen: The Foreign Mission School Controversy and American Ideals." *Journal of American Studies* 12, no. 3 (1978): 331–42.

———. *Rebuilding the Christian Commonwealth: New England Congregationalists & Foreign Missions, 1800–1830*. Lexington: University Press of Kentucky, 1976.

Andrews, Edward E. *Native Apostles: Black and Indian Missionaries in the British Atlantic World*. Cambridge MA: Harvard University Press, 2013.

Bacon, Leonard. *Sketch of the Rev. David Bacon*. Boston: Congregational Publishing Society, 1876.

Baird, W. David. *The Osage People*. Phoenix: Indian Tribal Series, 1972.

Beck, James R. *Dorothy Carey: The Tragic and Untold Story of Mrs. William Carey*. Grand Rapids MI: Baker Book House, 1992.

———. "Missions and Mental Health: Lessons from History." *Theory and Practice* 21:9–17.

Beecher, Lyman. *Autobiography, Correspondence, etc., of Lyman Beecher, D.D.* Edited by Charles Beecher. New York: Harper, 1865.

Berkhofer, Robert F. *Salvation and the Savage: An Analysis of Protestant Missions and American Indian Response, 1787–1862*. Westport CT: Greenwood, 1977.

Billings, John Shaw. *The National Medical Dictionary: Including English, French, German, Italian, and Latin Technical Terms Used in Medicine and the Collateral Sciences, and a Series of Tables of Useful Data*. 2 vols. Philadelphia: Lea Brothers. 1890.

Bliss, Edwin Munsell. *The Encyclopedia of Missions, Descriptive, Historical, Biographical, Statistical*. 2 vols. New York: Funk and Wagnalls, 1891.

Bowden, Henry Warner. *American Indians and Christian Missions: Studies in Cultural Conflict*. Chicago: University of Chicago Press, 1981.

Boyd, Colleen E., and Coll Thrush. "Introduction: Bringing Ghosts to Ground." In *Phantom Past, Indigenous Presence: Native Ghosts in North American Culture and History*, edited by Colleen E. Boyd and Coll Thrush, vii–xxxix. Lincoln: University of Nebraska Press, 2011.

Bradford, Alden. *A Discourse Delivered before the Society for Propagating the Gospel among the Indians and Others, in North America, November 4, 1830*. Boston: J. Putnam, 1830.

Bremer, Richard G. *Indian Agent and Wilderness Scholar: The Life of Henry Rowe Schoolcraft*. Mount Pleasant MI: Clarke Historical Library, Central Michigan University, 1987.

Brown, Barbara W., and James M. Rose. *Black Roots in Southeastern Connecticut*. Detroit MI: Gale, 1980.

Brown, Catharine. *Cherokee Sister: The Collected Writings of Catharine Brown, 1818–1823*. Edited by Theresa Srouth Gaul. Lincoln: University of Nebraska Press, 2014.

Brown, David. "Address of Dewi Brown, A Cherokee Indian." *Proceedings of the Massachusetts Historical Society* 12:30–36.

Brumberg, Joan Jacobs. *Mission for Life: The Story of the Family of Adoniram Judson, the Dramatic Events of the First American Foreign Mission, and the Course of Evangelical Religion in the Nineteenth Century*. New York: Free Press, 1980.

Butler, Jon. *Awash in a Sea of Faith: Christianizing the American People*. Cambridge MA: Harvard University Press, 1992.

Carey, William. *An Inquiry into the Obligation of Christians to Use Means for the Conversion of the Heathens*. Leicester, UK: Ann Ireland, 1792.

Cayton, Mary Kupiec. "Canonizing Harriet Newell: Women, the Evangelical Press, and the Foreign Mission Movement in New England, 1800–1840." In *Competing Kingdoms: Women, Mission, Nation, and the American Protestant Empire, 1812–1960*, edited by Barbara Reeves-Ellington, Kathryn Kish Sklar, and Connie A. Shemo. Durham NC: Duke University Press, 2010.

Champion, George, and Alan R. Booth. *Journal of the Rev. George Champion, American Missionary in Zululand, 1835–9*. Cape Town: C. Struik, 1967.

Champion, Sarah Elizabeth Booth, and George Champion. *Rev. George Champion, Pioneer Missionary to the Zulus: Sketch of His Life and Extracts from His Journal, 1834–8*. New Haven CT: Tuttle, Morehouse & Taylor, 1896.

Chapman, Carl Haley. *The Origin of the Osage Indian Tribe*. New York: Garland, 1974.

Clemmons, Linda M. *Conflicted Mission: Faith, Disputes, and Deception on the Dakota Frontier*. Saint Paul: Minnesota Historical Society Press, 2014.

Conforti, Joseph A. *Jonathan Edwards, Religious Tradition & American Culture*. Chapel Hill: University of North Carolina Press, 1995.

Connecticut Secretary of State. *State of Connecticut Register and Manual 1972*. Hartford: Secretary of State, 1972.

Copway, George (Kahgegagahbowh). *Life, Letters, and Speeches*. Edited by A.

LaVonne Brown Ruoff and Donald B. Smith. Lincoln: University of Nebraska Press, 1997.

Cornelius, Elias. *The Little Osage Captive: Account of an Osage Girl, Rescued by the Author from the Cherokee Indians and Named Lydia Carter*. New York: S. T. Armstrong, 1822.

Cott, Nancy F. *The Bonds of Womanhood: "Woman's Sphere" in New England, 1780–1835*. New Haven CT: Yale University Press, 1977.

Crews, Daniel C. *Faith and Tears: The Moravian Mission among the Cherokee*. Winston-Salem NC: Moravian Archives, 2000.

Degler, Carl N. *At Odds: Women and the Family in America from the Revolution to the Present*. New York: Oxford University Press, 1981.

De Jong, James A. *As the Waters Cover the Sea: Millennial Expectations in the Rise of Anglo-American Missions 1640–1810*. Laurel MS: Audubon, 2006.

Demos, John. *The Heathen School: A Story of Hope and Betrayal in the Age of the Early Republic*. New York: Alfred A. Knopf, 2014.

Densmore, Christopher. *Red Jacket: Iroquois Diplomat and Orator*. Syracuse: Syracuse University Press, 1996.

DeRogatis, Amy. *Moral Geography: Maps, Missionaries, and the American Frontier*. New York: Columbia University Press, 2003.

de Tocqueville, Alexis. *Democracy in America, Part the Second: The Social Influence of Democracy*. Translated by Henry Reeve. New York: J & H G Langley, 1840.

Dinnerstein, Myra. *The American Board Missions to the Zulu, 1835–1900*. Columbia University, 1971.

Dippie, Brian W. *The Vanishing American: White Attitudes and U.S. Indian Policy*. Lawrence: University Press of Kansas, 1991.

Drake, Daniel. *A Systematic Treatise, Historical, Etiological and Practical, on the Principal Diseases of the Interior Valley of North America: As They Appear in the Caucasian, African, Indian, and Esquimaux Varieties of Its Population*. Cincinnati: Winthrop B. Smith, 1850.

Duffy, John. *Epidemics in Colonial America*. Baton Rouge: Louisiana State University Press, 1953.

Durkheim, Emile, and Marcel Mauss. *Primitive Classification*. Chicago: University of Chicago Press, 1963.

DuVal, Kathleen. *The Native Ground: Indians and Colonists in the Heart of the Continent*. Philadelphia: University of Pennsylvania Press, 2006.

Edwards, Bela Bass. *Memoir of Rev. Elias Cornelius*. Boston: Perkins and Marvin, 1883.

Edwards, Jonathan. *The Life of David Brainerd*. Edited by John E. Smith. Vol. 7, *The Works of Jonathan Edwards*. New Haven: Yale University Press, 1985. First published 1749.

Elsbree, Oliver Wendell. *The Rise of the Missionary Spirit in America, 1790–1815.* Williamsport PA: Williamsport Printing and Binding, 1928.
Emmons, Nathanael, Jacob Ide, and Edwards Amasa Park. *The Works of Nathanael Emmons, D.D., Third Pastor of the Church in Franklin, Mass.: With a Memoir of His Life.* 6 vols. Boston: Congregational Board of Publication, 1860.
Faber, Michel. *The Book of Strange New Things.* New York: Hogarth, 2014.
Fenn, Elizabeth A. *Pox Americana: The Great Smallpox Epidemic of 1775–82.* New York: Hill and Wang, 2001.
Fiola, Chantal. *Rekindling the Sacred Fire: Metis Ancestry and Anishinaabe Spirituality.* Winnipeg, Manitoba: University of Manitoba Press, 2015.
Fogelson, Raymond D., and Paul Kutsche. "Cherokee Economic Cooperatives: The Gadugi." In *Symposium on Cherokee and Iroquois Culture,* edited by William N. Fenton and John Gulick. Washington DC: Government Printing Office, 1961.
Foreman, Carolyn T. "The Foreign Mission School at Cornwall, Connecticut." *Chronicles of Oklahoma* 7 (September 1927): 239–51.
Foreman, Grant. *Indians & Pioneers: The Story of the Southwest before 1830.* Norman: University of Oklahoma Press, 1936.
———. *Pioneer Days in the Early Southwest.* Cleveland: Arthur H. Clark, 1926.
Fowler, William Chauncey. *History of Durham, Connecticut, from the First Land Grant in 1662 to 1866.* Durham CT: Publication Committee, 1970.
Fredrickson, George. *White Supremacy: A Comparative Study in American and South African History.* New York: Oxford University Press, 1981.
Gabriel, Ralph Henry. *Elias Boudinot: Cherokee and His America.* Norman: University of Oklahoma Press, 1941.
Ganter, Granville. *The Collected Speeches of Sagoyewatha, or Red Jacket.* Syracuse: Syracuse University Press, 2006.
Gaul, Theresa Srouth. *To Marry an Indian: The Marriage of Harriet Gold and Elias Boudinot in Letters, 1823–1839.* Chapel Hill: University of North Carolina Press, 2005.
Gillespie, Joanna Bowen. "'The Clear Leadings of Providence': Pious Memoirs and the Problems of Self-Realization for Women in the Early Nineteenth Century." *Journal of the Early Republic* 5:197–221.
———. *The Life and Times of Martha Laurens Ramsay, 1759–1811.* Columbia: University of South Carolina Press, 2001.
Glatthaar, Joseph T., and James Kirby Martin. *Forgotten Allies: The Oneida Indians and the American Revolution.* New York: Hill and Wang, 2006.
Goodheart, Lawrence B. *Mad Yankees: The Hartford Retreat for the Insane and Nineteenth-Century Psychiatry.* Amherst: University of Massachusetts Press, 2003.

Graves, William White. *Annals of Osage Mission*. St. Paul KS: W.W. Graves, 1935.
———. *The First Protestant Osage Missions, 1820–1837*. Oswego KS: Carpenter, 1949.
Grimshaw, Patricia. *Paths of Duty: American Missionary Wives in Nineteenth-Century Hawaii*. Honolulu: University of Hawaii Press, 1989.
Gundlach, Bradley J. "Early American Missions from the Revolution to the Civil War." In *The Great Commission: Evangelicals and the History of World Missions*, edited by Martin I. Klauber and Scott M. Manetsch, 66–88. Nashville: B&H, 2008.
Hall, Timothy D. *Contested Boundaries: Itinerancy and the Shaping of the Colonial American Religious World*. Durham: Duke University Press, 1994.
Halsey, Francis Whiting. *Journal of Richard Smith*. New York: Scribner's, 1906.
———. *The Old New York Frontier: Its Wars with Indians and Tories, Its Missionary Schools, Pioneers and Land Titles, 1614–1800*. New York: Scribner's, 1901.
Hatch, Nathan O. *The Democratization of American Christianity*. New Haven CT: Yale University Press, 1989.
Hauptman, Laurence M. "The Oneida Nation: A Composite Portrait 1784–1816." In *The Oneida Journey*, edited by Laurence M. Hauptman and L. Gordon McLester III, 19–36. Madison: University of Wisconsin Press, 1999.
Hervey, William. *The Spirit of Missions, A Sermon Preached in Williamstown, Dec 13, 1829, and in Other Places*. Williamstown MA: Ridley Bannister, 1831.
Hoady, Charles J. *Colonial Records of Connecticut 1772–1775*. Vol. 14. Hartford CT: Hart, Case & Lockwood, 1887.
Holmes, Abiel. *A Discourse, Delivered before the Society for Propagating the Gospel among the Indians and Others in North America*. Boston: Belcher and Armstrong, 1808.
Hooker, Edward W. *Memoir of Mrs. Sarah L. Huntington Smith, Late of the American Mission in Syria*. 3rd ed. New York: American Tract Society, 1845.
Hopkins, Samuel, and Edwards Amasa Park. *The Works of Samuel Hopkins, D.D.* Boston: Doctrinal Tract and Book Society, 1854.
Hoyt, Dolly E. *Memoirs of Dolly E. Hoyt, A Member of the Union Mission Family: Who Died on the Arkansas River, While Ascending the Same, on Her Passage to the Osage Nation, the Place of Her Destination, AGED 23*. Danbury CT: O. Osborn, 1828.
Huntington, Susan. *Memoirs of Mrs. Susan Huntington Designed for the Young*. New Haven CT: A. H. Maltby, 1831.
Hutchison, William R. *Errand to the World: American Protestant Thought and Foreign Missions*. Chicago: University of Chicago Press, 1987.
Irwin, Lee. *Coming Down from Above: Prophecy, Resistance, and Renewal in Native American Religions*. Norman: University of Oklahoma Press, 2008.

Ives, Timothy H. "Reconstructing the Wangunk Reservation Land System: A Case Study of Native and Colonial Likeness in Central Connecticut." *Ethnohistory* 58:65–89.

Jensen, Richard E. *Pawnee Mission Letters, 1834–1851*. Lincoln: University of Nebraska Press, 2010.

Jette, Melinda Marie. Review of *Battle for the Soul: Metis Children Encounter Evangelical Protestants at Mackinaw Mission*, by Keith R. Widder. *Ethnohistory* 47:823–25.

Johnson, James. *The Influence of Tropical Climates on European Constitutions: Being a Treatise on the Principal Diseases Incidental to Europeans in the East and West Indies, Mediterranean, and Coast of Africa*. From the 3rd London ed. 2 vols. Philadelphia: B. & T. Kite, 1824.

Johnson, Paul E. *A Shopkeeper's Millennium: Society and Revivalism in Rochester, New York, 1815–1837*. New York: Hill and Wang, 1978.

Jones, Lot. *Memoir of Mrs. Sarah Louisa Taylor: Or, An Illustration of the Work of the Holy Spirit, in Awakening, Renewing, and Sanctifying the Heart*. New York Boston: J. S. Taylor, 1838.

Judson, Emily C. *The Kathayan Slave: And Other Papers Connected with Missionary Life*. Boston: Ticknor, Reed, and Fields, 1853.

Kellaway, William. *The New England Company 1649–1776, Missionary Society to the American Indians*. London: Longmans, 1961.

Keller, Charles Roy. *The Second Great Awakening in Connecticut*. Yale Historical Publications, Miscellany, 40. New Haven: Yale University Press, 1942.

King, John Owen. *The Iron of Melancholy: Structures of Spiritual Conversion in America from the Puritan Conscience to Victorian Neurosis*. Middletown CT: Wesleyan University Press, 1983.

Kling, David W. *A Field of Divine Wonders: The New Divinity and Village Revivals in Northwestern Connecticut, 1792–1822*. University Park: Pennsylvania State University Press, 1994.

———. 2003. "The New Divinity and the Origins of the American Board of Commissioners for Foreign Missions." *Church History: Studies in Christianity and Culture* 72:791–819.

Knowles, James D. *Memoir of Mrs. Ann H. Judson, Late Missionary to Burmah: Including a History of the American Baptist Mission in the Burman Empire*. 2nd ed. Boston: Lincoln & Edmands, 1829.

Konkle, Maureen. *Writing Indian Nations: Native Intellectuals and the Politics of Historiography, 1827–1863*. Chapel Hill: University of North Carolina Press, 2004.

———. "Recovering Jane Schoolcraft's Cultural Activism." In *The Oxford*

Handbook of Indigenous American Literature, edited by Daniel Heath Justice and James H. Cox, 81–102. New York: Oxford University Press, 2014.

Kotzé, D. J. *Letters of the American Missionaries, 1835–1838*. Cape Town: Van Riebeeck Society, 1950.

Lewis, Zechariah. *Letter to a Member of Congress, in Relation to Indian Civilization.* New York: D. Fanshaw, 1822.

Ludwig, Allan I. *Graven Images: New England Stonecarving and Its Symbols, 1650–1815.* Hanover NH: University Press of New England, 1999.

Macculloch, John. *An Essay on the Remittent and Intermittent Diseases.* Vol. 1. London: Longman, Rees, Orme, Brown, and Greene, 1828.

Martin, Joel W. "Almost White: The Ambivalent Promise of Christian Missions among the Cherokee." In *Religion and the Creation of Race and Ethnicity: An Introduction*, edited by Craig R. Prentiss, 43–60. New York: New York University Press, 2003.

———. "Crisscrossing Projects of Sovereignty and Conversion." In *Native Americans, Christianity, and the Reshaping of the American Religious Landscape*, edited by Joel W. Martin and Mark A. Nicholas, 67–92. Chapel Hill: University of North Carolina Press, 2010.

———. "Visions of Revitalization in the Eastern Woodlands: Can a Middle-Aged Theory Stretch to Embrace the First Cherokee Converts?" In *Reassessing Revitalization Movements: Perspectives from North America and the Pacific Islands*, edited by Michael E. Harkin, 61–87. Lincoln: University of Nebraska Press, 2004.

Mathews, John Joseph. *The Osages: Children of the Middle Waters.* Norman: University of Oklahoma Press, 1961.

McClinton, Rowena, ed. *The Moravian Springplace Mission to the Cherokees.* 2 vols. Lincoln: University of Nebraska Press, 2007.

McCoy, Isaac. *History of Baptist Indian Missions. Embracing Remarks on the Former and Present Condition of the Aboriginal Tribes: Their Settlement within the Indian Territory, and Their Future Prospects.* New York: W.M. Morrison, 1840.

McLoughlin, William G. "Cherokee Anomie, 1794–1810: New Roles for Red Men, Red Women, and Black Slaves." In *American Encounters: Natives and Newcomers from European Contact to Indian Removal, 1500–1850*, edited by Peter C. Mancall and James H. Merrell, 452–76. New York: Rutledge, 2000.

———. *Cherokees and Missionaries, 1789–1839.* Norman: University of Oklahoma Press, 1995.

Memoir of John Arch, a Cherokee Young Man, Compiled from Communications of Missionaries in the Cherokee Nation. 2nd. ed. Boston: Massachusetts Sabbath School Union, 1832.

Miles, Tiya. *The House on Diamond Hill: A Cherokee Plantation Story*. Chapel Hill: University of North Carolina Press, 2010.

Miller, Perry. *The Life of the Mind in America: From the Revolution to the Civil War*. New York: Harcourt, 1965.

Mills, Samuel J., and Daniel Smith. "Report of a Missionary Tour through That Part of the United States Which Lies West of the Allegany Mountains: Performed under the Direction of the Massachusetts Missionary Society." In *To Win the West: Missionary Viewpoints 1814–1815*, edited by Edwin S. Gaustad, 1–64. New York: Arno, 1972. First printed 1815.

Miner, Thomas, and William Tully. *Essays on Fevers: And Other Medical Subjects*. Middletown CT: E. & H. Clark, 1823.

Moore, Hannah. *Practical Piety: Or the Influence of the Heart on the Conduct of Life*. Boston: Monroe and Francis, 1811.

Moorhead, James H. "Between Progress and Apocalypse: A Reassessment of Millennialism in American Religious Thought, 1800–1840." *Journal of American History* 71: 524–42.

Morse, Jedidiah. *A Report to the Secretary of War of the United States, on Indian Affairs, Comprising a Narrative of a Tour Performed in the Summer of 1820, under a Commission from the President of the United States, for the Purpose of Ascertaining, for the Use of the Government, the Actual State of the Indian Tribes in Our Country*. New Haven: S. Converse, 1822.

———. *The First Annual Report of the American Society for Promoting the Civilization and General Improvement of the Indian Tribes in the United States: Communicated to the Society, in the City of Washington, with the Documents in the Appendix, at Their Meeting, Feb. 6, 1824*. New Haven: S. Converse, 1824.

Murphy, Lucy Eldersveld. *Great Lakes Creoles: A French-Indian Community on the Northern Borderlands, Prairie du Chien, 1750–1860*. New York: Cambridge University Press, 2014.

Nelson, Benjamin. "The Future of Illusions." In *Man in Contemporary Society: A Source Book Prepared by the Contemporary Civilization Staff of Columbia College, Columbia University*, 958–79. New York: Columbia University Press, 1956.

Newell, Harriet, and Leonard Woods. *Memoirs of Mrs. Harriet Newell: Wife of the Rev. S. Newell, American Missionary to INDIA, Who Died at the Isle of France, Nov. 30, 1812, Aged 19: Also a Sermon on Occasion of Her Death, Preached at Haverhill, Massachusetts*. 2nd ed. London: Booth, 1816.

Newell, Margaret Ellen. *Brethren by Nature: New England Indians, Colonists, and the Origins of American Slavery*. Ithaca NY: Cornell University Press, 2015.

———. "Indian Slavery in Colonial New England." In *Indian Slavery in Colonial*

America, edited by Allan Gallay, 33–66. Lincoln: University of Nebraska Press, 2009.

Nichols, David Andrew. *Red Gentlemen and White Savages: Indians, Federalists, and the Search for Order on the American Frontier*. Charlottesville: University of Virginia Press, 2008.

Noll, Mark A. *America's God: From Jonathan Edwards to Abraham Lincoln*. New York: Oxford University Press, 2002.

Nord, Paul. *Faith in Reading: Religious Publications and the Birth of Mass Media in America*. New York: Oxford University Press, 2004.

Nuttall, Thomas. *A Journal of Travels into the Arkansa Territory, during the Year 1819: With Occasional Observations on the Manners of the Aborigines: Illustrated by a Map and Other Engravings*. Philadelphia: T.H. Palmer, 1821.

Oberg, Michael Leroy. *Professional Indian: The American Odyssey of Eleazar Williams*. Philadelphia: University of Pennsylvania Press, 2015.

Parker, Robert Dale. *The Sound the Stars Make Rushing through the Sky: The Writings of Jane Johnston Schoolcraft*. Philadelphia: University of Pennsylvania Press, 2007.

Parmelee, D. L. *Discourse on the Semi-Centennial of the Litchfield County Foreign Mission Society*. Hartford CT: Goodwin, 1861.

Pastor's New Year's Greeting: No. XI, 1892, Memorial Presbyterian Church, Detroit, Michigan [In Memory of David Bacon and of Alice Parks, His Heroic Wife]. Detroit: O. S. Gulley, Bomman, 1892.

Pearce, Roy Harvey. *Savagism and Civilization: A Study of the Indian and the American Mind*. Baltimore: Johns Hopkins University Press, 1965.

Perdue, Theda. *Cherokee Editor: The Writings of Elias Boudinot*. Knoxville: University of Tennessee Press, 1983.

———. "Cherokee Women and the Trail of Tears." *Journal of Women's History* 1:14–30.

———. *Sifters: Native American Women's Lives*, edited by Theda Perdue, 77–91. New York: Oxford University Press, 2001.

Perdue, Theda, and Michael D. Green. *The Cherokee Removal: A Brief History with Documents*. New York: St. Martin's, 1995.

Peters, Laura, and Theresa Schenck. 2002. *My First Years in the Fur Trade: The Journals of 1802–1804*. Montreal: McGill-Queens University Press.

Pettit, Norman. "Introduction." In *The Life of David Brainerd*. New Haven: Yale University Press, 1985.

Peyer, Bernd. *The Tutor'd Mind: Indian Missionary-writers in Antebellum America*. Amherst: University of Massachusetts Press, 1997.

Phillips, Joyce B., and Paul Gary Phillips. *The Brainerd Journal: A Mission to the Cherokees, 1817–1823*. Lincoln: University of Nebraska Press, 1998.

Pierson, H. W. *American Missionary Memorial*. New York: Harper and Brothers, 1853.
Pilkington, Walter. *Journals of Samuel Kirkland: Eighteenth-Century Missionary to the Iroquoians, Government Agent, Father of Hamilton College*. Clinton NY: Hamilton College, 1980.
Prucha, Francis Paul. *American Indian Policy in the Formative Years: The Indian Trade and Intercourse Acts, 1790–1834*. Lincoln: University of Nebraska Press, 1970.
Pruitt, Lisa Joy. *A Looking Glass for Ladies: American Protestant Women and the Orient in the Nineteenth Century*. Macon GA: Mercer University Press, 2005.
Rabinowitz, Richard. *The Spiritual Self in Everyday Life: The Transformation of Personal Religious Experience in Nineteenth-Century New England*. Boston: Northeastern University Press, 1989.
Reeves-Ellington, Barbara, Kathryn Kish Sklar, and Connie A. Shemo. *Competing Kingdoms: Women, Mission, Nation, and the American Protestant Empire, 1812–1960*. Durham NC: Duke University Press, 2010.
Renda, Mary A. "Religion, Race, and Empire in the U.S. Protestant Women's Missionary Enterprise, 1812–1960." In *Competing Kingdoms: Women, Mission, Nation, and the American Protestant Empire, 1812–1960*, edited by Barbara Reeves-Ellington, Kathryn Kish Sklar, and Connie A. Shemo, 367–89. Durham: Duke University Press, 2010.
Richter, Daniel K. *Facing East from Indian Country: A Native History of Early America*. Cambridge MA: Harvard University Press, 2001.
Rogers, Richard Lee. "'A Bright and New Constellation': The Millennial Narrative of American Foreign Missions." In *North American Foreign Missions, 1810–1914: Theology, Theory, and Policy*, edited by Wilbert R. Shenk, 39–60. Grand Rapids MI: William B. Eerdmans, 2004.
Rohrer, James R. *Keepers of the Covenant: Frontier Missions and the Decline of Congregationalism, 1774–1818*. New York: Oxford University Press, 1995.
Rollings, Willard Hughes. *Unaffected by the Gospel. Osage Resistance to the Christian Invasion, 1673–1906: A Cultural Victory*. Albuquerque: University of New Mexico Press, 2004.
Ronda, James P. "Reverend Samuel Kirkland and the Oneida Indians." In *The Oneida Experience, Two Perspectives*, edited by Jack Campisi and Laurence M. Hauptman, 23–30. Syracuse: Syracuse University Press, 1998.
Rubin, Julius H. "The Deferred Ministry of James Lockwood Wright." *Publick Post* 94 (Summer 2001): 1–4. Proceedings of the Glastonbury Historical Society, Glastonbury CT.
———. "Mental Illness in Early Nineteenth-Century New England and the Beginnings of Institutional Psychiatry as Revealed in a Sociological Study

of the Hartford Retreat, 1824–1843." Ph.D. diss., New School for Social Research. Ann Arbor: University Microprint, 1979.

———. *The Other Side of Joy: Religious Melancholy among the Bruderhof*. New York: Oxford University Press, 2000.

———. *Religious Melancholy and Protestant Experience in America*. New York: Oxford University Press, 1994.

———. *Tears of Repentance: Christian Indian Identity and Community in Colonial Southern New England*. Lincoln: University of Nebraska Press, 2013.

Ruttenburg, Nancy. *Democratic Personality: Popular Voice and the Trial of American Authorship*. Princeton NJ: Princeton University Press, 1998.

Sabathy-Judd, Linda. *Moravians in Upper Canada: The Diary of the Indian Mission of Fairfield on the Thames, 1792–1813*. Toronto: Champlain Society, 1999.

Sargent, John. *Life and Letters of the Rev. Henry Martyn, B.D., Late Fellow of St. John's College, Cambridge, and Chaplain*. New ed. London: Seeley, Jackson, and Halliday, 1881.

Satz, Ronald N. "Cherokee Traditionalism, Protestant Evangelism, and the Trail of Tears, Part II." *Tennessee Historical Quarterly* 44: 380–401.

Schenck, Theresa M. *The Ojibwe Journals of Edmund F. Ely*. Lincoln: University of Nebraska Press, 2012.

Schoolcraft, Henry Rowe. *Personal Memoirs of a Residence of Thirty Years with the Indian Tribes of the American Frontiers*. 2 vols. Philadelphia: Waxkeep, 1842.

Schultz, George A. *An Indian Canaan: Isaac McCoy and the Vision of an Indian State*. Norman: University of Oklahoma Press, 1972.

Sexton, Ray O., and Richard C. Maddock. 1980. "The Missionary Syndrome." *Journal of Religion and Health* 19:59–65.

Sigourney, Lydia H. *Traits of Aborigines of America: A Poem*. Cambridge MA: Hillard and Metcalf, 1822.

Sill, E. N., and David Bacon. *Proceedings in Commemoration of the Fiftieth Anniversary of the Settlement of Tallmadge*. Akron OH: Beebe & Elkins, 1857.

Simmons, William S. *Spirit of the New England Tribes: Indian History and Folklore*. Hanover NH: University Press of New England, 1986.

Spence, Jonathan D. *The Question of Hu*. New York: Alfred A. Knopf, 1998.

Sprague, William Buell, and Leonard Woods. *Lectures on Revivals of Religion*. Albany, New York: Webster & Skinners, 1832.

Spring, Gardiner. *Memoirs of Rev. Samuel John Mills*. 2nd ed. Boston: Perkins & Marvin, 1829.

Starr, Edward C. *A History of Cornwall, Connecticut: A Typical New England Town*. New Haven CT: Tuttle, Morehouse & Taylor, 1926.

Stouffer, Samuel A., Edward A. Suchman, Leland C. DeVinney, Shirley A. Star, and Robin M. Williams Jr. *Studies in Social Psychology in World War II: The American Soldier.* Vol. 1, *Adjustment during Army Life.* Princeton: Princeton University Press, 1949.

Stout, Harry S., and D. G. Hart. *New Directions in American Religious History.* New York: Oxford University Press, 1997.

Strong, John. *The Unkechaug Indians of Eastern Long Island.* Norman: University of Oklahoma Press, 2011.

Taylor, Charles. *Sources of the Self: The Making of the Modern Identity.* Cambridge: Harvard University Press, 1989.

Tiro, Karim M. *The People of the Standing Stone: The Oneida Nation from the Revolution through the Era of Removal.* Amherst: University of Massachusetts Press, 2011.

Tracy, Joseph. *History of the American Board of Commissioners for Foreign Missions Compiled Chiefly from the Published and Unpublished Documents of the Board.* New York: M. W. Dodd, 1842.

Tuttle, Sarah. *Conversations on the Mackinaw and Green-Bay Missions.* Boston: T. R. Marvin for the Massachusetts Sabbath School Union, 1831.

Tyler, Bennet. *Memoir of the Life and Character of Rev. Asahel Nettleton, D.D.* Hartford: Robins & Smith, 1844.

Vanderpoel, Emily Noyes, and Elizabeth Cynthia Barney Buel. *Chronicles of a Pioneer School from 1792 to 1833: Being the History of Miss Sarah Pierce and Her Litchfield School.* Cambridge MA: Cambridge University Press, 1903.

Wallace, Anthony F. C. *The Death and Rebirth of the Seneca.* New York: Vintage Books, 1972.

Wardell, Morris. "Protestant Missions among the Osage, 1830-1838." *Chronicles of Oklahoma* 2 (September 1924): 285–97.

Weber, Max. "The Social Psychology of the World Religions." In *From Max Weber: Essays in Sociology,* edited by C. Mills Wright and H. H. Gerth, 267–301. New York: Oxford University Press, 1958.

Weddle, David L. "The Melancholy Saint: Jonathan's Edwards's Interpretation of David Brainerd as a Model of Evangelical Spirituality." *Harvard Theological Review* 81 (1998): 297–318.

Weigold, Isabel B. *Hannah Moore: A Biography of a Nineteenth-Century Missionary and Teacher.* New York: iUniverse, 2007.

Welter, Barbara. "She Hath Done What She Could: Protestant Women's Missionary Careers in Nineteenth-Century America." In *Women in American Religion,* edited by Janet Wilson James, 111–25. Philadelphia: University of Pennsylvania Press, 1980.

Westerkamp, Marilyn J. *Women and Religion in Early America, 1600–1850: The Puritan and Evangelical Traditions.* New York: Routledge, 1999.

White, Alain Campbell. *The History of the Town of Litchfield, Connecticut, 1720–1920*. Litchfield CT: Enquirer Print, 1920.

White, Ann. "Counting the Cost of Faith: America's Early Female Missionaries." *Church History* 57, no. 1 (March 1988): 19–30.

Widder, Keith R. *Battle for the Soul: Metis Children Encounter Evangelical Protestants at Mackinaw Mission, 1823–1837*. East Lansing: Michigan State University Press, 1999.

Willis, Thomas. *A Short Account of the Religious Exercise and Experience of Betty, An Indian Woman: One of the Last of an Ancient Tribe of Indians That Inhabited the South Side of Long-Island*. New York: Samuel Wood, 1830.

Wilson, James. *The Earth Shall Weep: A History of Native America*. New York: Grove, 1998.

Wilson, Terry P. *Bibliography of the Osage*, Native American Bibliography Series 6. Metuchen NJ: Scarecrow, 1985.

Winslow, Miron. *The Memoir of Mrs. Harriet L. Winslow*. New York: American Tract Society, 1840.

Woods, Leonard. *A Sermon Occasioned by the Death of Samuel Worcester*. Salem MA: Henry Whipple, 1821.

Wyss, Hilary E. *English Letters and Indian Literacies: Reading, Writing, and New England Missionary Schools, 1750–1830*. Philadelphia: University of Pennsylvania Press, 2012.

Yalom, Irving D. *Staring at the Sun: Overcoming the Terror of Death*. San Francisco: Jossey-Bass, 2008.

Young, Mary. "The Cherokee Nation: Mirror of the Republic." *American Quarterly* 33:504–24.

INDEX

ABCFM (American Board of Commissioners for Foreign Missions). *See* American Board of Commissioners for Foreign Missions (ABCFM)
acculturation, 28, 49, 106–7, 115, 121–23
Ackerknecht, Erwin Heinz, 66, 204n44
Agwrondougwas (Good Peter), xv
Alden, Bradford, 187–88
Algic Researches (Schoolcraft), 173
Allis, Samuel, 78
American Bible Society, 76
American Board of Commissioners for Foreign Missions (ABCFM): Brainerd Mission, 132–33; candidate selection process, 79, 171; closing Osage missions, 109–10; and the Cornwall Foreign Mission School, 112–13, 114; establishment of, 4, 81; Flat Head Indians missions, 78; Fond du Lac Mission, 181–83; gender role allocation, 191; and Hannah Moore, 91–92; Hawaiian missions, 93–96; Litchfield chapter, 55; position on marriage, 93; on racial discrimination, 115–16; South African missions, 89–90; and the UFMS, 117
American Fur Company, 170, 182
American huckster, 46
American Missionary Memorial (Pierson), 87–88
American Sunday School Union, 76
American Tract Society (ATS), 76
Anderson, Rufus, 124, 126, 127–29, 132
Andover Theological Seminary, 4, 12, 77
Andrews, Edward E., xv–xvi
Anishinaabe tribes, 170–71
Arch, John, 139–40
asylums: chronic patients at, 205n67; Hartford Retreat, 47, 53, 70–73; John Hu in, 100; K's treatment at, 99, 117; moral treatment of the insane, 71–72, 117
Atlantic world: and the Great Commission, 2–3; Native missionaries in, xv–xvi; and religious revivals, 7; views of Christian Indians in, 126
Attwood, Harriet, 81, 83–85, 125–26, 161
Ayer, Frederick, 166

Bacon, Alice Parks, 32–34, 37–38, 43–44, 46, 184, 190
Bacon, David: abandoning piety, 184; background of, 25–26; cultural nativism encountered by, 27, 35; in Detroit, 33–34; failures of, 24–25, 37, 40–42, 44–46, 166, 189–90; at Fort Miami, 34–37; gravestone of, 23; as an itinerant preacher, 41–42, 44; at Mackinaw, 23–25, 37–41; marriage, 32; millennial aspirations of, 23–24; perceptions of Native groups, 28, 30–32; spiritual pilgrimage of, 80; at Tallmadge (OH), 43–46
Bacon, Joseph, 25
Bacon, Leonard (David's brother), 24–25, 44–45
Bacon, Leonard (David's son), 25, 37, 43
Badger, Joseph, 41
Badger, Steven, 188
Baldwin, Charlotte, 96
Baptists, xvii, 3, 7, 79, 122, 162
Battle for the Soul (Widder), 170
Baxter, Richard, 8
Beach, Phoebe, 58
Beaulieu, Julia, 169
Beecher, Lyman, 54–56, 59, 110, 113
Berkhofer, Robert F., Jr., 106
Betty (Unkechaug Indian), xviii–xx
Bingham, Sybil, 96
Bishop, Delia, 95
Bishop, Elizabeth, 94–95
Bishop, Robert, 117–18
Black Roots in Southeastern Connecticut, 198n8
Bloom, Harvey Harris, 1
Boer War (1838), 90
The Bonds of Womanhood (Cott), 32–33

The Book of Strange New Things (Faber), 18–20
Boudinot, Elias (Buck Watie), 115, 144
Boudinot, Harriet Gold, 115, 144
Boyd, Colleen E., xiv
Brainerd, David: background of, 11–12; and the Brainerd Mission, 127; and death anxiety, 10–11; impact on Native Americans, 33; as model for gender differences, 94, 161; as model for missionary vocation, 8, 12–15, 25, 80, 91, 94, 161; model of evangelical personality, 13; as model of piety, 11–13, 30, 72, 75, 161, 181–82, 184, 189; and religious melancholy, 11–12, 77; and religious virtuosity, 13–14
Brainerd, Eliza, 60–61
Brainerd Journal, 139
Brainerd Mission: Brother Talmage controversy, 134; Catharine Brown at, 124, 127–30, 161; as a church community, 132–34, 189; David Brown at, 136; Dawzizi at, 144; and Elias Cornelius, 110–11; fictive kinship in, 132; founding of, 127, 132; impact of missionary women at, 128, 132; John Arch at, 139–40; Lydia Carter at, 111; organization of, 127; religious rituals and practices, 133; system of Native education, 126–27. *See also* Cherokee Nation
Brant, Joseph, xvi
Bremer, Richard G., 174
Brodhead, Daniel, 27–28
Brown, Catharine: background of, 126; at Brainerd Mission, 124, 127–30, 134–35, 161; dream of, 129; evangelical personhood of, 161; lifetime

vow of, 134–35; memoirs of, 124–26; piety of, 136–37; poem depicting, 123; work towards Christian Indian communities, 130, 131–32
Brown, David, 114, 123, 125, 126, 131, 135, 136–38
Brown, John (Yau-nu-gung-yah-ski), 126, 131, 134, 136
Brown, Sarah (Tsa-luh), 126, 131
Brüdergemeine, 133, 146, 155, 157–60
Bryant, William Cullen, 48
Buel, William, 70–71
Buffalo Creek reservation, 28–29
Bunce, Isaiah, 114–15
Bunyan, John, 76, 85
Butrick, Daniel, 140
Byhan, Dorothea, 142

Calhoun, John C., 51, 53, 111
The Call to the Unconverted (Baxter), 76
Candy's Creek Mission, 126–27
captives (Native American), 108, 110–11
Carey, Dorothy Plackett, 96
Carey, William, 2, 96
caritas (charity), 48, 57, 115, 153
Carter, Lydia (of Natchez), 111
Carter, Lydia (Osage captive), 110–11
Cass, Lewis, 173
Cayton, Mary Kupiec, 83
Cayuga tribes, 27–28
Chamberlain, Flora Hoyt, 130
Chamberlain, William, 130, 140
Champion, George, 89–90, 207n55
Champion, Judiah, 54
Champion, Susana, 89–90
Chapin, Israel, Jr., 27
Chapman, Epaphras, 53, 58, 59, 63, 65, 66, 67

Chapman, Hannah, 58
Chauncey, Nathaniel, xii
Cherokee Nation: and the Cornwall School, 113; cosmology of, 162; forced removal of, 121, 156–57, 161–62; and Hannah Moore, 91–92; hospitality practices, 153; intertribal warfare, 68, 101–2, 104–5; and John Arch, 139; and K, 99; land dispossession of, 161–62; missions to, 1–2, 4, 53, 55, 56; mixed-race plantation elite, 122–23, 141, 145–46, 147, 152; in the plan of civilization, 121–23, 137–38, 156–57; reception to missions, 162–63; and Springplace Mission, 142–44; women's roles in, 152, 162. *See also* Brainerd Mission; Brown, Catharine
Cherokees and Missionaries (McLoughlin), 122
Cherokee Sister (Gaul), 124
Chickasaw tribes, 4, 102
Chippewa tribes, 31, 35–36, 113, 170–71
Choctaw tribes, 4, 55, 102, 113
Chouteau brothers, 101
Christian anthropology, 48–50; and forced acculturation, 49, 106–7, 115; "noble/ignoble savage" stereotype, 48–49
Christian Examiner, 86
Christian Indian community: Catharine Brown's work towards, 130, 131–32; double discrimination faced by, 116; and ethnogenesis, xv; government plans for, 51–52; and métis culture, 122–23; and Moravian missions, 31, 142, 145, 146–47; and Native missionaries, xv–xvi, 157–60;

Christian Indian community (*cont.*) in Oneida tribes, xv; at Oothcaloga, 159–60; Sister Margaret Ann's work towards, 192

Christian Indian identity, 21–22; and anomie of Jane Schoolcraft, 179–81; and anomie of K, 99, 116–17, 119–20; of Catharine Brown, 129, 130–31, 132; following conversion, 108–9; goals in shaping, 193; hybridity in, 122–23, 138, 179–81; and mission schools, 106–7; and "professional Indians," 193–95; rhetoric of, 124–25; of Sister Margaret Ann, 150, 154, 158; as Writerly/Readerly Indians, 135–36, 137–38, 192

Christian Indian religious experiences: of Brainerd Mission scholars, 128–29; of Catharine Brown, 124–26; of John Arch, 139–40; of métis youth, 165–66; and millennial thought, xx–xxi; morphology of conversion in, 168; and power of agency, 131–32, 192; and Protestant cosmology, 106; and Protestant ethic, 108–9, 172; religious emotions, xvii, 148, 151–52, 161; in religious intelligence, xviii–xx; weeping, xvii, 128–29, 148, 151–52, 161

civilization, plan of. *See* plan of civilization

Clemmons, Linda M., 79

Clermont (Osage chief), 53, 102–3, 105

colporteurs, 76

Confidence Man. *See* "Professional Indians"

Conflicted Mission (Clemmons), 79

Conforti, Joseph A., 8, 12, 62

Congregational Church, xii, 7, 43, 54–56

Congress (U.S.), 50–51

Connecticut Evangelical Magazine (journal), 4, 8, 24, 25–26, 27, 32

Connecticut Missionary Society, 7, 23–25, 25–27, 33–35, 39–41, 42

Conversations on the Mackinaw and Green-Bay Missions (Tuttle), 166

Cooke, Juliette, 95

Cornelius, Ann, 197n2; gravestone of, x, xi, 197n3; questioned identity of, xi–xiii, xiv–xvi, 198n8; as a "vanishing American," xiii–xiv

Cornelius, Elias, 110–11, 128

Cornelius, George, xii–xiii

Cornwall (CT), 113

Cornwall Foreign Mission School: closing of, 115; and forced acculturation, 115; founding of, 112; goals for Native youth, 112–14; interracial marriage controversy, 114–15; K attending, 112, 116–17; students from Springplace Mission, 143–44

Costa-Grant, Paul, 197n2

Cott, Nancy, 32–33

Cram, Reverend, 30

Creek Path Mission, 126–27

Creek tribes, 4

Crutchfield, Joseph, 154, 156, 157, 158, 159

Crutchfield, Margaret Ann. *See* Vann, Margaret Ann "Peggy" Scott

Cuffee, Paul, xviii

cultural nativism, 27, 30, 35

D, Miss (missionary woman), 47, 53–54; background of, 54; in the Congregational church, 203n22; death of, 73; desire for missionary vocation, 56, 71, 72–73; families of, 71; at Hartford Retreat, 70–73;

malaria contracted by, 65–66; mental impairment of, 65–66, 68–73; return to Litchfield, 69–70; at Union Mission, 58; Union Mission's caring for, 68–70
Daggett, Herman, 113, 116
Dakayenesese (Old Isaac), xv
Dakota tribes, 55
Dawzizi (David Steiner), 144
Dean, James, xv
death anxiety, 10, 11, 15, 155–56, 177, 180
deaths: of Native students, 118–19; portrayed in religious intelligence, 60–61, 76–77, 85–86, 87–88; of Sister Margaret Ann, 160–61; of Union Mission members, 64, 67; of women missionaries, 85, 96
debt peonage, xii
De Jong, James A., 5
Delaware tribes, 31, 35–36, 102
Democracy in America (de Tocqueville), 46
democratic personality, 131–32, 156
Democratic Personality (Ruttenburg), 131
democratization of religion, 188
Demos, John, 117
de Tocqueville, Alexis, 46, 174
Detroit (MI), 33–34
devotional piety, 177–81; of Edmund Ely, 181–82, 184; gender differences in, 184–85
Diamond Hill plantation, 141
Dickinson, John, xii
Dingaan (Zulu chief), 89–90
"A Discourse Delivered" (Alden), 187
diseases: confusion on, 204n44; and Hannah Moore, 91; impact on Native Americans, 28; of Native students, 118–19; portrayed in religious intelligence, 60–61, 85–88; and religious melancholy, 47; at Union Mission, 64–65. *See also* malaria
disinterested benevolence, 5, 6, 8, 9, 12, 36, 61–62, 77, 79
Dissertation on Intermittent Fever in New England (Holmes), 70
doctrinal piety, 177–78
Doddridge, Philip, 76
Drake, Daniel, 65–66
Dunbar, John, 78
Durham (CT), x, xi–xiii
Dutch Reformed Church, 4, 57
DuVal, Kathleen, 101
Dwight, Timothy, 9, 110, 113
Dwight Mission, 53, 91–92

Eddy, Clary, 96
education families, 51–53
Edwards, Jonathan: and George Champion, 90, 207n55; influence of, xv, 5, 12, 14, 61; *Treatise Concerning Religious Affections*, 9, 76. See also *The Life of David Brainerd* (Edwards)
Eliot, John, 173, 188
Elk (Cherokee elder), 163
Elmwood Diary (Schoolcraft), 175–76
Ely, Catherine Goulais, 182
Ely, Edmund Franklin, 166, 181–84
Ely, Nathaniel, 194
Ely, Zebulon, 26, 32
Emmons, Nathanael, 5, 61
Episcopal Church, 54
An Essay on the Remittent and Intermittent Diseases (McCulloh), 66
ethnohistory, 10
ethnotheology, 162–63
evangelical personality (Brainerd's model), 13

evangelical piety: agency through, 91; American huckster as antithetical to, 46; of Catharine Brown, 130, 136–37; of David Bacon, 25, 30–31, 45–46; of David Brainerd, 10–12, 17, 25, 72, 94, 178–79; devotional, 17, 77–78, 94–95; and disinterested benevolence, 61–62; of Edmund Ely, 181–82, 184; in evangelical personhood, 10, 13; evangelizing through, 55; gender differences in, 184–85; of Gideon Hawley, 14–15; and individualism, 189; melancholy engendered by, 94–95; memoirs inspiring, 61, 75, 81–82; of Miss D, 56; and missionary vocation, 9; in Moravian theology, 146–47; portrayed in religious intelligence, 73–74, 75; rational theodicy of misfortune in, 176–77; of Sister Margaret Ann, 151; in spiritual pilgrimage, 8; and Union Mission, 63

evangelical religious personhood: agency through, 33, 91, 93, 131–32, 135–36; American huckster as antithetical to, 46; of Catharine Brown, 130–31, 135–36; and Christian Indian identity, 106, 119–20; David Brainerd's model of, 10, 13; dictates of, 188–89; in ethnohistory, 10; individualism in, 189; and millennial thought, 5; and the missionary vocation, 4–5, 9, 190–91; in Moravian missions, 145, 157; in morphology of conversion, 8; portrayed in religious intelligence, 75, 79; and religious melancholy, 73–74, 94; of Sister Margaret Ann, 151–57, 161; types of, 177–81; for women missionaries, 32–33, 94

Evarts, Jedidiah, 117
Evarts, Jeremiah, 67, 107, 119, 137, 140, 167
existential psychotherapy, 9–10

Faber, Michel, 18–20
Fairfield Mission, 31
federal government (U.S.), 50–51, 104, 121–22
Ferry, Amanda, 171
Ferry, William, 166, 167, 168–69, 172, 176
Finney, Charles Grandison, 166, 181, 214n26
First Ecclesiastical Society of Litchfield (Congregational church), 203n22
First Great Awakening, xvi, 8, 12, 191
Five Civilized Tribes, 4, 104, 113
Flat Head tribes, 78
Flavel, John, 76
Fond du Lac Mission, 181–83
Foote, Sarah Louisa, 81–82
Fort Miami, 34–37
Foster, Mary, 58
Foucquet, Jean-Francois, 100
Fowler, William Chauncey, xiv
Freneau, Philip, xiv
Fuller, Mrs. Stephen, 67
Fuller, Stephen, 58, 67
fur trade, 39, 101, 170, 182
"The Future of Illusions" (Nelson), 189

Gambold, Anna Rosina, 142, 145, 148–51, 154–55, 157, 159–60
Gambold, John, 142, 145, 148–51, 149, 154–55
Gaul, Theresa Strouth, 124
Gelassenheit, 190

gender: in the Cherokee Nation, 152; differences in missionary vocation, 79, 96–97, 184–85, 190–91; divisions among the Osage, 103; divisions at Springplace Mission, 144–45; divisions at Union Mission, 59; religious intelligence's impact on, 76; and "true womanhood," 33, 72, 83, 172, 191
Gillespie, Joanna Bowen, 81
Ginani Mission (South Africa), 89–90
Gold, Harriet, 115, 144
Good Peter (Agwrondougwas), xv
Goodrich, Elizur, xii
Gottlieb, Brother, 142
Goulais, Catherine, 182
Great Commission, xviii, 2–3, 5, 17, 24, 188–89
Green, David, 78, 92, 168–69
Griffin, Edward Door, 5, 88
Grimshaw, Patricia, 93–96

Hal-Bah-Chinto. *See* K (Osage youth)
Hall, Gordon, 81, 86
Hall, Isabella, 129
Hall, Moody, 127, 129
Harmony Mission, 53, 102
Hart, Levi, 26
Hartford Retreat, 47, 53, 70–73
Haudenosaunee (People of the Longhouse tribes), 27–28
Hawaii, 55, 93–96
Hawley, Gideon, xv, 14–15, 184
Haystack Prayer Meeting, 4, 80–81
Heathen School. *See* Cornwall Foreign Mission School
The Heathen School (Demos), 117
Hervey, William, 88–89

Hickok, Laurens P., 203n22
Hicks, Charles, 127, 139, 157, 158
Hicks, Leonard, 144
Hicks, Sally, 158
Hicks, William, 158
Hightower Mission, 126–27
History of Baptist Indian Missions (McCoy), 86
History of Durham Connecticut (Fowler), xiv
Hitchcock, Jacob, 92
Hobart, John Henry, 194, 195
Holiday, Mary, 167
Holmes, Abiel, 2–3, 187
Holmes, Abigail, 25
Holmes, Elkanah, 28–29
Holmes, Oliver Wendell, 70
Honaxii, John, 118
Hopefield Mission, 102
Hopkins, Samuel, 5, 61–62
Horton, Azariah, xviii
Hoyle, Lydia Huffman, 73
Hoyt, Ard, 133, 134
Hoyt, Dolly E., 58, 64, 65, 85
Hu, John, 100
Hudson (OH), 41, 42–43
Hudson, David, 41, 42–43
Huntington, Reverend, 54–55
Huntington, Sarah L., 77, 81
Huntington, Susan, 81

identity: American national, xvii–xviii; depicted in religious intelligence, 79; founded on religious values, 4–5; impact of missions on Native, 106–7, 122–23; impact of revivals on, 9, 78–79; and individualism, 189; and modern selves, 16–17; types of

identity (*cont.*)
    Protestant, 177–81. *See also* Christian Indian identity; evangelical religious personhood
"ignoble savage" stereotype, 48–49
imagined community, 7, 42, 188, 189
indentured servitude, xii
"An Indian at the Burying-place of His Fathers" (poem), 48
Indian Bureau, 50
"The Indian Burying Ground" (poem), xiv
Indian Canaan, 52–53. *See also* Christian Indian community
Indian Removal Bill (1830), 104
Indian Trade and Intercourse Acts, 36
individualism, 6, 189
An Inquiry into the Obligation of Christians (Carey), 2
intermittent fever. *See* malaria
interracial marriages, 114–15, 165, 174. *See also* métis (mixed-race) Native Americans
Iroquois tribes, 113
Irwin, Lee, 162
Ives, Timothy H., 197n2

Jackson, Andrew, 173
Jefferson, Thomas, 35–36
Johnson, Joseph, 188
Johnson, Sister, 65
Johnston, Jane. *See* Schoolcraft, Jane Johnston
Johnston, John, 174
Johnston, Susan (Ozhaguscodayway-quay), 174
Jones, Peter, xviii
Jourdain, Madeleine, 194–95
A Journal of Travels into the Arkansa Territory (Nuttall), 66

Judd, Laura Fish, 93
judicial slavery, xii
Judson, Adoniram, 80–81, 85–86
Judson, Ann Hasseltine, 81, 82, 85–86
Judson, Emily, 86

K (Osage youth), 21, 99, 192; at the asylum, 117; conversion of, 118; at Cornwall School, 112, 116–17; culture shock, 100; death of, 118–19; as diplomatic token, 105–6; lack of agency, 119–20; at Miami University, 117–18; religious mania crisis of, 100, 116–17; at Union Mission, 111–12
Kanonwalohale (Oneida village), xv, xvi
The Kathayan Slave (Judson), 86
Keepers of the Covenant (Rohrer), 12
Keller, Charles Roy, 60
Kickapoo tribes, 35–36, 102
Kingsbury, Colonel, 40
Kingsbury, Cyrus, 127, 132
Kirkland, Samuel, xiii, xvi–xxvii
Kling, David W., 13, 78–79
Konkle, Maureen, 173

Laird, Robert, 176
land dispossession: of the Cherokee, 161–62; of the Osage, 101–2, 104; in the plan of civilization, 36, 50; of the Seneca, 28–30; of the Unkechaug tribe, xviii
L'Arbre Croche, 23–24, 31, 34, 37–39
Lectures on Revivals of Religion (Sprague), 3
Leni Lenapes (Delawares), 11
Lewis, Zachariah, 49–50, 60
The Life of David Brainerd (Edwards), 12–13, 77–78, 178; influence on Henry Martyn, 76; as model for

missionary vocation, 8, 12–13, 77–78, 80; as model for piety, 15, 25, 61, 78, 181; popularity of, 76; and religious melancholy, 77
Lines, Sarah, 58, 64
"Lines Written under Severe Pain and Sickness" (Schoolcraft), 180
Litchfield (CT), 54–56, 203n19
Litchfield American Eagle, 114–15
Litchfield Foreign Missionary Society, 55
The Little Osage Captive (Cornelius), 110–11
Little Otter (Little Turtle), 34
longue durée, 17
A Looking Glass for Ladies (Pruitt), 82
Loomis, Elisha, 116, 117
Louisiana Purchase, 101, 104
Love, John, 12
Lovely's Purchase (1816), 102, 104
Lowry, Rachel, 136
Lyman, Sarah, 95

Mackinaw Island (Mickilimakinac), 23–24, 34, 37–41
Mackinaw Mission: candidate selection for, 171; founding of, 172; Julia Beaulieu at, 169; Mary Ann Willard at, 169–70; Me-sai-ainse at, 166–68; métis youth at, 170, 171–72; revivals at, 166, 168; school at, 172; and "true womanhood," 172
Mahican Stockbridge Mission, 14
Mahican tribe, xv, 11, 31
malaria: confusion on, 204n44; and David Bacon, 41; and Hannah Moore, 91; mental impairment, 65–66, 96, 100; and Miss D's mental impairment, 47, 68–73; and Susana Champion, 90; symptoms of, 65–66; treatments for, 70; at Union Mission, 65–67; virulence of, 66
Mancini, Jason, 197n4
Manifest Destiny, 47, 52, 187
marriage, 79, 84, 93, 114–15
Marshman, Joshua, 96
Martin, Joel, 127, 128, 129, 161–62
Martyn, Henry, 80
Mashpee Plantation, 14–15
Massachusetts Sabbath School Union, 166
McCain, Diane, 197n3
McClinton, Rowena, 145, 146
McCoy, Isaac, 51, 86
McCulloh, John, 66
McDonald, Sally, 158
McKenney, Thomas L., 111
McLoughlin, William G., 122
McNair, Delilah Amelia Van, 158
Meigs, Thomas, 111
melancholy. *See* religious melancholy
The Memoir of Catharine Brown (Anderson), 124–26, 161
The Memoir of John Arch (Arch), 139
The Memoirs of Mrs. Harriet Newell (Newell and Woods), 83–85, 125–26
Me-sai-ainse (Caroline William Rodgers), 166–68
Mesquakie tribes, 102
métis (mixed-race) Native Americans: benefits of missions to, 2, 183; Cherokee planter elite, 122–23, 141, 145–46, 147; double discrimination faced by, 116; encountering evangelical America, 181; ethnogenesis of, 170–71; at Mackinaw Mission, 170, 171–72; outside observations on, 172; and "professional Indians," 193; and settler colonialism, 165–66; at

métis (mixed-race) Native Americans (*cont.*)
  Union Mission, 105. *See also* interracial marriages
Miami, Fort, 34–37
Miami tribes, 34–37, 35–36, 101
Miami University (Oxford OH), 117–18
Miles, Tiya, 157
Milledoler, Philip, 57
Milledoler, Philip (Chief Tally's son), 105–6
millennial futurism, 126, 189
millennial thought: Cornwall School exemplifying, 114; and the Great Commission, 2–3, 5, 7; and missionary vocation, 5, 15; and the plan of civilization, 49; and the Redeemer's Kingdom, xx, 2, 7, 15, 23; and religious intelligence, 76, 79; in the Second Great Awakening, 5, 7; and Union Mission, 52–53
Miller, Perry, 2, 3
Mills, Samuel J., Jr., 4, 80–81, 86–87
Miss D. *See* D, Miss (missionary woman)
missiology of suffering, 96–97
missionary attitudes: in *The Book of Strange New Things*, 18–20; disdain for Native lifeways, 48, 183; toward Native education, 106; of Native receptivity, 7–8, 17–18
Missionary Herald, 157
missionary intelligence. *See* religious intelligence
missionary memoirs: of Catharine Brown, 124–26, 161; of Henry Obookiah, 113; impact on missionary vocation, 12–13, 85, 125–26; inspiring piety, 61, 75, 81–82; of John Arch, 139–40; *The Memoirs of Mrs. Harriet Newell*, 83–85; of missionary women, 81–86
missionary spirit: burdens of, 93–97; of Catharine Brown, 124–26, 131–32; Cornwall School exemplifying, 114; David Bacon exemplifying, 25; David Brainerd exemplifying, 10; Emily Judson's defense of, 86; ideals of, 9, 20, 59; and the Puritan mandate, 4; religious intelligence's impact on, 60–61, 76, 98, 110–11, 166–67, 190; and religious melancholy, 73–74, 96; and the Second Great Awakening, xvii–xviii; and the vanishing American trope, 1–3, 20, 47; William Hervey exemplifying, 88–89
missionary syndrome, 98
missionary theology, 78–79
missionary vocation: agency through, 191–92; candidate selection process, 26, 79, 171; comparisons to World War II soldiers, 97; confrontation with failure, 20–21, 46, 73; and the education family, 63; and evangelical personhood, 4–5, 119; fate of idealism, 14–15, 75; gender differences in, 79, 96–97, 184–85, 190–91; hardships and early death, 8, 37–40, 65, 66–67, 90, 96; impact of memoirs on, 12–13, 85, 125–26; impact on Native identity, 100; Miss D's desire for, 72–73; and missionary syndrome, 98; motivations for, 9–10, 13, 56, 88–89; religious intelligence portrayals of, 60; and religious melancholy, 73; special burdens for women, 73–74, 93–97, 190; and "true womanhood," 83, 191; utopian ideals, 6, 9, 57, 188–89

Mission Herald (journal), 4
missions: approaches to education, 106–7; to the Cherokees, 1–2, 126–27; as education families, 51–53; failures and hardships, 6, 24–25, 37–40, 107–10, 187–88; federal government's use of, 50–51; fictive kinship in, 57, 94, 132, 150; gender divisions in, 51; in the Great Commission, 2–3; and the Haystack Prayer Meeting, 80–81; impact on Native identity, 100; to Long Island tribes, xviii–xix; métis youth at, 165–66, 170; as model communities, 51–52, 59–60; Native responses to, 24, 27, 29–30, 31–32, 35, 37, 105, 162–63; to the Oneidas, xv–xvii; to the Osage, 1, 56–60; and the "perishing heathens" trope, 1–2, 49–50; and the plan of civilization, 49–53, 121; religious intelligence promoting, 60–61; and the Second Great Awakening, 3–4; in South Africa, 89–90
mixed-race planter elite (Cherokee), 122–23, 141, 145–46, 147
Mohawk tribes, xv, 27–28, 31
Mohegan tribes, 77, 113
Monroe, James, 50
Moore, Hannah, 90–93, 178–79, 191
Moorhead, James H., 188
Moor's Charity School (Lebanon CT), xvi
moral geography, 42, 46; Hudson (OH), 41, 42–43; Tallmadge (OH), 43–46, 189, 190. *See also* Indian Canaan
moral piety, 177–78
moral treatment of the insane, 71–72, 117
Moravian missions: *Anbeten*, 149; beliefs and rituals, 133, 145, 146–48, 149, 151, 152–53; *Brüdergemeine*, 133, 146, 155, 157–60; *caritas*/charity, 154; Christian tribalism, 146–47; *Das Sprechen*, 150, 155; Fairfield Mission, 31; fraternal correction in, 146–47; gendered division of labor in, 144–45; history of, 146; *Idea Fidei Fratrum*, 149; penitential sense of life, 147–48; religious paternalism of, 146–47, 153–56; and religious personhood, 145, 157; and Sister Margaret Ann, 140–41; on slavery, 156. *See also* Springplace Mission
morphology of conversion, xvi, 5–6, 13, 32–33, 168
Morse, Elizabeth, 96
Morse, Jedidiah, 51–52
Mosely, Eleazer, xv
My First Years in the Fur Trade (Nelson), 172

Nanga, 31
Nanticoke tribes, xv, 31
Narragansett tribes, 113
Natick tribes, 188
Native Americans: acculturation through youth, 106–7; cultural nativism, 27, 30, 35; and debt peonage, xii; federal government policies toward, 50–51; forced removal of, 104, 156–57, 161–62; land dispossession of, xviii, 28–30, 36, 50, 101–2, 104, 161–62; and the plan of civilization, 35–36, 122; responses to missions, xv, 20–21, 108–10; settler colonialism impacting, 165; viewed by Christian anthropology, 47–50. *See also* métis (mixed-race) Native Americans

Native Apostles (Andrews), xv–xvi
Native ghosts, xiv
The Native Ground (DuVal), 101
Nelson, Benjamin, 189
Nelson, George, 172
Nettleton, Asahel, 5, 8–9, 91
New Divinity movement: and the ABCFM, 4; and the Connecticut revival, 5–9; and Long Island missions, xviii–xix; and the missionary spirit, 9; teachings of, xvi, 7, 61–62. See also *The Life of David Brainerd* (Edwards)
Newell, Harriet Attwood, 81, 83–85, 125–26, 161
Newell, Samuel, 80–81, 84
New England Company, xv
New York Missionary Society, 28
Nichols, David Andrew, 35
"noble savage" stereotype, 48–49
Nott, Rosanne Peck, 81
Nott, Samuel, 26, 86
Nuttall, Thomas, 66

Oaks, Charles H., 169
Oberg, Michael Leroy, 193–95
Obookiah, Henry, 113
Occom, Samson, xix, 188
Ojibwe tribes: David Bacon's mission to, 23–24, 34, 37–39; Edmund Ely's mission to, 181–84; and Jane Schoolcraft, 179–80; missions to, 2, 55; rejecting praying religion, 182–83; responses to missions, 37, 38–39, 182–84
Old Durham Cemetery, x, xi
Old Isaac (Dakayenesese), xv
Oneida tribes: Ann Cornelius as possible member, xiv–xvi; and the Cornwall School, 113; intratribal factionalism, xv–xvi, 194–95; missions to, xv–xvii; and the War of Independence, 27–28
Onondaga tribes, 27–28
"On Reading Miss Hannah Moore" (Schoolcraft), 178
On Religious Affections, 9
Oothcaloga village, 159–60
Oquaga (village), xv
Osage tribes, 100–105; closing of missions to, 109–10; forced removal of, 104; gender divisions in, 103; intertribal warfare, 68, 101–2, 104–5; and K, 99; land dispossession, 101–2, 104; missions to, 1, 52–53, 55, 56–60, 102; responses to missions, 105–10, 208n22; social organization, 102–3. See also Union Mission
The Other Side of Joy (Rubin), 190
Ottawa tribes, 35–36

Palmer, Marcus, 58, 59, 109
Panoplist (journal), 4
Parker, Samuel, 78
Parks, Alice. See Bacon, Alice Parks
Parks, Beaumont, 33–34
Parmalee, Levi, xii–xiii
pastoral care: at Moravian missions, 150, 155; at Springplace Mission, 147, 150; at Union Mission, 63, 67. See also religious paternalism
Paths of Duty (Grimshaw), 93–96
Pawnee tribes, 78
Peck, Rosanne, 81
Pemenechaugun, 38–39
People of the Longhouse tribes, 27–28
Perdue, Theda, 129–31, 162
"perishing heathens" trope: in American nationalism, 46; and

the Great Commission, 2–3; Lydia Carter exemplifying, 111; and the missionary spirit, xx, 1–3, 9, 20, 47–48; in religious intelligence, 49–50, 166–67; and revivals, 115
Personal Memoirs (Schoolcraft), 173
personhood. *See* evangelical religious personhood
Pettit, Norman, 10–11
Phantom Past (Boyd and Thrush), xiv
Pierce, Sarah, 54, 56
Pierson, H. W., 87–88
piety. *See* evangelical piety
pilgrimage. *See* spiritual pilgrimage
The Pilgrim's Progress (Bunyan), 76, 85
Place At The Oaks (Osage village), 102–3, 104–5
plan of civilization, 121–22; in Christian anthropology, 49–50; fur traders opposing, 39; in Manifest Destiny, 47, 52, 187; Native support for, 126, 136, 137–38, 156–57; role of missions in, 49–53, 113–14; Thomas Jefferson's support of, 35–36; transformations associated with, 122
Potawatomi tribes, 35–36, 102
Potter, Laura, 137
Practical Piety (Moore), 179
praying religion, 182–83
Presbyterians, 57, 168
"Professional Indians," 193–95
Protestantism, xvii–xviii, 2, 5, 33
Pruitt, Lisa Joy, 82
Purchase, Lydia, 73–74

Quapaw tribes, 101
The Question of Hu (Spence), 100

Rabinowitz, Richard, 177

racial discrimination, 115–16, 138
Ranson, John, 64
rational theodicy of misfortune, 20, 147–48, 176–77
Redeemer's Kingdom of God. *See* millennial thought
Redfield, Abraham, 58, 107
Red Jacket (Sagoyewatha), 27, 28–30
Reece, Charles, 127
Reeve, Tapping, 54
religious ecstasy: of Alice Bacon, 32; of Catharine Brown, 128–29; of David Brainerd, 10, 11–12; and evangelical personhood, 13, 15; of Mary Ann Willard, 169–70; of Me-sai-ainse, 168; portrayed in religious intelligence, 80, 84; of Sister Margaret Ann, 151
religious intelligence: Christian Indians in, xviii–xxi, 21–22, 123–24, 135–36; conversion narratives, 166–70; endless chain of, 16, 75–76, 96, 126, 161, 190; fostering missionary spirit, 60, 98, 110–11; and the Great Commission, xviii–xx; hardships and death portrayed in, 62, 67, 75, 76–77, 85–88; Henry Obookiah's memoirs, 113; impact of *The Life of Brainerd* on, 12–13, 178–79; by Jane Schoolcraft, 174–76, 178–80; *The Memoirs of Mrs. Harriet Newell*, 83–85; millennial narratives, 79; Native Americans portrayed in, 166–67; obituary of Eliza Brainerd, 60–61; periodicals, 4, 8; "perishing heathens" trope in, 49–50; and religious melancholy, 73, 96; of Sister Margaret Ann, 157. *See also The Life of David Brainerd* (Edwards); missionary memoirs

Religious Intelligencer, 112, 157
religious melancholy: of Alice Bacon, 46; of Catharine Brown, 128–29; of David Bacon, 24; of David Brainerd, 11–12, 13, 77; and despair, 6, 9; engendered by piety, 10–11, 94–95; and evangelical personhood, 10–11, 13, 73–74; of Gideon Hawley, 14–15; of Harriet Newell, 83–85; of Julia Beaulieu, 169; of K, 116–17; of Me-sai-ainse, 167–68; of Miss D, 47, 53, 65, 72; and the missionary spirit, 181; morphology of conversion, 32–33; physical symptoms of, 95–96; portrayed in religious intelligence, 80, 81–82, 86–87
Religious Melancholy and Protestant Experience in America (Rubin), 178
religious paternalism: at Brainerd Mission, 139; of David Bacon, 36–37; at Hartford Retreat, 72; in Moravian missions, 146–47, 153–56, 159–61; at Springplace Mission, 150, 153–56, 159–61; at Union Mission, 63. *See also* pastoral care
Religious Remembrancer, 144
religious virtuoso, 13–14
Renda, Mary A., 191
Report on Indian Affairs (Morse), 51
Requa, George, 58, 67, 69
Requa, Mrs. George, 65, 67
Requa, William, 58, 59, 119
revivals: in Connecticut, 5, 7–8, 54–56; and the Haystack Prayer Meeting, 80–81; impacts on missionary vocation, 171; at Mackinaw, 166, 168; millennial aspirations of, 3; New Measures, 172; and "perishing heathen" trope, 115; and religious identities, 17, 78–79. *See also* Second Great Awakening
Revolutionary War, xiii, 27–28, 121
Rice, Luther, 80–81
Richards, Clarissa, 95
Ridge, John, 144
Ridge, Major, 127, 157, 159
Ridge, Susanna, 157, 158, 159
The Rise and Progress of Religion of the Soul, 76
Robbins, Thomas, 41
Rodgers, Caroline William (Me-sai-ainse), 166–68
Rogers, Lewis, 118
Rohrer, James R., 12
Rollings, Willard Hughes, 101, 109–10
Ross, John, 127
Ross, John Osage, 111
Ruttenburg, Nancy, 131, 191

Sagoyewatha (Red Jacket), 27, 28–30
Salter, Richard, 25
Salvation and the Savage (Berkhofer), 106
Sargent, John, 80
Sauk tribes, 102
Schenck, Theresa M., 183
Schoolcraft, Henry Rowe, 172–77, 179–80
Schoolcraft, Jane Johnston, 166, 173, 174–77, 178–81, 184, 192
Schoolcraft, John, 180
Schoolcraft, William Henry "Willy," 174, 175–76, 192
Scott, Betsy, 141, 150
Scott, Elizabeth, 158
Scott, Margaret Ann. *See* Vann, Margaret Ann "Peggy" Scott
Scott, Sarah Hicks, 141

Scott, Walter, 141
Scudder, Catherine H., 87–88
Second Great Awakening: in Connecticut, 5, 54–56; Cornwall Foreign Mission School, 112–13; and *The Life of David Brainerd*, 12; millennial ideals, 7–8; moral machinery of, 3, 5–6; New Divinity theology, 5; origins of, xvii–xviii; sense of self in, 191; and voluntary societies, 3–4
Seminole tribes, 4
Seneca tribes, 26, 27–28, 28–30, 113, 201n17
separate creation, 30, 35, 38–39; racial polygenesis, 163
Sequoyah, 122, 136, 138
Sergeant, John, Jr., 26
settler colonialism, xiii–xiv, 7, 21, 48, 138, 165, 184
Shawnee tribes, xv, 35–36, 101, 102
Sherman, John, 25
A Short Account of the Religious Exercise and Experience of Betty (Willis), xviii
Sigenog, 38–39
Sigourney, Lydia H., 140
slavery, 92, 108, 141, 156
smallpox, xiii
Smith, Daniel, 87
Smith, Eli, 77
Smith, Ned, 197n4
Smith, Sarah L. (Huntington), 77, 96
Sources of the Self (Taylor), 17
Spaulding, John, 58, 59
Spence, Jonathan D., 99–100
Spencer, Elihu, xv
spiritual pilgrimage: of Catherine Brown, 124–26, 128–31; of Christian Indians, xx–xxi, 192; of David Brainerd, 10; of David Hudson, 42; of Edmund Ely, 182; in evangelical personhood, 13, 32–33; following new birth, 6; of Gideon Hawley, 14–15; of John Arch, 139–40; of Mary Ann Willard, 169–70; of Mesai-ainse, 167–68; morphology of conversion in, 168, 169–70; in New Divinity teachings, xvi; piety in, 8; portrayed in religious intelligence, 79, 80; of Sister Margaret Ann, 142, 161
The Spiritual Self in Everyday Life (Rabinowitz), 177
Sprague, William, 3, 5
Spring, Gardiner, 87
Springplace Mission: and Cornwall Foreign Mission School, 143–44; farm at, 142, 145; fictive kinship at, 150; gendered division of labor at, 144–45; and James Vann, 142; and millennial futurism, 189; and mixed-race Cherokee elite, 145–46; and Oothcaloga, 159–60; religious paternalism at, 159–61; school at, 142–45; and Sister Margaret Ann, 147–58; and Sister Margaret Ann's baptism, 149–50; and Sister Margaret Ann's conversion, 148–51; Sister Margaret Ann's death at, 160–61; system of education at, 147
Staring at the Sun (Yalom), 10
Starr, Ephraim, 43
Stockbridge tribes, 113
Strong, John, 197n4
Strong, Nathan, 5, 24
Stuart, Robert, 176
Sullivan, John, 27–28
"Sweet Willy" (poem), 175
A Systematic Treatise (Drake), 65–66

Tallmadge (OH), 43–46, 189, 190
Tallmadge, Benjamin, 43, 44–45
Tally (Osage chief), 99, 102–3, 105–6, 119, 120
Talmage, Brother, 134
Taloney Mission, 126–27
Taylor, Charles, 17
Taylor, Sarah Louisa (Foote), 81–82
Tears of Repentance (Rubin), 146–47
"technique of Jesus," 19–20
theology of consolation, 65, 82. *See also* pastoral care
Thrush, Coll, xiv
Thurston, Lucy Goodale, 93
Todd, Eli, 70–72
Touchstone of Sincerity (Flavel), 76
Tracey, Uriah, 31
Trade and Intercourse Acts, 50
transmoral conscience, 17
treaties: Osage treaty (1808), 102; Treaty of 1817, 104; Treaty of Paris (1783), 28
Treatise Concerning Religious Affections (Edwards), 76
"true womanhood" ideal, 33, 72, 83, 172, 191
Trumbull, Benjamin, 26
Turnip Mountain Mission, 126–27
Tuscarora tribes, 27–28, 113
Tuttle, Sarah, 166
Tyler, Bennett, 9

UFMS (United Foreign Missionary Society). *See* United Foreign Missionary Society (UFMS)
Unaffected by the Gospel (Rollings), 101, 109–10
Union Mission: caring for Miss D, 68–70; deaths at, 64–65, 67; failures of, 107–10; farm at, 59; fictive kinship in, 57; founding of, 53, 56–60, 62–65, 102, 105; hardships faced by, 62–68, 73; intertribal warfare, 68; issues recruiting scholars, 105–10; K at, 99, 111–12, 118–19; Lydia Carter at, 111; members of, 64; mission family's journey to, 62–65; as a model community, 59–60; Native responses to, 105–10, 208n22; objectives of, 52–53, 105, 108, 116; organization of, 58, 59; pastoral care, 63, 67; purchasing Indian captives, 108; and religious intelligence, 62; school at, 59, 105–10; and the Verdigris village attack, 104–5
United Brethren (Unitas Fratrum). *See* Moravian missions
United Foreign Missionary Society (UFMS): and ABCFM, 117; and the Cornwall Foreign Mission School, 112, 114; establishment of, 4; Miss D's asylum admission ruse, 71; missions of, 49–50, 52–53, 102. *See also* Union Mission
Universal History (Pierce), 56
Unkechaug tribes, xviii

Vaill, Asenath, 58, 73
Vaill, H. C., 55
Vaill, Sarah, 69
Vaill, William F., 58–59, 63–65, 67, 73, 99, 105, 107–8, 112, 117–18
"vanishing American" trope: Ann Cornelius exemplifying, xiii–xiv; embraced by Henry Schoolcraft, 173; K's death confirming, 118–19; and the missionary spirit, 47–50; and the plan of civilization, 49–53;

and religious intelligence, xviii, 166–67
Vann, Betsy Scott, 141
Vann, Clement, 157, 158
Vann, James, 141–42, 145, 150
Vann, John, 144
Vann, Margaret Ann "Peggy" Scott, 140–41; background of, 141, 152; baptism of, 149–50; Christian Indian community work of, 192, 213n103; conversion of, 148–51; death of, 160–61; evangelism of, 150–51, 157–58; marriage to James Vann, 141, 142, 147, 150; marriage to Joseph Crutchfield, 154; at Oothcaloga, 159–60; and slavery, 156; at Springplace Mission, 147–48; as a Writerly Indian, 156–57
Vann, Wali, 141, 142, 149, 157, 158
Van Renssalaer, Stephen (Osage youth), 106, 112, 117–19
Verdigris (Osage village), 102–3, 104–5
Vermont Missionary Society, 3
Vinall, Job, 53, 66
voluntary societies, 3–4, 5–7, 55. *See also* American Board of Commissioners for Foreign Missions (ABCFM); United Foreign Missionary Society (UFMS)

Wallace, Anthony F. C., 28
Wangunk tribes, xii, xiv
War of Independence, xiii, 27–28, 121
Washington, George, 27
Watie, Buck (Elias Boudinot), 115, 144
Watie, Dawnee, 144
Watie, Stand, 144
Wea tribes, 35–36
Weber, Max, 13–14, 20, 147–48

Wesley, John, 12
Wheelock, Eleazar, xvi, 125
White Path (Nunnatsunega), 163
Whitney, Mercy, 95
Widder, Keith R., 170, 171
Wiley, Reverend, 92
Willard, John, 169
Willard, Mary Ann, 169–70
Williams, Eleazer, 193–95
Williams, Eunice, 193
Williams, Loring S., 127
Williams College, 80–81
Willis, Thomas, xviii
Wills Town Mission, 126–27
Winslow, Harriet, 85
women: agency of, 32–33, 83, 191; appeal of missionary vocation to, 60; at Brainerd Mission, 128, 132; of the Cherokee mixed-race elite, 152; in the Cherokee Nation, 122, 162; fate of idealism for, 93–94, 97; friendship and support among, 94, 95, 191–92; at Hartford Retreat, 72; illnesses and death endured by, 85, 94–97; impact of religious intelligence on, 75–77; in interracial marriages, 174; maternal depletion, 85, 93, 94; memoirs of, 81–86, 124–26; missiology of suffering, 96–97; and missionary syndrome, 98; in Osage tribes, 103; portrayed in religious intelligence, 79; and religious melancholy, 73–74; special burdens of, 38, 73–74, 82–83, 85, 90, 93–97, 184–85, 190; "true womanhood" ideal, 33, 72, 83, 172, 191
Woodruff, Alexander, 58
Woods, Leonard, 4

Worcester, Samuel, 4
World War II, 97
"Writerly Indians," 136, 156–57, 192
Wyandot tribes, 35–36
Wyss, Hilary E., 135

Yalom, Irving D., 9–11

Zeisberger, David, 145
Zion's Herald, 123
Zulus, 89–90

OTHER WORKS BY JULIUS H. RUBIN

―――――――――

*Religious Melancholy and Protestant
Experience in America*

*The Other Side of Joy:
Religious Melancholy among the Bruderhof*

*Tears of Repentance:
Christian Indian Identity and Community
in Colonial Southern New England*

www.ingramcontent.com/pod-product-compliance
Lightning Source LLC
Chambersburg PA
CBHW030410100426
42812CB00028B/2898/J